Contents

Acknowledgements

The ideas and understandings shared in this book have been developed through our work with children, students, teachers and colleagues over the years. Many of the teachers have attended language, literacy and special educational needs courses at Canterbury Christ Church University College. We are indebted to them all, and wish to acknowledge in particular the contribution of our colleague, Peter Dorman, Principal Lecturer in ICT at Canterbury Christ Church University College, for writing the chapter 'ICT: enabling literacy and learning'.

The book has been partly informed by work undertaken at Southborough CP, Tonbridge, Belvedere Junior, Bexley, Platt CP, Maidstone and Southlake Primary, Thamesmead. We are grateful for the support and tolerance offered by our families during the process of producing this book.

The views represented in this book are those of the authors and are not intended to represent the views or policies of any particular body or LEA.

Preface

> An inclusive education is one which seeks to respond to individual differences through an entitlement of all learners to common curricula. (Armstrong and Barton 2000)

This book attempts to respond to this definition of inclusion by examining the principles of the literacy curriculum and a range of pedagogic practices. The complex relationships between inclusion, literacy and learning are acknowledged and it is argued that quality learning in language and literacy can work towards increased equity and involvement within the classroom community.

In exploring the requirements of the National Curriculum, the expectations of the National Literacy Strategy and the social nature of learning, it is recognised that inclusive educational practice in literacy is a developing process. As a consequence, this text is organised to enable schools and teachers to examine underlying principles, evaluate their own provision, and energise development and change.

We accept the diversity of individuals, their different interests, enthusiasms, strengths and needs, as well as their entitlement to a rich language and literacy curriculum. We seek to create inclusive practice by profiling the process of effective and affective learning. Our hope is that this book will support both teachers and student teachers in making literacy learning a vital, interactive, enjoyable and inclusive educational experience.

Teresa Grainger and Janet Tod
Canterbury
October 2000

Inclusive Educational Practice
Literacy

Teresa Grainger and Janet Tod

David Fulton Publishers

London

David Fulton Publishers Ltd
The Chiswick Centre, 414 Chiswick High Road, London W4 5TF
www.fultonpublishers.co.uk

First published in Great Britain in 2000 by David Fulton Publishers

Note: The rights of Teresa Grainger and Janet Tod to be identified as the
authors of this work have been asserted by them in accordance with the
Copyright, Designs and Patents Act 1988.

David Fulton Publishers is a division of Granada Learning Limited, part of
Granada plc.

Copyright © Teresa Grainger and Janet Tod 2000

British Library Cataloguing in Publication Data
A catalogue record for this book is available from the British Library.

ISBN 1-85346-658-1

Typeset by Kate Williams, Abergavenny
Printed and bound in Great Britain

Language, literacy and learning in context

In the 1990s the education profession experienced unprecedented government imposition and increasing regulation. The National Literacy Strategy (NLS) prescribed both content and teaching methods, and the National Curriculum affirmed the significance of this tool, 'designed to raise standards in all primary schools in England' (Department for Education and Employment (DfEE) 1999a). The new National Curriculum also requires further attention to speaking and listening and includes a statutory inclusion statement. It would not be surprising, therefore, if teachers feel caught in a catch-22 situation, like Rodge in Michael Rosen's poem, with so many initiatives, expectations and targets to contend with.

Yet teachers are creative professionals, who can draw on their experience and commitment to the children to respond flexibly. There is plenty of scope for schools and teachers to make literacy learning vital, experiential and effective, to respond to learners' needs, and build on community practices in a balanced and inclusive manner. This chapter explores the current context and offers a balanced way forward through encouraging teachers to remind themselves what they already know about language, literacy and learning and to more confidently and imaginatively assert their professionalism.

The National Curriculum

Aim 1: The school curriculum should aim to provide opportunities for all pupils to learn and to achieve.

Aim 2: The school curriculum should aim to promote pupils' spiritual, moral, social and cultural development and prepare all pupils for the opportunities, responsibilities and experiences of life.   National Curriculum (DfEE 1999a)

These clearly stated academic and social aims of the National Curriculum are consistent with both the English requirements and the 'statutory inclusion statement on providing effective learning opportunities for all pupils' (DfEE 1999a). It is encouraging that both academic and social aims appear to be given equal credence in the document, in addition to an overt commitment to inclusion. This represents a marked change from imposing strategies for raising academic standards alone in an environment of competition and comparison. The new National Curriculum, at least on paper, inherently recognises the necessity to offer *all* learners a quality education that includes personal and social development. This supports lifelong learning and the development of learning communities and seeks to value human difference and diversity. Teachers have always valued the uniqueness of individuals and the importance of children's emotional and social engagement in learning. The National Curriculum's slightly changed orientation, therefore, represents an opportunity to welcome the children and their learning back into the educational equation. While the government's agenda may be to create 'good citizens and voters', the second National Curriculum aim can be used to create effective learners and participants. This new National Curriculum hints at an opportunity for teachers to exchange the 'setting and selection' that characterised the search for academic excellence, and develop inclusive learning contexts that foster increased equity and social inclusion.

However, such a promise cannot be easily realised, and this book does not seek to provide a panacea for marrying the academic and social aims of the curriculum. What it does seek to do is to encourage learning and pedagogy to take centre stage, and to acknowledge that the members of the cast are diverse learners, who have the right to the same high quality literacy education. While some actors may need extra rehearsals or a revised script, members of the cast can only get their equity cards through participation and interactive engagement. This book therefore is concerned with learning principles and processes, and the pedagogical practices and routines that characterise both effective and affective literacy provision.

English in the National Curriculum

The new programmes of study and attainment targets (ATs) continue to reflect the language modes: speaking and listening, reading and writing, and in principle very little has changed from the last statutory orders (DES 1995) although the programmes of study for reading and writing are now intimately related to the *National Literacy Strategy Framework for Teaching* (NLSF) (DfEE 1998b): 'the Framework provides a detailed basis for implementing the statutory requirements of the programmes of study for reading and writing' (DfEE 1999a). However, this close affiliation is not entirely a perfect match. In general, the National Curriculum is more conscious of the different language modes while the NLSF focuses more on the study of texts and the study of language. The clearest divergence in the two documents is in the continuing statutory requirements for speaking and listening, which can only be partly covered through the NLSF. Four strands are noted, namely speaking, listening, group discussion and interaction and drama activities. Given the recent emphasis on the literacy hour, schools may need to re-examine their planned provision of progression in speaking and listening. Drama in particular receives a higher profile than ever before, with the explicit requirements centred around improvising, performing and writing in role, as well as appraising and responding to drama. The stress on improvisation and in role work is a real strength, since classroom drama involves entering and creating possible worlds in order to explore issues in the real world. This engaging learning medium is a powerful tool for learning, which can contribute significantly to literacy and personal and social skills and the development of reflection, as well as developing imagination in action. Teaching classroom drama is a demanding and exciting challenge for many in the profession, and offers teachers a creative way forward, particularly in relation to providing purposeful contexts for writing.

In relation to writing, the National Curriculum emphasis is still on range and purpose, language structure, spelling and standard English. The writing process continues to be recognised, but in contrast to the NLSF children's ability to choose their own form and content is a statutory requirement at Key Stage (KS) 2. Given the imitative modelling so prevalent in the NLS objectives, this should help writers move towards increasing independence and ensure that teachers offer time for extended and purposeful writing. In the programmes of study for reading, playscripts are added at KS2 to line up with the NLSF, as are 'texts where the use of language benefits from being read aloud and re-read' at KS1. Few other real changes are evident, although there is some rewording to create a common vocabulary with the framework document. Moving image texts (e.g. television, film, multimedia) are noted in passing as possible to study at KS2. However, considering the importance of visual literacy skills and children's considerable interest in and knowledge of the media, it is surprising that viewing texts, critical reflective reading of media texts and media education itself are not included. Despite these omissions there are few real changes overall, which may encourage teachers to consolidate literacy provision while they attend to speaking and listening opportunities and integrate drama into the curriculum. What is clear is that speaking and listening, reading and writing need to be flexibly integrated in order that each may be fully developed and a balance needs to be achieved.

Issues of inclusion

The statutory inclusion statement within the new National Curriculum sets out three principles that are stated as essential to developing a more inclusive curriculum. These are:

- setting suitable learning challenges;

- responding to pupils' diverse learning needs;

- overcoming potential barriers to learning and assessment for individuals and groups of pupils.

National Curriculum (DfEE 1999a)

Teachers are guided to adopt a flexible approach towards choice of content, knowledge, skills and understanding from the curriculum, including that from an earlier key stage if appropriate. The term 'diverse learner' is used in the National Curriculum to include pupils with special educational needs (SEN), pupils with disabilities, pupils from all social and cultural backgrounds, pupils of different ethnic groups, including travellers, refugees and asylum seekers, and those from diverse linguistic backgrounds. There is an emphasis on human rights and equal opportunities, and teachers are required to take specific action to address these diverse learning needs through:

- creating effective learning environments;

- securing pupil motivation and concentration;

- providing equality of opportunity through teaching approaches;

- using appropriate assessment approaches;

- setting targets for learning.

National Curriculum (DfEE 1999a)

It is these key issues in relation to inclusion that this book seeks to address. It offers teachers an integrated and interactive perspective on literacy and hopes to re-energise teachers by building on what they know, extending both their understanding and their repertoire of creative activities that prompt motivation and involvement and allow them to target appropriate and effective learning.

Although teachers are required to set suitable learning challenges and adopt strategies that enable diverse needs to be met, it is acknowledged that for some children there will be some residual barriers to learning and assessment. Pupils included in this category are those with:

- special educational needs – sensory, emotional, language and communication;

- pupils with disabilities;

- pupils who are learning English as an additional language.

For these pupils the emphasis is on removing or reducing social or cultural, biological or psychological barriers to learning, such that access to the curriculum is facilitated and participation in learning is increased. The aim is to increase social inclusion and reduce exclusion from the curriculum. The emphasis on 'identifying barriers' and creating inclusive educational contexts is a welcome development from the pervasive practice of allocating funding to individuals who are deemed to have failed and need 'additional or extra' individual provision or are excluded from mainstream education. However, although teachers welcome the principle of inclusion, the challenge of promoting educational inclusion while simultaneously meeting national targets is considerable. A priority must be to establish quality provision and a common curricula for all. The NLS goes some way towards creating such a common curriculum in English but needs to be imaginatively developed and interactively shaped in the classroom.

Teachers' knowledge about language, literacy and learning

Teachers need to remind themselves what they already know about language and learning, the relationship between thought and language, texts and contexts, interaction and experience. Such knowledge and beliefs have been shaped and developed through years of teaching and reflection, reading and research, innovation and in-service education and training (INSET). Teachers' philosophies underpin their practice and prompt them to make principled and informed decisions in the moment-to-moment interactions in the classroom. However, such knowledge and understanding is not static; it is constantly evaluated and refined in the light of new experience and in response to insights and alternative curriculum demands. Primary teachers need to be language and learning experts as well as literacy experts, not only seeking to raise the assessed standards of schooled literacy, but also working to sustain and develop children as lifelong learners and reflective thinkers. The development of children's literate competence and confidence is essential, alongside their creative and critical faculties, their desire to learn and their increasing independence as learners.

In the classroom the teacher scaffolds the children's learning in a manner that enables them to complete tasks they could not manage alone (Bruner 1986; Rogoff 1990). Working within what Vygotsky (1978) called the 'zone of proximal development', the teacher mediates the task and offers the support that the child needs in order to become competent. Through this interactive encounter, the teacher prompts the child to draw on their relevant knowledge and skills, loans his or her consciousness and gradually transfers responsibility for managing problem solving to the child. So fine-tuned intervention and guidance are required, and a better balance needs to be maintained between whole-class and individual interactions, to enable teachers to scaffold learning appropriately. 'Learning intentions may be common to all, but what is also important is that all children develop certain attitudes, understandings and strategic approaches to learning and literacy'(Dombey 2000). The models of literacy instruction used in the classroom are based on different approaches to learning. Rogoff *et al.* (1996) describe three such models:

- an 'adult run' model of instruction, which focuses on the expert's transmission of knowledge;

- a 'child run' model of instruction, which focuses on the child's exploration of knowledge;

- a 'community of learners' model of instruction, which focuses on collaboration and joint knowledge construction.

This last model of learning involves mutual responsibility within the community of learners despite '... some asymmetries in roles and responsibilities' (Rogoff *et al.* 1996). Education, in this model is clearly an 'act of participation' and not 'something done to you' (Marshall 1998). The transmission model holds out limited scope for the learner, whereas a more interactive pedagogy, which is contingent on the children's active involvement, offers more hope for lifelong participation in, and the shaping of, one's own learning.

Interactive teaching and learning does not merely involve children in responding to their teacher, but demands a fuller participation in the sense that children are expected to bring their own interests, ideas and questions to each learning encounter, and their perceptions and actions shape their teacher's contribution. High levels of 'involvement', which encompass curiosity, imagination, communication and self-management, are required and develop deep-level learning, which affects the deeper structures on which competencies are based. Such involvement enables children to move 'forward to basics' (Leavers 2000). Pupil participation and quality interaction are widely recognised as crucial features in effective education (e.g. Cambourne 1995; Cole 1995; Geekie *et al.* 1999), and although this does not mean that children learn only through interaction, it is clear that learning is social and collaborative in nature. So in a classroom community of learners, responsibility for learning is shared.

> I have come increasingly to recognise that most learning in most settings is a communal activity, a sharing of the culture. It is not just that the child must make his knowledge his own, but that he must make it his own in a community of those who share his sense of belonging to a culture. It is this that leads me to emphasise not only discovery and invention, but the importance of negotiating and sharing – in a word of culture creating as an object of schooling and as appropriate step *en route* to becoming a member of the adult society in which one lives out one's life.
>
> (Bruner 1986)

Such a social, participation based perspective not only leads to more efficient learning but will also produce better learners (Cambourne 2000). It should also enable literacy learning to be a rich interactive experience, and children to, for example, explore the structure of words with delight and interest, experience a character's inner motivation with enthusiasm and feel sufficiently empowered to offer their own perspective. In essence, this will echo the involvement, motivation, concentration and self-direction that we recognise in young children's play. This collaborative and interactive conception of learning has the potential to promote more inclusive pedagogical practices and underpins teachers' knowledge about language literacy and learning.

Language, literacy and learning – teachers know that:
- literacy learning needs to be a motivating interactive experience;
- language, literacy and communication are most powerfully learnt in the context of purposeful use;
- literacy learning involves: engagement in literate practices, the teaching of language conventions, consideration of the nature, structure and purpose of texts and a metacognitive stance;
- literacy learning needs to recognise and build on the social and cultural diversity in the classroom and the ever-changing needs of the children;
- all aspects of literacy learning need to be planned for and imaginatively developed;
- a wide range of printed, oral, media, electronic, handwritten and physical texts need to be included;
- the integration of the language modes is central to developing each;
- literacy learning is a product of community.

Alongside knowledge about language, literacy and learning teachers use their knowledge of individuals, their interests, social and cultural experience and particular strengths and learning needs. Such knowledge is identified through sensitive assessment, observation and interaction and integrated into planning. This knowledge is used to structure appropriately challenging and motivating work for all children and to establish effective learning environments in which the contributions of all are valued, and learners are expected to take an active part. This dynamic view of literacy teaching and the concept of full involvement in a community of learners deserves a clearer profile in all discussions of inclusive educational practices.

The National Literacy Strategy

> There is a very wide scope for teachers to select texts, to devise and choose appropriate tasks and activities and to develop personal styles of teaching suited to them and their own classes. Of course, the NLS is bound to evolve as schools implement it in different local contexts.
>
> (Stannard 1997)

As Stannard, Director of the NLS, recognises, teachers use their professional knowledge and understanding flexibly to adapt the NLS and do 'intelligently implement well-designed models'. Beard (1999) describes this process. The evolutionary nature of the NLS has not however been brought to the foreground in the educational press, and the 'non-negotiable' nature of the framework has been voiced much more frequently and assertively. Professional confidence and flexibility are critical to the successful development of literacy teaching, since learning theories and the learner's needs must be acknowledged and used to shape the delivery of the NLSF in the wider context of National Curriculum requirements. Inevitably, the many elements of the NLSF, and its attendant literacy hour, have been disseminated and interpreted in various ways, but the core features of the strategy still remain the same.

Core Features of the NLS
Reading/writing connection
Range of literacy genre and non-fiction text types
A shared framework of teaching objectives
Clear conceptual content and language skills
Range of teaching methods
Pace and progression

Many teachers have welcomed these features, particularly the clarity of the framework, the acknowledgment of the relationship between reading and writing, the additional funding and the high profile that has been afforded literacy (e.g. Fisher and Lewis 1999; Anderson *et al.* 2000; Smith and Whitely 2000). In addition, in the original pedagogical intentions of the NLS, elements of the social model of learning highlighted earlier can be seen. The processes of shared and guided reading and writing are premised on interaction and depend for their success on the quality of these dialogic interchanges. Through shared reading and writing, access to challenging text is offered with considerable support from the teacher, who models the meaning-making process, teaches the text type and makes the learning strategies explicit through engagement in comprehension or composition. In guided text work, the teacher scaffolds the learning in a more finely tuned manner with a small group, who share their insights or challenges together. In independent reading and writing, the children have more control over the process, having internalised their knowledge and understanding, if handover of learning has taken place (Vygotsky 1978). The teacher's involvement cannot be equated with instruction and exposition alone, since instruction itself will be contingent on the responses offered, as a communal approach to meaning making is established and the children's questions and interest will shape the teacher's responses. Through this process meaning is negotiated. As Clay (1991a) has demonstrated, to develop children's literacy we need to:

- read *to* children and immerse them in experience of language and literacy;

- read/write *with* children;

- provide opportunities for children to read/write *by* themselves.

This journey from dependence, through interdependence and finally to independence is travelled in school and out, not in literacy hours, but through '24 hour literacy' (Whitehead 1999). This is partly shown in Figure 1, which highlights the need for a range of literacy practices in school that support learners in moving over the bridge to increased independence, bringing their own literacy experience with them and crossing the rivers of range on the way. In addition, the National Curriculum programmes of study for AT1 need to be planned and integrated into literacy hour work and cross-curricular opportunities need to be seized so that as well as the literacy hour, other practices are included (all of which are within the NLSF document itself), namely: the practice of reading to the class; pupils' own independent reading for interest and pleasure; and extended writing for older pupils.

The NLS, while it profiles interactive classroom routines and activities, is clearly dependent on the teacher's imaginative ability to make this literacy learning, relevant, engaging and responsive to the children. The assessment of children's competences, difficulties and interests also has a significant role to play in this engaging enterprise.

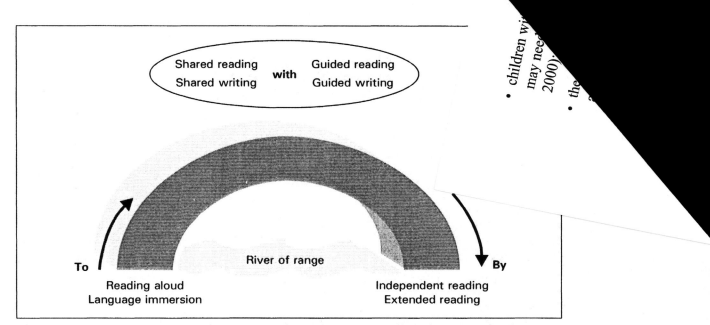

Figure 1 The Bridge to Literacy: from dependence, through interdependence to independence

Critiques of the NLS: principles and practice

The NLS has come under considerable criticism, and if a balanced and inclusive curriculum is to be offered, teachers need to be aware of these critiques, placing them alongside their own experience and knowledge of language, learning, literacy and children. As Dombey (1998b) argues, the NLSF is 'a bold pedagogic statement, a pedagogy of untried uniformity', which can be read as denying children's diverse out-of-school experiences and ignoring the fact that literacy practices are changing. The purposeful nature of literacy learning and the role that different literacy practices can play in the social and emotional lives of children are also arguably underplayed in the NLSF. Literacy learning occurs in the social context of the classroom, but children must have opportunities to build on their literate competencies gained elsewhere. In addition, the human dimension to literacy learning needs to be recognised. It is widely acknowledged that humans make progress as language learners when they feel free to experiment and when they feel confident that their efforts will be received with interest and approval. Affective and cognitive development are integrated, and recent research has shown an incontrovertible link between how pupils perceive themselves as learners and their subsequent capacity to achieve (e.g. Black and William 1998). Some pupils who receive negative feedback from teachers learn that it is better not to try than to repeatedly experience the sense of failure associated with doing their best and not succeeding. Broadfoot (1998) suggests that this tendency to stop trying is increasing, as more emphasis is placed on formal tests and reporting comparative results. Considerably more attention needs to be given to the impact of children's psychological state on their capacity to learn, and on their relationship with their teacher (Pollard 1996), particularly in the current climate in which some teachers are clearly feeling deskilled and demotivated themselves (Frater 2000). Is teachers' knowledge of children currently too focused on their National Foundation for Educational Research (NFER) results, Standard Assessment Task (SAT) scores and writing targets? Or are individuals' personalities, enthusiasms and interests given due weight alongside their cognitive competence and apparent intellectual achievements?

A variety of specific criticisms have been levelled at the NLS and these are now examined in more detail. It is argued that:

- the model of literacy in the NLS is limited, functional and mechanistic, and does not encompass twenty-first century literacies (e.g. Cox 1998; Dombey 1998b; Hilton 1998; Whitehead 1999);

- the speed of implementation gave limited time to evaluate the National Literacy Project, the forerunner of the NLS, and created pressure and stress for teachers (e.g. Dadds 1999; Smith and Whitely 2000; Waugh 1999; Goodwin and Routh 2000);

th special difficulties have shown rather less improvement than their classmates, and additional support (e.g. Sainsbury 1998; Byers 1999; Jones 1999; Smith and Whitely

whole-class shared work of 30 minutes' duration is too sedentary, with insufficient appropriate interaction for bilingual learners, boys or children with particular learning difficulties (e.g. HMI 2000; Smith and Whitely 2000);

- the *Progression in Phonics* pack (DfEE 1999b) and the *Additional Literacy Support* (ALS) (DfEE 1999e) materials are not supported by any research to demonstrate their efficacy, and they imply that to raise attainment simply requires various methods to teach the same skill (e.g. Solity *et al.* 1999; Solity 2000);

- the NLS is focused on construction and correctness in writing at the expense of the content and meaning of the language used (e.g. D'Arcy 2000);

- there is an over-reliance on less than worthwhile worksheets and a preoccupation with discrete exercises (e.g. Whitehead 1999; Frater 2000; HMI 2000);

- word, sentence and text levels are taught separately and not incorporated into the teaching of composition – likewise, reading, writing, speaking and listening are not integrated (e.g. Frater 2000; HMI 2000);

- there is insufficient time being given to shared, and guided writing and particularly to extended writing (e.g. Campbell 1998, 1999; Barrs 2000; HMI 2000);

- practice is focusing on the didactic teaching of reading and writing conventions and strategies and teaching is becoming a matter of telling (e.g. Clarke 2000; Dadds 1999; Hilton 1998);

- literacy activities outside the literacy hour have been sidelined, including reading aloud and drama (e.g. Anderson *et al.* 2000; Frater 2000).

- the principles of the NLS do not build on the principles of good early years literacy practice (e.g. Clarke 2000; Whitehead 1999).

- the imposition of the NLSF may be deskilling and demotivating primary teachers (e.g. Whitehead 1999; Frater 2000).

While some of these criticisms are directed at the principles of the NLS, others focus on practices that have developed as a consequence of literal interpretations of the framework. As the former HMI, Frater (2000), has noted, a conscientious and literal reading of the NLSF as an actual plan is a misguided reading of the document, although such a reading is an understandable one, given the climate of accountability, league tables and inspections by the Office for Standards in Education (OFSTED). The NLSF is really a *basis for planning* the delivery of the National Curriculum, not the plan itself. However, this 'checklist for coverage' can fruitfully be used alongside the teacher's knowledge about language, learning and literacy to plan rich coherent language experiences that integrate the ATs across genre based units of work and create communities of teachers and learners who learn together about the power, purpose and pleasure of language.

The challenge of balance in the new millennium

In preparing children to play a full part in society in the twenty-first century, whether locally, nationally or globally, teachers need to respond creatively and critically to both the new National Curriculum (DfEE 1999a) and the NLS (DfEE 1998b). To do this they must lean upon and extend their knowledge of language and learning, recognise the strengths and constraints of current curricula and feel confident enough to exercise their professional judgement. If inclusion can offer increased empowerment through full collaboration and effective learning, then teachers too need to feel included and empowered to take more ownership of the current agenda, and to shape their classroom culture and community accordingly. Balancing the learners' needs with National Curriculum statutory requirements (both the English content and the inclusion demands), alongside the NLS teaching objectives and knowledge about how children learn, are exciting and exhausting professional challenges. Flexible creative approaches that retain a clear sense of balance are needed. Such approaches are explored and expanded on in this book within a focus on literacy learning. The balancing act, noted below, highlights a number of contrasting strands that need to enrich and complement each other.

> **The challenge of balance**
> Knowledge about language and creative language use
> Direct instruction and interactive teaching
> Tailored text extracts and whole affective texts
> Curriculum content and learning processes

Achieving a balance between knowledge about language and creative language use

> The more prescriptive a curriculum, the greater the need to be explicit about creativity and not leave it to chance.   (The Design Council, quoted in DfEE 1999c)

Children need to develop their knowledge about language and to be helped to make their implicit knowledge explicit. The NLSF provides considerable clarity about the linguistic knowledge required at text, sentence and word level, and the new English Orders affirm this, as do the criteria for assessment in the SATs. However, while important, this kind of linguistic analysis pays little or no attention to the content and meaning of a piece of writing, and fails to show 'how a text is constructed through the thoughts and feelings of the writer and also how a text is interpreted through the thoughts and feelings it evokes in the mind of a reader' (D'Arcy 2000). These different perspectives on writing need to be balanced in both teaching and assessment, so that knowledge about text types and literary forms is both taught and learnt in a manner that encourages flexibility, judgement and imagination, and helps to foster the personal voice of the writer. Children need to be encouraged to express themselves freely and creatively, and to be introduced to forms that they can mirror or harness for their own purposes. A related balance between accuracy and fluency must also be established to encourage motivation, imagination and a bias towards the innovative.

Teachers' subject knowledge may well be a cause for concern (Alexander *et al.* 1992; Bennett and Turner-Bisset 1993; Waugh 1998), but the assumption that increasing teachers' knowledge of written forms and features will on its own improve standards is short-sighted. What is needed is the ability to *apply* this knowledge in the context of meaningful whole-text activities. For content knowledge (knowing what) needs to be integrated with procedural knowledge (knowing why) and applied in the context of knowledge about learning and the learners. So effective language use and reflection upon it must be profiled, and writing from the 'inside out' must be honoured as well as writing from the 'outside in'. A much clearer balance is needed between form and freedom, structure and innovation in literacy learning. The DfEE document *All Our Futures: Creativity and Culture in Education* (1999c) is useful here and deserves a higher profile and the widest readership. Bridges also need to be built between the widely accepted and required pedagogical practices, such as shared writing and imitative modelling, and more open-ended activities such as story-telling, poetic exploration and drama.

Achieving a balance between direct instruction and interactive teaching

Establishing a balance between direct instruction and interactive teaching is also central to effective and inclusive literacy learning. Both are valuable and appropriate in different teaching contexts, but as Wood (1988) has argued, effective instruction is contingent instruction. Such instruction may well be explicit, but it is clearly also responsive. Whole-class/small-group interactive teaching premised on the social nature of learning should enable each child to participate as an active constructor of meaning. In the learning community, the children's attitudes and authentic responses are valued and shaped through dialogue and interaction. So in cooperatively working with more knowledgeable others, enquiry and resolution can be learnt through interaction. Explicit exposition and teacher modelling do not need to be at odds with this climate of mutual responsibility and endeavour, providing a balance is maintained. Teachers can promote investigative and collaborative approaches to learning in which explanation and direct instruction play their parts at pertinent moments. The degree to which the pedagogical practices of the literacy hour are truly interactive, collaborative and productive needs to be constantly examined, for an interactive model of teaching and learning is a complex and demanding one. But teaching cannot, and should not, become merely a matter of telling, nor do the children need 'slick performers and dutiful delivers of the literacy hour' (Whitehead 1999). What is needed is knowledge about how children learn, about the children themselves, and about language and literacy. A coherent and creative community based model of literacy teaching and learning can be built on such knowledge.

Achieving a balance between tailored text extracts and whole affective texts

The range of textual resources for literacy learning must adequately reflect a balance between the culture and interests of the children and the range of literary genre and non-fiction text types stipulated within the National Curriculum and NLSF. The role of quality texts in learning to read and write is widely acknowledged (Barrs and Thomas 1991; Martin and Leather 1994; Graham 2000) and this is recognised in both documents. However, the *quality* of resources is not given sufficient profile, and engaging moving image texts and powerful picture books need to be woven in as popular, relevant and affective multimedia resources in the twenty-first century. Families in all their diversity need to be reflected, and issues of equality brought to the fore in the process of selecting suitably motivating whole texts that offer enough intrinsic pleasure to make them worth rereading or studying in detail. By contrast, much of the material produced by publishers in response to the literacy hour is highly tailored and contrived, with decontextualised extracts of texts, photocopiable resources and a wealth of activities for individual independent work. While some publishers' resources can offer ideas to integrate into a unit of work, they need to be confidently manipulated and not used merely for their extrinsic illustrative value of, for example, a grammatical feature. Tailored schemes that claim to cover the termly genre requirements have also been produced and purchased in large numbers (Goodwin and Routh 2000), but such texts, and any programme based on disembodied extracts, must be carefully evaluated by teachers. Most cannot hope to motivate pupils in the same manner as high quality affective literature and interesting non-fiction materials. 'Off-the-shelf' resources, tailored to fulfil requirements, may apparently ensure coverage and reduce teacher workload, but they can also serve to reduce both teachers' and children's emotional and creative involvement in literacy learning. Commercial resources, if not flexibly handled, can increase conformity and reliance, undercut professionalism and exclude children from pleasurable and purposeful language learning and emotive, satisfying and meaningful texts.

Achieving a balance between curriculum content and learning processes

The current pressures on teachers are phenomenal; the accountability noose, which is lashed to high stakes assessment, performance targets and OFSTED, is pulled tighter each year. In a system that has set national standards for improvement and made these educational goals a political imperative, measurable outcomes inevitably skew provision. Yet schools and teachers can create a pathway between the imposed curriculum content and the learning processes that enable this content to be understood and transformed for later use. Successful language and literacy learning involves helping children think about *how* they learn as well as what they learn (Palinscar and Brown 1984). This metacognitive awareness is gained through reflection and can enable children to achieve a deeper understanding of the processes involved, since through a developing metalinguistic awareness, an increasingly conscious control over learning is developed (e.g. Bereiter and Scardamalia 1987). To enable this to happen teachers and children need a shared language with which to talk about language: a metalanguage in effect. Interaction in the classroom can, and should, enable both the learning agenda and the learning processes to be shared. Curriculum content does need to be taught, but, as has been noted, there are limitations to the content in both the National Curriculum and NLSF, especially with regard to twenty-first century literacies, the texts of popular culture, and meaning based approaches in writing. However, to develop thoughtful participation and active thinkers, teachers must also model and teach practical metacognitive strategies and increase children's metalinguistic knowledge and understanding. There are many links between approaches to teaching thinking and teaching literacy. These include the need for explicit and flexible teaching, interaction, task open-endedness and the active and creative role of the learner. The language of reflection and evaluation has been shown to raise standards (e.g. Fisher 1998; Corden 2000; Williams 2000) and teachers need to establish 'thinking classrooms' rather than merely teaching thinking skills (McGuiness 1999). Such classroom communities will focus on learning processes, pedagogical practices and literacy routines that characterise effective and inclusive literacy practice.

Despite a current culture of prescription and the weight of endless objectives, the act of teaching remains a creative one. In revisiting the five key areas for addressing inclusion in the National Curriculum (DfEE 1999a) – creating effective learning environments, securing pupil motivation and concentration, providing equality of opportunity through teaching approaches, using appropriate assessment approaches, and setting targets for learning – teachers need to harness the power of creativity once again. This book seeks to remind teachers of their imaginative capacity, to reassert what they know, to recognise the current challenges but not be constrained by them. Creative inclusive education has the potential to rejuvenate the teaching profession.

Inclusive Educational Practice – Literacy: Principles

Ten Little Schoolchildren, by Trevor Millum

10 little schoolchildren
standing in a line
one opened her mouth too far
and then there were 9.

9 little schoolchildren
trying not to be late
one missed the school bus
then there were 8

8 little schoolchildren
in the second eleven
one twisted an ankle
then there were 7

7 little schoolchildren
trying out some tricks
one went a bit too far
then there were 6

6 little schoolchildren
hoping teacher won't arrive
one flicked a paper dart
and then there were 5

5 little schoolchildren
standing by the door
one tripped the teacher up
and then there were 4

4 little schoolchildren
longing for their tea
one's kept in after school
and then there were 3

3 little schoolchildren
lurking by the loo
teacher saw a puff of smoke
then there were 2

2 little schoolchildren
think that fights are fun
one got a bloody nose
and then there was 1

1 little schoolchild
playing in the sun
whistle blew buzzer went
then there were none!

Millum's poem fittingly reflects the diversity inherent in the behaviours and intentions in 'school children' and their vulnerability to temporary or permanent exclusion from the curricula, culture and community of their school.

> Inclusion is a process, not a fixed state. The term can be used to mean many things including the placement of pupils with SEN in mainstream schools; the participation of all pupils in the curriculum and social life of mainstream schools; the participation of all pupils in learning which leads to the highest possible level of achievement; and the participation of young people in the full range of social experiences and opportunities once they have left school. For most children placement in a mainstream school leads naturally on to the other forms of inclusion. Thus, for the great majority of children with SEN, there is never any need to consider provision outside the mainstream.
>
> (DfEE 1998c)

The requirement that the values of equity and inclusion should be realised in the context of the National Literacy Strategy, where the curriculum has been determined and academic outcomes prescribed, appears to offer yet another challenge for teachers. It is a challenge that offers the opportunity to redress the balance between prescription and innovation, and to value, nurture and monitor the processes of learning with as much enthusiasm as is currently afforded the level of output. This

---

'Ten Little Schoolchildren', by Trevor Millum, from *Warning, Too Much Schooling Can Damage Your Health* © Stanley Thornes, 1989.

chapter briefly reviews educational perspectives on inclusion with a view to identifying critical issues and development opportunities.

Background to inclusion

The historical trend in educational policy designed to address the education of young people with disabilities and difficulties has been that of segregation, integration and inclusion. The Pre-Warnock (1974) period of provision for children deemed to fall outside the normal range of ability, attainment or behaviour was characterised by psychometric assessment, normative referencing, categorisation, labelling and developments in 'specialist' teaching. The recommended placement for such children was in special schools or units, which resulted, for many, in their exclusion from the cultures, curriculum and community of local mainstream school provision. Following the Warnock Report (DES 1978) and the 1981 Education Act 'integration' took over as the dominant model for educational placement. This period was influenced by a commitment to children with SEN to be educated in mainstream settings, albeit with certain provisos. The contribution of social, institutional and curricular factors to learning difficulties was emphasised with the consequent developments of differentiation and whole-school policies for SEN. The realisation that some individuals needed 'extra or different' resourced provision within the context of a National Curriculum's integrated settings prompted the introduction of the Code of Practice in 1994. This code attempted to balance whole-school and individual specialist provision by introducing a five-stage model of identification and assessment with provision being enhanced by Individual Education Plans (IEPs) at Stage 2 and beyond. Concern about educational outcomes, costs, societal inequalities, moral imperatives and political preferences prompted the adoption of inclusion as the educational ideology for the approaching new millennium.

Philosophical perspective

Although the concept of inclusion in education is not new (Clough 1998) the recent policy changes for SEN have undoubtedly been triggered by the United Nations Educational, Scientific and Cultural Organisation (UNESCO) Salamanca Statement (1994). This followed a World Conference on Special Needs Education, which called for inclusion to be the 'norm'. The conference further adopted a new 'Framework for Action', which would require all children to be accommodated in ordinary schools regardless of their physical, intellectual, social, emotional, linguistic or other conditions.

> Regular schools with this inclusive orientation are the most effective means of combating discriminatory attitudes, creating welcoming communities, building on an inclusive society and achieving education for all; moreover they provide an effective education to the majority of children and improve the efficiency and ultimately the cost effectiveness of the entire education system. (Centre for Studies in Inclusive Education (CSIE) 1995: 8)

Central to the ideology of inclusive education is the belief that education makes a powerful contribution to the social construction of inclusive communities and an inclusive society. Inclusive education is concerned with human rights in relation to access and participation to appropriate mainstream community based education, and equal opportunity to engage in lifelong learning and employment opportunities.

While a government commitment to educational inclusion has been welcomed by teachers there are concerns about the ideological perspectives. These concerns need to be openly discussed in staffrooms if effective inclusive practices are going to be realistically developed within a spirit of ownership and collaboration.

1. Is the ideology sound? Is the notion of 'an inclusive society' a realistic aim? Is inclusion 'morally necessitated and structurally indicated' (Clough 1999). If we get the structures right and develop inclusive schools will humanity follow or will individuals show a preference for 'the selfish

gene' and 'survival of the fittest'? What are the anticipated characteristics of individuals who make up inclusive communities and an inclusive society? If an inclusive society cannot be realised is it morally right to experiment with radical educational change on the basis of hope and rhetoric?

2. If the ideology of inclusion centres around a human rights agenda does an *individual* right to an appropriate education override an ideological commitment to inclusion (Croll and Moses 2000)? The government perspective gives *individual* rights priority.

> Our policy for schools will be consistent with our commitment to rights for disabled people more generally. But we must always put the needs of the child first and for some children specialist and perhaps residential provision will be required.　　　　　(DfEE 1997)

This concern for individual rights has also triggered debate about 'justifiable' exclusion/segregation of children from mainstream education, as those who:

- need combined educational and care placements – a 24-hour curriculum;

- opt not to be included, including:
- some individuals with sensory difficulties (e.g. deafness), who choose schooling that offers sign language as the predominant form of communication (Corker 1998);
- individuals who are, for some period of their lives, unable to respond to inclusive classroom practices such as interactive teaching, collaborative learning and problem solving such as those who experience significant emotional difficulties, language difficulties or mental health problems;

- exhibit behaviour that interferes with inclusion for others.

> We have always recognised that for some special needs such as emotional and behavioural difficulties [EBD], special schools will often be more appropriate.
>
> > Jacqui Smith, Schools Minister, introducing
> > the draft new code of practice (7 July 2000)

3. If individual rights take precedence over collective rights to belong to an inclusive society can inclusion and choice coexist (Riddell 2000)? Do parents and individuals have a choice of school within the ideology of inclusion? The government seems to think so:

> Where parents want a mainstream setting for their child our policy is to try to provide it. Equally when parents want a specialist setting for their child it is important that their wishes are respected ... we are advocating inclusion by choice and have underlined that there remains a continuing and vital role for special schools.
>
> > Jacqui Smith, Schools Minister, written answer to
> > the House of Commons (1 February 2000)

4. If individual rights take precedence over the ideology of an inclusive society, and choice of school coexists with inclusion, is the inclusion movement being seriously undermined? Or was it never that serious in the first place?

5. The ideological model of educational inclusion is based on the social construction of barriers to learning and participation. It follows that segregation and exclusion can be deconstructed such that access and participation to education will ensue. However it has been questioned whether a social model of disability is sufficient to tackle issues of participation and access or whether a bio-psycho-social model is more appropriate. If this is the case then specialist expertise and competencies as describe in the Teacher Training Agency's (TTA) specialist standards for teachers of SEN (TTA 1999) need not be an anathema for inclusionists.

6. Is there research evidence to support the ideology of educational inclusion? This is problematic in that ideological inclusionists do not always direct their research towards questioning whether or not educational inclusion works for children with diverse needs. It is argued by inclusionists

that inclusion is morally and socially justified and should not be undermined by outcomes based research. Instead inclusion research has largely been concerned with methodologies (comparative case studies, action research, discourse analysis) that examine the development of processes of inclusion rather than outcomes: 'the charge that [research] is based on ideal types and idealised models rather than the realities of schools is not altogether without foundation' (Clark *et al.* 1999, referring to Lingard 1966). Many of the claims made by inclusionists – that special schools offer a restricted curriculum, that the employment of learning support assistants (LSAs) for individual children is not effective, that specialist teaching and expertise is not normally justifiable on the grounds that diversity is a resource and 'in most schools the expertise to teach all pupils effectively is usually available amongst the teaching staff' (Ainscow 2000) – have not been developed from rigorous evidence based research. Of course, *some* special schools may offer a restricted curriculum, but this is unlikely in an OFSTED era; *some* LSAs may foster dependency in their pupils, but does this suffice as a justification for the abolition of *all* special schooling or individual support?

7. Advice to teachers arising from ideological principles of inclusion includes: interactive teaching techniques and the use of inclusive questioning techniques, collaborative problem solving, planning in action, and so on (Ainscow 2000). While such techniques underpin good teaching and foster the development of active participation and engagement, we still need to *ensure* that the diverse needs of all learners are met. It is possible that some children with language, communication or emotional difficulties may not be enabled to learn and participate by these techniques. This is not necessarily a justification for specialist schooling or segregated provision, but we must be careful to ensure that individual rights to a quality education are not sacrificed to a belief system based on human rights. Diverse learners will respond differently to inclusive practices and it is unlikely that 'one size will fit all' (Hornby 1999). It is important, therefore, that in responding to national requirements schools and teachers adopt an imaginative and evaluative stance to their practice, to support effective school development and their own professional standing.

8. Inclusion subscribes to concepts of empowerment, engagement, access, participation and collaboration, but has been a top-down generated policy with little consultation with teachers, pupils and their parents. Schools will need to ensure that this balance of power is redressed when they seek to translate given policy into practice in their own setting.

Political perspective

The government has transplanted some aspects of the ideology of inclusion into the existing body of educational policy, which is characterised by standards raising and accountability. The Programme of Action for meeting special educational needs (DfEE 1998c) described the proposed plan for the development of practice for SEN pupils, which can be framed into Inclusive Educational Practice by Table 1.

At this stage of development of policy to support inclusion it can be seen that the key indicators are:

- increasing the numbers of SEN pupils in mainstream schools;
- monitoring the progress of SEN pupils in mainstream schools;
- high expectations for all pupils;
- changing the role of special schools so that they are linked with mainstream schools to support increased inclusion;
- promoting social inclusion and reducing social exclusion by developing social inclusion programmes for disruptive pupils;
- reducing discriminatory practices and promoting equality of opportunity for all pupils regardless of age, gender, ability, ethnicity, attainment and background;

Table 1 Inclusive Educational Practice (DfEE 1998c)

Inclusive	Promoting **inclusion** wherever possible to be supported by additional targeted funding (1999–2000) and research projects. Overall increase of funding for SEN to schools via 'Fair Funding' policy. Local education authorities (LEAs) to publish a budget statement for each school to identify budget allocation for SEN and value added data and numbers of SEN admissions. LEAs to publish their policies on inclusion with possible goals being: • as many children as possible educated in mainstream schools; • effective reintegration of pupils from special schools; • pupils with SEN to spend maximum time in mainstream classes; • pupils in mainstream schools to have access to expertise from special schools; • encourage links with mainstream for pupils in special schools or units; • LEAs to monitor admission and outcomes of pupils with SEN (value added). Curriculum flexibility at KS4 to provide opportunities for work-related learning. Social Inclusion programme to help schools cope with disruptive pupils and ensure excluded pupils receive a full-time education
	• Training for LSAs to support class teachers (including to support Social Inclusion). • Good practice on LSAs to be published. • Funded training for early years staff in SEN to include early identification and intervention.
	Multi-agency partnership • Publish guidance on regional coordination arrangements; • work jointly with Department of Health to consider speech and language provision; • improve career guidance for pupils with SEN.
Educational	**High expectations** (standards raising) for all pupils via: • National Literacy Strategy (NLS); • National Numeracy Strategy (NNS); • target setting (to include SEN pupils); • LEA Education Development plans to include proposals for raising achievement of pupils with SEN; • funding to support out-of-school hours learning activities; • High quality early years education via Early Years Development and Child Care plans; • Sure Start programmes for children aged 0–3 and their families; • smaller infant class sizes.
Practice	**Shift focus in meeting SEN from procedures to practical support and from remediation to prevention and early intervention** • revised code of practice (CoP) to remove current Stage 1, reduce school based elements from 3 to 2, Support and Support Plus, plus LEA guidance on what is normally provided. 'need for adequate record keeping but IEPs are generally most helpful when they are "crisply written" focusing on three or four short term targets for the child, typically targets relating to key skills such as communication skills, literacy, numeracy, behaviour and social skills.'

- developing a more inclusive curriculum (DfEE 1999a), which additionally seeks to promote spiritual, moral, social and cultural development
- fostering community and multi-agency relationships.

The new National Curriculum contains two additional important developments which support inclusion:

- an apparently equal emphasis on learning and achievement *and* the development of spiritual, moral, social and cultural development via the curriculum for personal, social and health education (PSHE) and citizenship;
- a statutory statement on inclusion.

This curriculum seeks to promote the development of individual well-being by providing opportunities for spiritual, moral, social, cultural, physical and mental development. Additionally it seeks to develop a productive economy, sustainable development, a healthy and just democracy, and equal opportunity for all. Self, family and other relationships, diversity and the environment should be valued. The overall aim is that individuals should make a positive contribution to economic, social and cultural change. This document signalled a changed perspective on SEN in that this group was contained within 'diverse' learning needs. One way of thinking about educational inclusion in the context of current government policy, albeit simplistic, is to consider the following grid:

INCLUSION

	ACCESS Reduce barriers?	ENGAGEMENT Build bridges?
	LEARNING	PARTICIPATION
ACADEMIC	High expectations, curriculum entitlement	Inclusive practices
SOCIAL	PSHE	Citizenship

Whereas policies for integration were concerned with 'access' to learning, inclusion is concerned with access *and* engagement and learning *and* social participation. There are opportunities within the new National Curriculum, as can be seen from the grid above, to meet the requirements for inclusion. Having established policies and practices to enable pupils to *access* the curriculum (e.g. via differentiation, use of visual aids, learning support, and so on) there is now a need to develop strategies to encourage greater engagement and participation at both academic and social levels. There is optimism from the new National Curriculum (DfEE 1999a) that social and emotional learning should be linked to academic aspects of learning to provide a more coherent and balanced educational experience for children. Inclusive teaching, collaborative learning and target setting that includes social and emotional aspects of development and learning are priority areas for school development.

Despite this development in curriculum design and delivery that underpins the new National Curriculum, there remain concerns about the government policy for inclusion which include:

1. Inclusion is set within a competitive standards raising agenda. Will inclusive practice be valued as much as position in league tables? Will a strategic response be developed that pays lip service to the principles of inclusion?

2. Will the evaluation of inclusive practices, undertaken against OFSTED criteria at *whole-school* level (OFSTED 1999) suffice to assess the effect of inclusive practices on *individual* pupils? 'Feeling included' and 'being included in peer social interaction' may not be tapped by measures that seek to assess academic outcomes and examine school policy documents. Inclusion occurs at different levels of school management and practice: indicators of inclusion for different levels have yet to be decided against which schools can evaluate their practice.

3. Primary stakeholders (children and their parents) have not been consulted on inclusion. It is important that they do not remain unheard voices in a policy that claims to encourage involvement and participation.

4. Some aspects of the curriculum are very prescriptive, including much of NLS and ALS (DfEE 1999e). Teachers and LSAs must balance their roles and be creative in trying to cope with prescribed practice and the principles of inclusive practice.

5. Inclusion is framed within a political model for change rather than an educational one. This time framing, geared to link with election periods, is likely to lead to an emphasis on surface short-term outcomes rather than longer term outcomes. Within this model there is a risk that 'inclusion' could be considered to be successful simply because more children with SEN are placed in mainstream settings, when in fact the real test of inclusion should also be made in relation to longer term measures such as inclusion of individuals in the community and world of work.

6. The government has allowed inclusion and choice of school to coexist. If single sex schools, grammar schools, church schools, special schools and so on remain an option then this could seriously undermine the planned link between educational policy and the creation of an inclusive society.

7. Inherent in inclusive practice are notions of collaborative working, community links and multi-agency planning. Time will be needed for this. As yet a change to inclusive practice has not included this as a requirement and so it is likely to remain unresourced.

8. The notion of 'community school' as the focus for inclusive education (CSIE 2000) suggests that the influence of technology and different modes and places for learning may not have been fully considered. This restriction of the 'place' of learning, rather than the meeting of ideals of a quality education and social inclusion in a variety of contexts, may mean that current policy for inclusive education may need to be updated in the near future.

Teachers are on the whole committed to the principles of inclusion but have reservations about the realisation of inclusive practice (Croll and Moses 2000). Table 2 reflects some questions posed. It is important that schools afford opportunities for discussion concerning these issues on inclusion so that all staff can exchange and share views and agree a way forward. Table 2 could be used as a basis for a staff development session.

Table 2 Teachers' reservations (from teachers attending SEN INSET sessions at Canterbury Christ Church University College, 1999–2000)

Areas of debate arising from current policy	Individual perspective and concerns	Examples given by teachers
Inclusive policy for education has been informed from a human rights agenda: inclusion is morally necessitated. The aim is to develop a society in which all learners are valued and participant members.	In planning for inclusion which takes priority - the needs of the group or the needs of the individual? If individual needs take priority and some individuals are perceived to need 'different' education (e.g. individuals with severe sensory or emotional difficulties) does this happen at the cost of developing an inclusive society? Is the aim for an inclusive society or a less exclusionary society?	Given that the literacy hour is designed with zero exclusion in mind but also has as an aim to 'increase time spent actively learning literacy' is it justifiable to: i) exclude an individual pupil who is persistently disturbing the class from participating in the hour? ii) consider educating some pupils with considerable access and participation difficulties in a different setting so that their chances of learning literacy are increased?
Choice v/s inclusion	Does the notion of a 'community school' restrict, or conflict with, the notion of parental choice?	How should I react to a parent who wants his/her child to go to a residential special school on the grounds that he/she will have a 24-hour curriculum which will give him/her more learning time and more chance of mixing socially with his/her peers?
Theoretical models on which practice is based. The dominant model for inclusion in the UK is the social model of disability, which is concerned with 'reducing barriers' to learning and social participation.	Is the adoption of a sociological model of disability a necessary or sufficient condition to fully meet the needs of individual pupils? For many children difficulties in learning arise from biological and psychological factors. If social deconstruction and reconstruction of disability could be achieved via initiatives for inclusion, would equity for individuals be achieved? Is inclusion for individuals about removing barriers *and* building bridges?	I have a pupil in my class who has chosen to exclude himself from learning and social activities. In this case, when a pupil has a long history of emotional and behavioural problems, is it possible that his psychological problems are preventing him from taking advantage of what we feel is a more inclusive school than many?
Are the social and academic aims of inclusive education of equal importance as is suggested by the two expressed aims of Curriculum 2000?	Evidence from the literature suggests that for many individuals there are social benefits to being placed in mainstream settings. The belief that inclusive education is the best way of improving attainment for individuals has yet to be validated by research.	We have a pupil with Aspergers who is unable to benefit from the interactive teaching within the literacy hour because he does not share the perspectives of his peers. He is very bright and an excellent reader. We feel that he experiences such difficulties in social situations that at times this interferes with his learning and so there is a justification for not trying to tackle academic and social aspects of learning at the same time.

Areas of debate arising from current policy	Individual perspective and concerns	Examples given by teachers
Should individuals be supported to learn or should learning support be integral to school practice for all pupils?	What is the purpose of learning support for individual pupils. If LSAs are to become less involved with individuals does this reduce the 'different' or 'otherwise extra' provision they need and the close monitoring of their responses to class teaching?	In our school the LSAs take responsibility for individual monitoring of pupil responses to their IEP. I can see that some pupils can become dependent on individual LSA support but that is monitored via the IEP targets, which describe the conditions under which the target is achieved. Dependency on the LSA can occur but teacher attention to one individual is necessarily limited by class size. In a class of 30 that works out to approximately eight minutes per individual per day.
Outcomes: long or short term?	As the long-term aim of inclusion is to promote equity and social participation is it reasonable to suggest that any one individual could achieve those long-term aims via a variety of educational experiences including a period of special school placement e.g. in a unit where specialist provision is available for EBD so that the pupil could, in time, be able to respond to the opportunities offered by mainstream inclusive setting?	We have a pupil in our school who has experienced disrupted home placements and has been 'in and out of care'. Given the poor long-term outcomes for looked-after children, we feel that he needs time in a small-group specialist setting and some one-to-one relationship experience which, he has been so far denied. If he can't relate on an individual level how can he function effectively in a group?
Specialist or mainstream provision?	Is teaching for diversity any more than 'good' teaching? If all teachers adopted inclusive teaching strategies would that be sufficient to meet individual pupil needs?	I have a pupil with a language difficulty who has been assessed as needing 'different and extra' provision via her IEP. None of our teachers meet the TTA specialist standards for specialist teaching of such pupils and we have found that good teaching as described by Ainscow (2000) does not make up for lack of specialism in this area.
Equity through valuing diversity or 'normalisation'?	Should we seek to assess and value different outcomes for individual pupils or try to encourage pupils towards NLS, NNS outcomes irrespective of time taken?	I have a pupil in my class for whom the pace and content of the NLS is simply out of his reach. We have designed targets based on Qualifications and Curriculum Authority (QCA) additional targets but this seems to be just a way of saying that the pupil shares the curriculum. The targets might be relevant for the government but not for the pupil.

Practice based perspectives

The consistent theme running through guidelines for practice (DfEE 1999a; OFSTED 1999; CSIE 2000) is that inclusion needs to pervade the culture and thinking of educational policy and provision if real change is to be achieved. In essence, as described in the *Index of Inclusion* (CSIE 2000), there needs to be development that will:

- create inclusive *cultures* by building community relationships and establishing shared inclusive values which will guide school development;
- produce inclusive *policies* by developing a school for all and organising support for diversity;
- evolve inclusive *practices* by orchestrating learning and mobilising resources.

Within this framework the Index of Inclusion contains a list of indicators and questions designed to support school development for inclusion.

Although provision for SEN pupils is subsumed within a dominant philosophy of inclusive practice for *all* learners, the government continues to recognise that some pupils will require 'additional or different' provision in order to meet their needs. It is emphasised, however, that such provision should be delivered within the context of the inclusive curriculum and should not be seen as compensatory or exclusionary. The 'Critical Success Factors' (DfEE 2000) are that such provision should ensure that:

children's needs are met; SEN should be identified early, intervention should exploit good and best practice; the wishes of the child should be taken into account; SEN professionals should work in partnership with parents, there should be a multi-disciplinary approach to the resolution of issues; interventions should be reviewed regularly, and the LEA must make assessments within prescribed time limits. (DfEE 2000)

The draft revised SEN Code of Practice (DfEE 2000) recommends a 'graduated response' to pupils' special educational needs: 'For the vast majority of pupils it is the actions taken by their class teachers in ordinary settings which are the key to helping them make progress and to raising achievement'. The five stages of the 1994 code is replaced by two stages: School Action (school alone); and School Action Plus (school plus external agencies, which may include the possibility for statutory assessment, which may lead to a statement of special educational need). It is anticipated that this model will reduce the level of statementing overall and be consistent with the government's commitment to increased inclusion.

Children's needs are grouped into broad areas: communication and interaction; cognition and learning; behaviour, emotional and social development; and sensory and/or physical. It is anticipated that action to meet pupils' special educational needs in the context of the inclusive curriculum will fall into four broad strands:

- assessment planning and review (e.g. more detailed monitoring of pupils' classroom performance, individualisation of planning, specialist expertise in assessment, etc.);

- grouping for teaching purposes (e.g. small groups with additional, possibly specialist support, out of hours provision, etc.);

- additional human resources (e.g. volunteers, specialist support, outside expert help, etc.);

- curriculum and teaching methods (inclusive curriculum plus focused differentiation; enabling devices, information and communications technology (ICT), augmented forms of communication, individualised teaching programmes, etc.).

Schools and LEAs are required to organise these strands of action in such a way that they can call on progressively more powerful interventions to meet increasing need. Decisions are based on two thresholds: the first strengthens strategies already available to classroom teachers; the second focuses on providing support and intervention across wide areas of the curriculum through intensive assessment and planning, access to adult support and targeted tuition. Between these two thresholds is an area labelled 'increasing levels of special educational need'. In this area action is focused towards providing interventions for those more limited aspects of learning and skills where pupils experience greatest difficulty; e.g. through the involvement of external specialists in assessment and tuition or in class support for those areas. Table 3 suggests how this might take place. Some indication of what the thresholds and response might look like for different areas of SEN are given in the draft revised Code documentation (DfEE 2000), which may prove useful for mainstream teachers.

In practice then, teachers are required to continue with the NLS but provide for diverse learners via a continuum – that of developing inclusive cultures, policies and practices and of providing 'different or additional' provision with increasing individualisation and additional support. While the new Code seeks to improve practice for pupils with SEN within the context of an inclusive curriculum it remains to be seen whether teachers and schools will be supported, trained and resourced to manage these changes.

Many of the 'practice' based developments for inclusion have not been grounded in research and it remains to be seen if individual pupils receive a quality education from a mixture of inclusive and specialist provision. Much will depend on the confidence, knowledge and flexibility of the profession to balance prescription and creativity in practice.

Table 3 Matching action to levels of special educational need (DfEE 2000: 13, Table 3.1)

	Assessment & planning	Grouping for teaching purposes	Human resources	Curriculum and teaching methods
Lower threshold of special educational need	Assessment by class/subject teacher and special educational needs coordinator (SENCO); continuous assessment and curriculum assessments may be supplemented by standardised and/or diagnostic tests. IEP setting 'SMART' targets (some may be shared with other pupils in a Group IEP). Regular reviews. Parents informed & may be involved in supporting targets in the home.	Pupils based in the ordinary classroom. Grouping strategies used flexibly within the classroom. Out of hours learning opportunities (homework, clubs, lunchtime clubs etc.) provided where possible.	Main provision is by class/subject teacher. SENCO involved in assessment and planning rather than teaching. Pupil support used routinely and some adult support may be provided on an ad hoc basis (e.g. if teaching assistant or parent is assistant or parent is already working in the classroom). Specialist teachers or educational psychologist may be involved in providing advice on strategies.	Emphasis on differentiation for curriculum access. Possibly some specific reinforcement or skill-development activities in support of IEP targets.
Increasing levels of special educational need	External services (specialist support service, educational psychologist) undertake specialist assessment leading to a more specifically focused IEP. Parents involved in supporting targets in the home.	Pupil based predominantly in the ordinary classroom, supported through flexible grouping strategies. There will also be access to individual or small group tuition to support IEP targets, delivered within the classroom, through limited periods of withdrawal and/or through out-of-hours provision.	Main provision is by class/subject teacher. Pupil support used routinely in the classroom with some limited targeted adult support provided by LSA or other adult. Individual or small group tuition provided by LSA (under guidance), specialist teaching (or other specialist) and/or SENCO.	Emphasis on increasing differentiation of activities and materials. Some individual programming to support specific targets. Access to ICT and to specialist equipment and materials as necessary.
Higher threshold of special educational need	Involvement of both educational and non-educational professionals in assessment and planning. Longer term plan for provision, supported by shorter term IEPs. Parents involved in both long- and short-term planning.	Pupil works predominantly in small groups or on an individual basis in the ordinary classroom, in a withdrawal situation, in a resource base and/or through out-of-hours provision.	Pupil support used routinely in the ordinary classroom with sustained targeted support provided by LSA or other adult. Individual or small group tuition is provided by LSA (under guidance), specialist teacher (or other specialist) and/or SENCO.	Increasingly individualised programme (though within the context of an inclusive curriculum). May involve the use of specialist teaching and/or communication techniques, supported by appropriate equipment and materials.

Inclusive Educational Practice: literacy

Inclusive education seeks to give every child a 'chance' and needs to acknowledge the fact of difference: historically, philosophically and practically. For children's lived experience is highly specific and is not able to be assumed or prejudged. As the ethnographic work of Brice-Heath (1983) has shown, long before schooling, language and culture at home structure and shape ways of making meaning. Each family's literacy practices and their values shape the course of the child's literacy development 'in terms of the opportunities, recognition, interaction and models available to them' (Hannon 1995). Literacy is not a singular competence, but a social activity that can be described in terms of sets of social practices.

> People have different literacies which they make use of, associated with different domains of life, these differences are increased across different cultures or historical periods.   (Barton 1994)

In the different domains of life (e.g. home, school, church, work), individuals use different technologies (e.g. television, computer, pen and paper, telephone) to serve different purposes. So a shift is needed away from the single model of literacy enshrined in the NLS towards an acknowledgement of, and respect for, community literacy practices (Street 1997) and an awareness of the multiple, often overlooked literacies in children's lives. As Au (1993), Gee (1996), Brice-Heath (1983) and others have shown, when mismatches occur in the way literacy is defined at home and school the chances for school success are severely compromised. The match and mismatch in language and literacy between home/community and school are vitally important in responding to the specific needs of all children, but in particular to those who experience difficulties with literacy and schooling. Children need to be able to 'develop critical and creative thought in the language of their own communities', as well as 'master the literacy and language constructions of the elite, so that they are empowered to challenge the dominant discourses of society' (Hilton 1994). This ideological model of literacy emphasises its variability in different contexts and social practices (Street 1993), and acknowledges that languages and literacy are inescapably tied to the production, reproduction and maintenance of unequal power relations (Lankshear 1997). Cummins identified four structural elements of schooling, which he argues influence the extent to which students from minority backgrounds are empowered or disadvantaged. These are:

- the incorporation of minority students' culture and language;

- inclusion of minority communities in the education of their children;

- pedagogical assumptions and classroom practices;

- assessment of minority students.   (Cummins 1986)

In Barton's research (1994), which started from people's *uses* of literacy, and not from their formal learning of literacy, it is again clear that literacies are not valued equally. They vary in purpose and in whose purpose they serve. Some are imposed from the outside while others are self-generated. Another related distinction is drawn between dominant and vernacular literacies; between those that originate from the dominant institutions of society and those that have their roots in everyday life. Inclusive educational practice has to recognise the existence of multiple literacies used in different domains of twenty-first century life and the complex relationship between literacy and culture that shapes these. Such anthropological models of literacy highlight the need to develop community links to sustain and support parental interest and enable teachers to build on the cultural knowledge, wide linguistic competence, interest and enthusiasms of the children they teach.

Teachers must wet their bodies in the waters of children's culture first – then they will see how to teach reading and writing.
                                                                       (Freire 1985)

Children use a variety of texts and technologies in making their out-of-school journeys into literacy, (Meek 1992, Minns 1990) and these many texts too must be acknowledged and integrated into the curriculum. The popular culture industry interests and engages children and this assuredly affects the literature they choose and the stories they write (Hilton 1996). Moreover, and more significantly, it influences their developing sense of self, so media texts should be used as rich and meaningful material in the classroom for creative and critical reading encounters. Such texts are often multimodal (e.g. television adverts, comics, picture fiction, film) and require different reading patterns, which are increasingly visual and multidimensional. Despite the clear lack of recognition of these within the National Curriculum for KS1/2, the audiovisual texts of television, film and video and computer-generated images are shaping what it means to be literate in the twenty-first century (Kress and Van Leween 1996). There is a clear tension between the current tendency to narrow down the curriculum and this ever-widening range of textual forms. This may widen the gulf still further between 'schooled literacy' and the breadth of literate practices engaged in by children outside school. In banning Pokémon in school, for example, a currently significant literate practice is excluded, and the children's competence in this regard ignored. This will not help children develop a metalanguage to talk about such texts reflexively, nor construct texts for their own purposes, nor 'help them to read the word and the world' (Freire 1985). The development of critical literacy should be a common goal for all learners, not merely the basic measurable and limited literacy of national requirements. What follows from these arguments is that as Baynham states,

> Literacy cannot be taken as a given, a known technology from context to context. Literacy practices remain to be discovered, investigated, researched.   (Baynham 1995)

In order to establish an inclusive approach to the multiple literacies in which their children engage, teachers need themselves to become ethnographers and enquirers into these literacy practices (Brice-Heath 1983), and build on these literacies in the classroom.

Inclusive Educational Practice – Literacy: Institutional self-review

- Have there been opportunities for staff openly to discuss their hopes and concerns for inclusion?
- To what extent have school perceptions and policies for inclusion been discussed with governors, parents/carers, pupils and representatives from the local community?
- Is the development of inclusive practice seen as a shared responsibility of all staff?
- Is there a strategy to allow pupils to receive additional or different support without being consistently excluded from one subject area or class group?
- Are support policies concerned with reducing barriers to learning and social participation?
- To what extent have differences in attainment and participation between groups (e.g. boys/girls) been successfully addressed?
- In what ways does the school identify and value the language and literacy practices in the community?
- How encompassing is the school's language and literacy policy? To what extent is schooled literacy alone taught?
- How are the texts of popular culture used in literacy teaching?
- How is children's literate competence and extensive knowledge of such texts harnessed, celebrated and critically extended through the school?
- What strategies are employed to make the curriculum more culturally relevant and socially/ linguistically responsive to the children?
- Is the personal, social and emotional development of the children carefully planned for and the significant relationship with their teacher consciously shaped in human terms, or only from the perspective of instruction?

Inclusive Educational Practice – Literacy: Ideas for action

- Plan a careful programme to help staff recognise and respond to the many languages and multiple literacies used in the community. An effective partnership will use a range of strategies.

- Focus on pedagogy and the social nature of teaching *and* learning in school professional development. Establish current knowledge understanding and practice and seek to extend this.

- Work towards producing an inclusive teaching and learning policy as a staff. Share this appropriately with both parents and children.

- Encourage children to bring literacy texts and artefacts from home to school, e.g. comics and magazines, catalogues, home writing, videos, photographs, treasured possessions, toys. Base literacy work around these artefacts.

- Encourage children to take literacy texts and artefacts from school to home to inform parents about literacy practices in school, e.g. the class anthology, a class or personal diary or learning log, a class photo album, storysacks, curiosity kits, cards, letters, tapes.

- Establish a programme for teachers to examine their own classroom interactions and literacy practices.

- Create opportunities for children to use the texts of popular culture for their literacy learning e.g. researching Pokémon or producing their own 'interest' magazines.

- Profile the recognition of multiple literacies through displays that demonstrate, for example, the value of oral storytelling or televisual literacy.

- Keep families and the community informed about school language and literacy activities through a variety of media, e.g. newsletters, posters, children's own school newspapers, community magazines.

- Encourage families to contribute 'home' examples and perspectives to their child's record of achievement or portfolio.

- Seek personal, emotional and cultural connections in literacy work.

Inclusive educational practice in literacy needs not only to widen the brief of diversity and difference to include all learners, but also to reflect an emphasis on the processes that underpin effective learning. As Figure 2, a framework for inclusion, suggests, all learners need to participate thoughtfully, effectively and affectively to learn, and the pedagogic practices employed by teachers are central to this. Perhaps the importance of learning and pedagogy for children who experience difficulty or disability has been undermined, for example, during periods of SEN provision that directed attention towards individual deficits (pre-Warnock 1978) or towards curriculum access (post-1981 Education Act). However, inclusive education can respond to individual differences by offering a rich language and literacy curriculum, which is shaped by creative and responsive teachers and built on sound pedagogic principles.

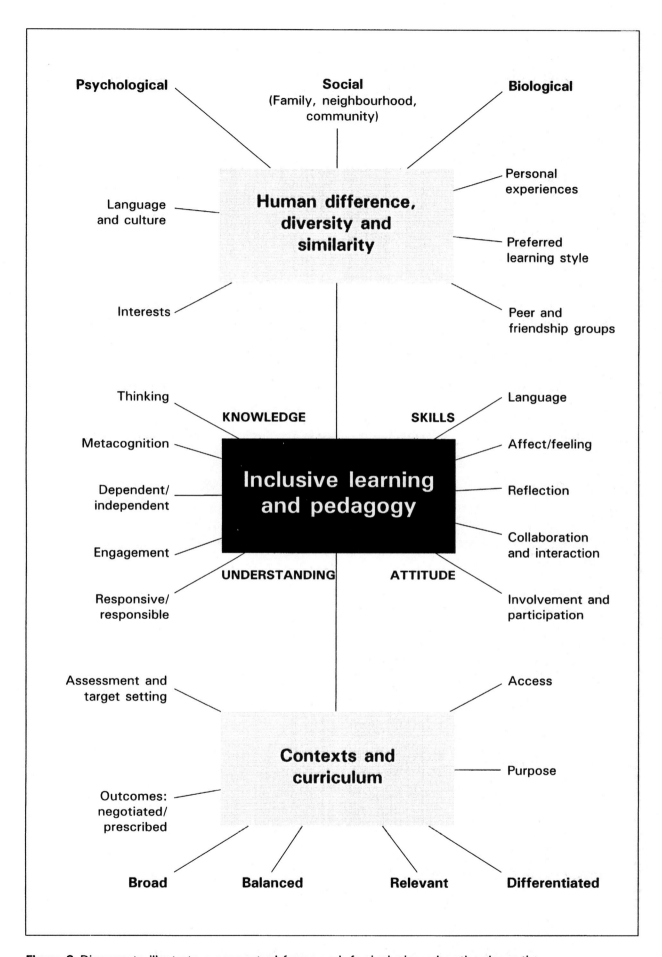

Figure 2 Diagram to illustrate a conceptual framework for inclusive educational practice

Assessment and target setting: Principles

A Boy's Head, by Miroslav Holub

	There is a river
In it there is a space ship	that flows upwards.
and a project	There is a multiplication table.
for doing away with piano lessons.	There is anti-matter
And there is	And it just cannot be trimmed.
Noah's ark	I believe
which shall be first.	that only what cannot be trimmed
And there is	is a head.
an entirely new bird,	There is much promise
an entirely new hare,	in the circumstance
an entirely new bumble-bee.	that so many people have heads.

Of course targets alone will not raise standards in schools. They are the next step in improving development planning ... They are a further management tool which head teachers and governing bodies can use.
(DFEE 1997)

But does target setting sit comfortably with the management of inclusive educational practice and to what extent do targets that are set for individuals take note of the promise for learning inherent in Holub's 'A Boy's Head'? Assessment for target setting in literacy is undertaken at different levels for different purposes. There is a requirement for schools to develop targets that support the achievement of national targets for literacy and also to develop targets for individual learners that are intended to be compatible with, but may be distinct from, these whole school targets (QCA 1999a). It is useful to conceptualise target setting based on Norwich's notion of needs:

- *Common needs* – arising from characteristics shared by all (the need to belong, for achievement, have effort recognised, etc. – whole-class targets)

- *Exceptional needs* – arising from characteristics shared by some (this would indicate small group targets)

- *Individual needs* – arising from characteristics different from all others (e.g. a child may have a particular sensory difficulty – individual targets)   (Norwich 1996)

In identifying these needs, a range of assessment tools can be harnessed to create medium term learning intentions, specific learning objectives and pupil targets, which take into account the curriculum and current priorities, individual differences and the complex nature of learning. The key principles which underpin effective assessment must be acknowledged from the outset:

- Assessment should build on and develop existing practices for assessment.

- Assessment should be clearly linked to purpose: i.e. assessment should be focused towards assessing the processes of access, engagement, participation, and response.

'A Boy's Head', Miroslav Holub, from *Selected Poems*, translated by Ian Milner and George Theiner (Penguin Books 1967) © Miroslav Holub 1967, translation © Penguin Books 1967, reproduced by permission of Penguin Books Ltd.

- Assessment requires both individual and social levels of analysis; interdisciplinary perspectives and inter-professional collaboration will be necessary for some individual pupils.

- Assessment should seek to identify barriers to learning that arise from biological, psychological and sociocultural factors.

- Assessment should seek to identify how barriers to learning might be reduced for learners and bridges built.

- Assessment should be focused towards identifying pupil differences *and* similarities, so that common/shared features can be communicated and used as a resource to support inclusive learning.

- Assessment should note, value and use learner characteristics and responses.

- The learner should be a valued contributor to their own assessment.

Summative/formal assessment

Summative assessment, in the form of national statutory tasks and tests (SATs) (and to an increasing extent the QCA optional tests for Years 3, 4 and 5) are of increasing significance and influence in the current accountability culture. Yet the National Curriculum Task Group on Assessment and Testing (TGAT) report stated clearly:

> The assessment process itself should not determine what is to be taught and learned. It should be the servant and not the master of the curriculum. (Black *et al.* 1988)

However, guidance has been issued to schools (DfEE 1997) concerning target-setting procedures to meet national literacy and numeracy targets. The target for literacy is that 80 per cent of 11-year-olds will reach Level 4 in English by the year 2002. National target setting has prompted schools and LEAs to develop a strategic response, which has been seen by many to conflict with a requirement to develop inclusive educational practices. The classroom consequences of this narrow assessment of performance within the SATs are considerable. Concern has been expressed that 'high stakes' testing inevitably leads to a narrowing of the curriculum, and 'surface' rather than 'deep' learning takes place since teachers teach to the test (Airasian 1988; Harlen and James 1997). Additionally, the remarkable recent practices of targeting those children who are just below the threshold in order to improve published results can surely not be justified in terms of equal opportunities or inclusion. Such a strategy encourages selection and streaming of children into those who 'will' achieve Level 4, those who 'could' with extra targeted support, and those who are 'unlikely or unable to'. This latter group are likely to be those designated SEN or experiencing learning differences and/or difficulties. Indeed it could be argued that Warnock's 20 per cent of pupils who have 'learning needs' have been reconstructed by the 80 per cent target setting procedures. Although the 80 per cent 'average' targets could be met by LEAs it does not follow that all learners, particularly those who experience underachievement at all levels, will have benefited from being included in a national procedure to raise standards. Concern about the rising number of SEN pupils who are deemed to need 'extra or otherwise different' provision (Marks 2000) reflects that national targets may prove to be an exclusionary and costly strategy.

> Defining improvement as the extent to which children perform successfully at an external test assumes that the test was valid and reliable and did not advantage or disadvantage particular pupils according to race, gender, class or any other factor ... Year on year comparisons can only prove valuable if there has been a period of stability with tests remaining constant and unchanging in their level of difficulty and in their basic demands. This has certainly not been the case so far since the introduction of National Curriculum's associated testing. (Clarke 1998)

The SATs, snapshots of children's learning that are shared with parents and the nation, are used to judge school effectiveness and are regarded as quantitative performance criteria. However, recent criticisms of SATs have highlighted their limitations, particularly in relation to writing (Fox 1994, 2000; D'Arcy 2000). The use of judgements of best-fit to descriptors of performance for acknowledges is difficult since some of the writing dimensions are muddled, for example under quality and style, various statements are included about meaning, syntax, genre and vocabulary! In addition, many features are missing including length of writing, the child's control and use of the writing process and their boldness and risk taking. Fox (2000), in critiquing the writing SATs at KS1, creates a new framework in line with the existing criteria (and word, sentence and text level), which includes a significant dimension: 'the overall communication of meaning'. This gives credit to writing that is lively, imaginative and coherent. The meaning and purpose of writing at KS2/3 is also sidelined, at the expense of linguistic construction and correctness (D'Arcy 2000). The assessor's attention is therefore directed towards looking *at* the words, not *through* them.

> My prime concern ... is the way in which pupils' performance as writers – and generalisations about their performance – is to be so narrowly assessed through focusing on surface features of text, meanwhile ignoring the meanings which that text seeks to convey.   (D'Arcy 2000)

The concept of 'style' is therefore reduced to whether the sentences children choose are 'grammatically complex' enough, and the meaning and purpose of the writing is sacrificed on the altar of literary techniques. In assessing writing it is now common practice for teachers to set a termly writing task, which is analysed, annotated and moderated as evidence of current attainment and included in the child's portfolio. The tendency to use the level descriptions to undertake this is increasing, yet they were explicitly 'not designed to level pieces of work' (School Curriculum and Assessment Authority (SCAA) 1995). Some areas of writing are ignored and limited evidence is provided on the child's overall confidence, ability to use the writing process or their growing reflectiveness as writers. However, the moderation process is useful in that it encourages a dialogue and provides a clearer notion of development.

Other forms of formal assessments, such as standardised reading tests, also serve to highlight the relative status afforded 'objective tests' as opposed to teachers' rounded professional judgements. While it is clear that reading is a complex skill and no test can provide a full picture of a reader's skills, knowledge, understanding and attitude, schools still seem to rely on such standardised tests and the reading ages they produce. This is a 'misleading concept, obscuring more than it reveals' (DES 1975), which certainly has no diagnostic function and does not seek to identify strengths or weaknesses. Furthermore, many of the reading tests still in use are culturally and linguistically biased.

Ongoing day-to-day assessment

Evidence of children's learning in literacy should be recorded in 'words not numbers' (Barrs 1990), from both target-led assessment and ongoing records gathered in informal and semi-formal contexts. A strength of informal assessment, however, is that it allows teachers to note developing behaviours and strengths, and does not merely seek to demonstrate 'attainment': what a child has achieved in relation to a specific learning objective. It offers a holistic and developmental picture that can enrich the teacher's understanding of the child's learning and be placed alongside target-led assessment. Systems for monitoring and assessing progress and involving both the parents and the child, can help teachers shape and develop their teaching. A range of ongoing approaches is helpful to make a full assessment of children's literacy development. These include informal observation and conversations, conferences and more detailed diagnostic assessments such as a miscue analysis or a running record. Record-keeping formats, such as *The Primary Language Record Handbook for Teachers* (Barrs *et al.* 1998), can be particularly valuable for organising and structuring ongoing assessment.

Informal observation

During classroom activities there are opportunities to observe children engaged in reading, writing, speaking and listening. Much of this will be unrecorded, yet will add to the teacher's awareness and understanding of, for example, a child's attitude to reading, or ability to play imaginatively and cooperatively in the role play area, or use of a range of writing materials at the writing table. Through questioning in whole-class work and in all classroom interaction, the teacher can gather evidence of the children's thinking, although focused individual questions can backfire if the child lacks the confidence to voice their views. As with all observation, teachers must recognise that the information gathered offers not only data about individual learners, but also reflects the quality of classroom practice. To be really useful it is appropriate to target children in particular contexts, perhaps recording a brief note of the positive skills demonstrated and particular difficulties encountered. Three examples are offered to highlight observation for assessment in different contexts.

Observation in guided reading

In this group context, after introduction of the book, the teacher is able to focus on individual children as they read independently to see the strategies they are employing. For example, in searching for an answer to a set question, the teacher may observe whether the child is using the contents and/or index, scanning to locate the section, skimming through the information, and making a more detailed reading. The child's understanding of the information read, shared in the discussion, will complete the observational record. Briefly noting what two or three members of the group can do and still find difficult can help shape the following guided session.

Observation in writers' workshop

As the class settle to write, a targeted observation of individuals or a group may indicate their interest and motivation, use of planning strategies, interaction, and so on. Such an observation may prompt a later conversation with the writer/s to establish their views about the challenge of beginning writing; it may also challenge the teacher to provide more time for preparation and oral drafting.

Observation in classroom drama

During drama, the teacher works in and out of role, so there are times when observation of targeted individuals is possible. Classroom drama involves developing six areas of learning simultaneously; the imagination, personal and social skills, drama processes, language, reflection and the content of the drama (Grainger and Cremin 2000). Only three need to be explicitly identified as objectives for each lesson. For example, in a lesson about Grace Darling the teaching objectives might be:

- to show empathy and sensitivity to others (personal and social);
- to learn more about Grace's role in the shipwreck of the *Forfarshire* (the content of the drama);
- to use a range of different spoken registers (language).

Observational notes in the form of verbatim quotes and comments may be used alongside writing in role, e.g. in Grace's diary, to record children's learning in drama. Over time, assessment can encompass all the areas of learning in drama.

Literacy conferences

> This is a useful way of involving the children in self evaluation and enables them to make a real contribution to the assessment of their own progress.
> (Browne 1996)

Opportunities to discuss literacy learning with individuals are immensely valuable; they can integrate self-assessment, acknowledge the relationship between reading and writing, explore the role of speaking and listening and allow targets to be negotiated, not imposed. Termly conferences can be very effective tools for assessment and, if the ethos is supportive enough, can be conducted in small guided group contexts. Preparation for a conference is essential. Children may be asked to bring, for example, their reading record, home–school contact book, current reading book, writing folder, spelling journal or learning log. They may also be encouraged to identify aspects of their work that they are pleased with, or some area in which they need help, so work on reflective thinking and self-assessment supports conferencing directly. Conferences can enable an assessment of attitude and motivation to be made and can track back through recent work to gain a more holistic picture of the child's progression and development. They can focus exclusively on reading or writing in response to need and would usually include a record of the child's self-assessment, range and preferences, skill and strategies and targets. Such conversations involve the negotiation of meaning by both teacher and child to create quality interactive opportunities for 'feedback' and 'feed forward' (Black *et al.* 1988). To extend children's thinking and metacognitive awareness in this context, teachers need to establish a joint focus, share a clear structure with the child, personalise the conversation, give clear positive affirmation of development and listen and negotiate explicit targets on the basis of the evidence and in relation to the medium term learning intentions.

If the teacher's response to the children's views about texts and their writing is genuine and is not focused on the technical aspects alone, but critically centres on meaning and thinking about language, then the children become more willing to talk about their work and reflect upon it. Thinking time needs to be built into conferencing. The affective dimension of learning is honoured in a literacy conference and must be an essential consideration in assessing and targeting children's progress.

Running records/miscue analysis

Both these procedures share the purpose of diagnosing and analysing the reader's strategies and approaches to text as well as assessing comprehension. More importantly, techniques like these reveal profiles of strengths and weaknesses and differentiate between varieties of errors. They are useful for children about whom there is some concern and particularly for creating needs based grouping for guided reading. Some schools use the KS1 SAT texts (Levels 2 and 3) and the accompanying prepared passages/assessment sheets for running records; others have created their own prepared passages/record sheet from familiar texts in the classroom. Assessment of need in this detailed manner can enable the teacher to, for example, gather together all those children who are over-dependent on contextual and syntactic strategies and need to be taught to use more grapho-phonic strategies in their reading.

Miscue analysis, invented by Goodman (1973) is a procedure that provides 'a window onto the reading process'. It is most useful for older children whose reading is a cause for concern. Through a step-by-step process, a child's specific strengths are identified and maximised. The text chosen (unknown) is supposed to be of sufficient difficulty to ensure miscues will be produced. These are then categorised under various headings including omissions, insertions, substitutions and self-corrections. A number of variations of the procedure exist, which all attempt to simplify it for easier use in the classroom (e.g. Barrs *et al.* 1988; Arnold 1982; Sheridan 1982; Moon 1984; Graham and Kelly 1997; Wilde 2000). In essence, the teacher selects a text, photocopies it, explains the process to the child and listens to the child, helping where necessary and noting all miscues. Finally the teacher asks the child about what has been read. The miscues are noted in, or translated into, standard symbols (if a tape has been used) and these are then analysed to identify:

- positive strategies, which do not change the meaning of the text – e.g. reading on in order to work out a word, self-correcting;

- negative strategies, which do change the meaning – e.g. reading words uncorrected despite the disruption to the meaning, reading non-words or grapho-phonically similar words that do not make sense.

In noting the patterns of errors, teachers are able to identify areas that need further teaching and explicit intervention and development.

The running record is a simplified version of a miscue analysis and was devised by Clay (1985) and is used in KS1 SATs, although in this context the errors are scored rather than analysed in detail. It is most useful with younger learners. A record is made summarising the strategies the child is using (contextual, syntactic, grapho-phonic), and the child's comprehension, response, fluency, self-correction and expression. In essence the procedure involves the following:

- the teacher selects a known/familiar text, and copies a passage from it;
- the teacher reads aloud from the section just before the selected passage;
- the child takes over, and the teacher tries not to intervene but helps if needed;
- the teacher records miscues on his or her own copy;
- the teacher discusses the text to establish the child's understanding;
- miscues are analysed;
- targets are set.

The miscues are recorded by:

/	for each word read correctly	Ph	phonic substitutions
O	for omitted words	G	graphic substitutions
T	for told words	S	syntactic substitutions
H	for hesitation	C	contextual substitutions

Versions of a 'miscue analysis' for writing have also been devised (Bearne 1997; Fox 2000), which, like reading miscue, look at a piece of writing for meaning, at the level of the text and at sentence and word level. Again it is a lengthy procedure, but a valuable one for carefully analysing those children whose work gives particular cause for concern. Bearne (1997) suggests observing the child at times during the writing and then spending time hearing the child read their writing and discussing it with them. Observational notes on their readiness to start, ability to settle and use of word book or friend could be recorded. In the discussion the teacher elicits the child's responses to questions about the process of writing, purpose/intention, audience and form, and avoids pointing to areas for improvement. The analysis of the writing could be in relation to a framework (Barrs *et al.* 1988; Fox 2000; Graham 1995) or in relation to Bearne's (1997) recommendations. However the writing is analysed, conclusions drawn need to feed into future action.

Miscue analysis in writing

- Writing behaviour
- The process of writing
- Purpose/intention

- Audience/readership
- Structure/form
- Technical features

(Bearne 1997)

Self-assessment

For formative assessment to be productive, pupils should be trained in self-assessment so that they can understand the main purposes of their learning and thereby grasp what they need to do to achieve.
(Black and William 1998)

Children's reflective capabilities are a significant dimension of learning, for it is through reflection and talk that understandings are synthesised, affirmed and set within a wider context. Reflecting on ideas, on process and product, and articulating their thinking, however tentative, can help children take more responsibility for their learning, and appreciate the active part they can play in it. This reflectiveness relates to the 'learner's developing capacity to reflect on her/his language and language uses' (Barrs *et al.* 1988). The capacity to reflect consciously on what is known and to begin to make evaluative comments needs to be taught, modelled and planned in an integrated manner, not seen separately as merely one aspect of assessment procedures, or a routine exercise to be gone through.

Individual and shared reflection underpin effective learning, and self-assessment is built on this informed and reflective stance. Self-assessment can help children gain a better understanding of what they have achieved and what they want to achieve and this supports their move towards increasing independence. As the 1998 National Curriculum document noted, 'it should be given due weight as part of the evidence towards the teachers' internal assessment' (DES 1988a). Children need to be given time and support if their reflective capacity is to be honed, and they are to take more responsibility for the evaluation of their own work. It will help if they regularly:

- consider the extent to which they achieved the learning objectives set;

- identify and discuss what they learned (e.g. in this week, in this unit of work, about traditional tales);

- think about what they have enjoyed and what they found more difficult;

- negotiate their targets for development.

It is recognised that cognitive skills such as language competence and memory, and psychological development (children who fear failure or who prefer to attribute their difficulties to factors outside themselves), will place constraints on the ability to self-reflect. However, reflection and self-assessment can take many forms and may involve representing thinking in a variety of ways, for example through drawings and diagrams. Literacy conferences and guided learning contexts offer ideal opportunities to profile self-assessment and record the children's views, negotiating appropriate ways forward. However, whole-class opportunities for reflection/evaluation also need to be seized, for example in discussing a child's piece of writing, or modelling response partnerships.

In addition, in regularly sharing the termly learning intentions with the class and in stating the learning objectives of, for example, a unit of work, a teaching session or a piece of work, the teacher is making explicit to the children the focus of the work, and the criteria by which it will be assessed. The purpose of the work needs to be meaningful and clearly explained to the class, as research into effective teachers of literacy clearly highlighted (Medwell *et al.* 1998). Children can become involved in identifying success criteria through discussion with the teacher, prompted perhaps through the question 'How will I know you have achieved it?' The discussion that ensues can help learners to articulate the nature of the task before them, and become more conscious of the complex word, sentence, and text level features within it. If the objective is framed in 'child-speak' (Clarke 1998) and a clear purpose for the work is given, then children can more easily evaluate their own or others' achievement. This structured approach, however, suits highly focused tasks but needs to be supplemented. Children do demonstrate achievement outside the aims set, and this must be recognised and celebrated alongside intended learning outcomes. As always with inclusive educational practice, balance in terms of pedagogical practice is a key issue.

The challenge of target setting

There are a wealth of challenges involved in target setting. These include:

- Targets linked to a curriculum based on learning objectives tend to reflect an approach to learning that is 'hierarchical and reductionist, adopting a step by step approach to learning and embracing a product ideology' (Goddard 1977).

- By stressing the need to write to 'specific, measurable, achievable, relevant and timely' (SMART) targets (Lloyd and Berthelot 1992), LEAs and schools have encouraged an emphasis on the skills and knowledge aspects of learning. Understanding and attitude, which may be considered to be equally important – particularly for transfer of learning and the development of autonomy – are not so easily translated into SMART format as desired outcomes cannot be always be specifically prescribed in advance (Tod *et al.* 1998). An over-emphasis on curriculum based SMART targets may be giving learners a measurable, but impoverished, education.

- By setting learning outcomes in advance as targets, non-targeted learning that arises from literacy experience, for example a creative or emotional response, is likely to remain undocumented and even unrecognised.

- In order to support the target-setting process, QCA (1998c) have developed 'P' scales for SEN pupils, which dovetail into existing schemes (Early Learning Goals, Base Line Assessment and National Curriculum learning outcomes). These have been further broken down into smaller steps (PIVATS) to support the inclusion of pupils with complex learning needs (Attfield 2000). This suggests that an 'inclusive curriculum' can be created by simple adaptation to what is in place and that learners will feel included even if they are working on targets that have been broken down so much that they bear little resemblance to their original source.

- Targets place an emphasis on product at the expense of process. They emphasise the 'what' but not the 'how', and are not therefore necessarily enabling for pupils with diverse needs. For example, pupils with language difficulties are often given literacy targets that cover the written aspects of literacy rather than speaking and listening simply because written language skills are easier to assess.

- The incessant national drive to raise literacy standards can narrow mindsets and focus assessment and target setting on merely the manageable or assessable areas of literacy learning.

- Targets over the year need to be set in all three language modes, or integrated targets used.

- Target setting can become unmanageable in large classes unless the paperwork, planning and recording are feasible, integrated targets are set, and a whole-school approach is adopted.

- The use of given targets (e.g. using NLS teaching objectives) and commercially produced target planners risks pupils being continually assessed against 'normative' models. This use of 'norm' comparison has been criticised on the grounds that it contributes to the exclusion of those pupils who fall outside the normal range (Booth 2000).

- Target setting and achievement in inclusive settings should pay credence to issues of involvement and ownership. Currently target-setting procedures for schools are prescribed by the government and translated to schools by their LEAs as imposed requirements.

In essence schools need to self-assess and retain what they consider to be the strengths of their current target-setting procedures for literacy. They also need to identify whether their practices for target setting conflict with the development of inclusive practices and use the information from the exercise to make changes to their procedures.

Models for target setting

There are various approaches to target setting depending on the strategic response decided on by the school to meet LEA/national targets. Most schools have to balance planning to meet overall school targets with planning to raise individual attainment, particularly for SEN pupils who receive additional resourcing. Figure 3 describes two approaches. The top-down model starts with an identification of school needs and follows with an attempt to identify which groups can be given additional support in order to enable them to cross into the predicted 'Level 4' criteria. Those deemed to fall outside this category are given IEPs that can often contain targets taken from lower age group curriculum levels or 'P' levels (QCA 1998c). The bottom-up model starts with the individual's current level of functioning and seeks to move all pupils forward from the baseline by giving each pupil short-term easily achievable targets that feed into medium and longer term class and group targets. Both approaches have pitfalls. The top-down model is focused towards 'average 80 per cent' attainment with an emphasis on individual provision for those pupils who experience difficulties with literacy.

The bottom-up model involves teachers in considerable target setting and monitoring and may be unmanageable. Neither model operates an inclusive approach to target setting, which is why some literacy practitioners are developing alternative approaches such as that described in Figure 4.

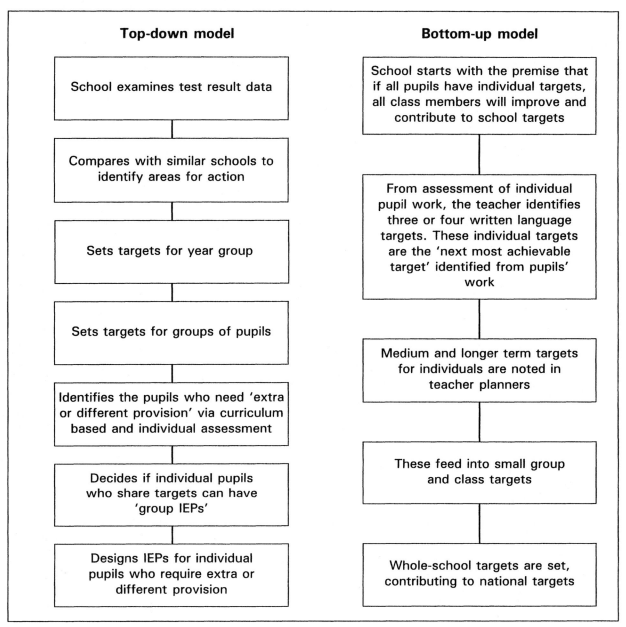

Figure 3 Models for target setting

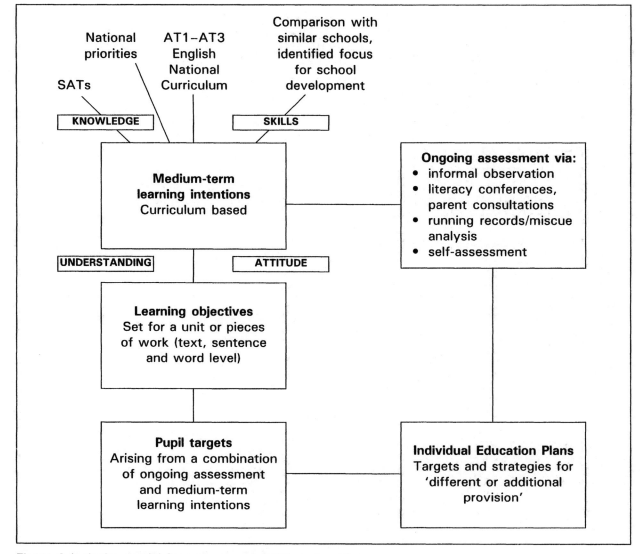

Figure 4 Inclusive model for assessment and target setting

This model acknowledges the diverse range of information that feeds into the medium term learning intentions. It will include government priorities, curriculum requirements and the school development plan as well as information gathered from ongoing assessment tools such as literacy conferences, parent consulations and observation. So the medium term learning intentions can critically encompass not only knowledge and skills but also understanding and attitude. The learning objectives derived from these overall intentions will relate to a unit of work or to individual pieces of work and need to be explicitly shared with the children.

The pupil targets, whether individual or small group, arise from a combination of ongoing teacher assessment and the medium term intentions. Such targets are often therefore broader and richer than specific learning objectives that are related to individual pieces of work. The specific learning objectives are essential in order to work towards the medium term learning intentions and are planned by the teacher. The pupil targets however will be negotiated and agreed through literacy conferences, guided work and/or parent consultation.

Assessment and target setting: Institutional self-review

- Are summative measures driving curriculum content and formative assessment? What can be done to mediate/mitigate this situation?

- To what extent are each class's medium-term learning intentions balanced across reading, writing, speaking and listening, and at text, sentence and word level?

- Are the learning objectives attached to individual pieces/units of work made explicit and shared with the children?

- Is each learning objective and its purpose made clear to the children?

- How is the involvement of the learner harnessed to encourage reflection and self-evaluation?

- How are personal targets negotiated and monitored for balance?

- How are parents and children involved in the target setting, assessment and review process?

- How are children's attitudes and motivation in literacy learning recognised, recorded and developed?

- How frequently are focused diagnostic tools employed to establish in more detail particular children's strategies and the difficulties they encounter?

- In what ways do the personal targets or learning objectives encourage the development of collaborative learning skills?

- How are diverse and different outcomes recognised and valued?

Assessment and target setting: Ideas for action

Model and teach reflection and evaluation

In shared and guided contexts and through the plenary in the literacy hour and in other contexts, model the process of reflection. Embed this in purposeful contexts and ensure that reflection involves learning through language and learning about language, and all the language modes.

Profile peer assessment

Use a range of peer assessment strategies through sharing and reflecting on work collaboratively. These might include talk detectives, storytelling reviews, response partners, reading partners or review pairs. Honour and recognise their comments.

Integrate learning intentions

One way of supporting the development of inclusive teaching is to consider how literacy, PSHE and citizenship intentions can be linked and to share teaching ideas, choice of texts, activities, etc. Examples are given in Table 4, but the opportunities for this type of integration across the curriculum are rich and varied.

Table 4

Learning targets relating to the teaching objectives of the NLSF (QCA 1999a)	Non-statutory guidelines for pupils KS2 pupils in PSHE and citizenship	Activity/teaching method to support meeting of 'integrated intention'?
Recognise the way writers present issues and points of view in fiction and non-fiction texts (Year 4, term 3).	Realise the consequences of anti-social and aggressive behaviours, such as bullying and racism, on individuals and communities.	Develop a unit of work on Anne Fine's *The Angel of Nitshill Road*.
Understand how different layers of meaning are created e.g. through the use of different viewpoints, narrators, characters, and use of such features in their own writing (Year 6, term 1).	Resolve differences by looking at alternatives, making decisions and explaining choices.	Use forum theatre regularly in drama to create particular scenes. In this, individuals intervene in it and reflect on choices, decisions and different perspectives.
New NC Speaking and Listening Programmes of Study (POS) (DfEE 1999a)		
Ask relevant questions. Clarify, extend and follow up ideas. Respond to others appropriately taking into account what they say.	Talk about their opinions and explain their views on issues that affect themselves and society.	Hold a debate on an issue identified by the class or in drama develop a whole-class improvisation in which the key issue is explored in role.
Deal politely with opposing points of view and enable discussion to move on.	Pupils should be taught that their actions affect themselves and others, and to care about other people's feelings and try to see things from their point of view.	Develop empathy and understanding through working in role alongside the teacher (also in role), challenging others' views in the fictional context.

Identify clear learning intentions in the medium-term plan

Start the assessment process with two or three clearly stated major learning intentions related to the genre focus and NLSF text, word and sentence level recommendations for the term. Include AT1 too.

Plan work with specific learning objectives

Based on the major learning intentions in the context of the NLSF, plan work with clear learning objectives that work towards achievement of the class's learning intentions. These objectives may relate to a week's work and/or to individual pieces of work.

Plan for breadth in learning objectives

Monitor whether the learning objectives set for work reflect all three attainment targets and encompass a balance of work at text, sentence and word level.

Profile the purpose of learning objectives

State the purpose of the learning objective in shared work and revisit it in the lesson plenary, with the children providing evidence of what was learned, what they found hard, how they solved the challenges they met and significantly what was the purpose of the work. Make connections to other work explicit; for example, 'It is important for us to explain our views, then the reader will understand why Jan Mark is your favourite author. Try to give two or three reasons at least'.

Record the stated learning objective

Children can record the learning objective on each piece of work or the teacher can note this in the class learning log (a big book, prominently displayed). The objective can be stated as an aim: for example, 'Aim: to find synonyms for speech verbs'; or 'Aim: to make the reader afraid of The Demon Headmaster'. These can also be written as a question: 'Can we find synonyms for speech verbs?'; 'Can we make the reader feel afraid of The Demon Headmaster?'

Reflect on the learning objective

In reviewing the work the learning objective is revisited explicitly. Children can indicate their evaluation of a piece of work in several ways: through smiley faces; or through review pairs, in which children meet to discuss the learning objective and their work; or through response partners, when after reading each others' work, children respond orally and/or in writing.

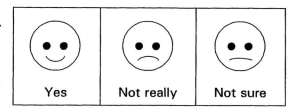

Marking the learning objective

The teacher's response should be targeted to include explicit reference to the objective, or may just be a signature to affirm the self-/peer evaluation recorded. Much will depend on the nature of the task. If it is an extended piece of writing, a fuller response to the writer and the content is essential to give value to writing as communicating meaning, and not merely demonstrating use of a particular linguistic skill.

Identify personal targets

These are related to the major learning intentions, and are focused individual or small group targets. Timescales will vary but are likely to be half termly: and related to all three language modes. These are negotiated and agreed through literacy conferences, guided work and/or parent consultation.

Use an evaluation stamp for personal target setting

In setting personal targets use an evaluation stamp to highlight targets achieved and a new target to work towards. Use this for personal target setting when conversation and negotiation of targets is not possible. One school designed their own, highlighting positive achievement, the target/s and giving space for the children to comment.

Belvedere Junior School evaluation stamp

Record personal targets accessibly

Keep these available and profiled, for example on placemats, on target cards, in flap inside the writing folder, in learning logs or on stickers.

Review personal targets for breadth

Review a sample of individual targets from both more and less experienced learners. Is breadth in evidence? Have text, word and sentence level targets been balanced over time?

Keep parents informed and involved

However regularly the targets are set, ensure they are communicated to home through, for example, homework target cards, home–school reading records, letters home for signature or consultation sessions. Suggest strategies for parental support.

Children write their own reports

Before parents' consultation evenings or at the end of term, the children write their own brief report. This is used as evidence at the consultation session. The literacy section might include:

```
We have studied several forms of writing, including _____

My favourite piece of written work was _____ because _____

My best book was _____ by _____

because _____

My recent targets were to _____

I am better at _____

I still need to work on _____
```

Design target focused consultation meetings

Agree targets with parents at consultations. For example:

```
Child's contribution:
I think I have done well at _____
I think I need to work at _____

Parents' contribution:
Experience of language/ICT at home: _____
Languages spoken: _____
Observations and concerns: _____

Teacher's contribution:
Progress in earlier targets: _____
Suggestions for future targets: _____

Agreed targets:
1. _____
2. _____
```

Plan termly literacy conferences

These could be individual or small group and seek to include: the child's views; self-assessment; range and preferences; skills and strategies; attitude and interest; a review of targets.

Establish school resources for diagnostic assessment

Create resource packs for undertaking running records/miscue analyses and agree set writing tasks for use on an annual basis in year groups, so moderation and some comparison can be developed.

Establish weekly reviews

Seek to review the week, reflecting on positive learning experiences and challenges, orally or in a letter home (Figure 5). These may not be focused on targets but profile reflection on learning. This can be undertaken for just one half-term period and their use reviewed with parents and the children.

Develop a past and present chart

Create a chart listing what the class knew about a genre/author/a topic (e.g. entymology) before working on it. This could be from the initial brainstorm on 'what I think I know about ...'. With the class, complete the second column of this 'then and now' chart to highlight progress made.

Write letters about literacy

With a new class the teacher asks them to write personal letters to him/her about their literacy, stating, for example, their likes and dislikes, range and preferences, recent improvements, favourite book, best piece of writing, parents' views. This could focus on one of the language modes only.

My week at school

This week I am especially pleased with my work on: _____

_____

because: _____

_____

Something I could have done better this week was: _____

_____

because: _____

_____

Next week I will aim to try to improve: _____

_____

by: _____

Did you achieve last week's aim? _____

How? _____

Parent's signature and comment _____

_____

_____

Figure 5 A weekly review form

Make a poster profiling evaluation questions

To support reflection and evaluation, use the poster as a prompt for teaching, modelling and discussion in whole-class and guided group work. Questions might include (adapted from Clarke 1998):

- What were you doing?

- Why were you doing this? What was the purpose of the work?

- What did you find easy?

- What was more difficult?

- What did you *do* when you were stuck?

- How did you cope? (Did you, for example, ask a friend? Or use a dictionary, spelling book, poster, or word wall? Or do something yourself? Or remember what I had said?)

- What are you most pleased about?

- What have you learnt that's new to you?

- What questions do you have about this?

Create learning logs

These self-assessment journals can take many forms and may focus on, for example, reading. Like reading journals they serve as a commentary on children's reading experiences and enable the child to develop 'relationships on papers' (Barrs and Pidgeon 1998) with their teacher. The learning log could be more general, however with sections including: records of reading/writing; evaluations of oral work, such as drama and storytelling; words to learn; weekly reviews; intentions and desires; personal past and present charts; and so on.

User attitude questionnaires

Undertake questionnaires (Figures 6, 7, 8) to collect the children's views and attitudes to one of the language modes. These can be collated to ascertain patterns or trends which need attention. A sample across the school could also be collected.

Talking/listening questionnaire

How did you learn to talk? _____
_____

Are you ever afraid/nervous about talking? _____
When? _____
_____

What do you talk about at home? _____
At school? _____

Do you talk differently to different people or in different places? _____
_____

Do you think you are a good talker/listener? _____
Why? _____
_____

Who do you know who is a good talker/listener? _____
Why? _____
_____

What do you think teacher's/my views are about talking/listening? _____

Why do we talk/listen to each other? _____

Figure 6 Talking/listening questionnaire

Reading questionnaire

Tick all those that apply:

☐ I read well   ☐ I am OK at reading   ☐ I am not very good at reading   ☐ I read because I enjoy it

☐ I often choose to read   ☐ I read because I have to   ☐ I sometimes choose to read   ☐ I rarely choose to read

	Often	Sometimes	Rarely	Never
I read to myself at home	☐	☐	☐	☐
I like listening to stories/poetry	☐	☐	☐	☐
I read comics/magazines	☐	☐	☐	☐
I read parts of newspapers	☐	☐	☐	☐
I read factual books	☐	☐	☐	☐
I read stories	☐	☐	☐	☐
I read poetry	☐	☐	☐	☐
I read television listings	☐	☐	☐	☐
I go to the library	☐	☐	☐	☐

My favourite books are: _____

My favourite author is: _____

The book I enjoyed most recently is _____

My favourite place to read is _____

How do you know which books to read? _____

Do you read with anyone at home? Who? _____

What do you read at home? _____

Why do you think reading is important? _____

Figure 7 Reading questionnaire

Writing questionnaire

Tick one:　　☐ I write well　　☐ I am OK at writing　　☐ I am not very good at writing

Is there anything you particularly like about writing? _____

_____

Is there anything you particularly dislike about writing? _____

_____

Which activities help you most as a writer?

☐ Being able to choose what to write about　　☐ Brainstorming and planning

☐ Drafting and revising　　☐ Editing and proofreading

☐ Teachers' comments on your work　　☐ Friends' comments on your work

☐ Clear learning objectives

Number your first and second choices. How do these help you? _____

_____

_____

What are your favourite kinds of writing? _____

_____

_____

Describe one piece of writing that you have been very pleased with recently, and explain why you chose this piece. _____

_____

_____

_____

_____

Do you write at home at all? What kinds of writing? _____

_____

_____

Figure 8 Writing questionnaire

Speaking and listening: Principles

School Inspection, by Raymond Wilson

'Well, what do you say?' the Inspector asked
'Just speak up! There's no need for thinking'.
'But if I don't think, how can I know
What to say? Mary answered him, blinking.

'Just blurt it out, girl! Say what you think,
Without caring what words you may use.'
'But how can I speak', said Mary, until
I've decided which words I should choose?'

'Simply say what you mean,' the Inspector groaned,
'Without all this absurd delay.'
'But how can I *tell* what I mean, Sir,
Till I've heard what I've had to say!'

As this poem amusingly demonstrates, speaking, listening and learning are closely related. Opportunities for developing speaking and listening need to be planned into the curriculum, both to develop children's confidence and competence as communicators and to enrich their ability to learn *through* talk.

> Oracy is a condition of learning in all subjects, it is not a frill but a state of being in which the whole school must operate.
>
> (Wilkinson *et al.* 1965)

The spoken word is the most accessible medium for learning and personal development. In their early years, children learn to talk through interaction with adults in a range of purposeful contexts (McTear 1981). However, the oral development documented at home is not fully sustained in school, and evidence suggests that levels of self-initiated conversation, negotiation and decision making frequently plummet in early schooling (Tizard and Hughes 1984; Wells 1985). Clearly different adult:child ratios and physical features exist in school, as well as different roles and responsibilities. Yet if teachers find out about the home language practices of their pupils, this knowledge can enable them to develop their talk further and communicate in ways that build on children's collaborative language experience and cultural practices (Brice-Heath 1983). Children need to become actively involved in their own learning and to share and shape their views and understanding through interaction with ideas and with people. Such collaborative learning encourages involvement and engagement, helps to motivate learners and can help teachers respond to individual needs.

All children have the right to participate and even those who have problems with oracy itself still benefit from interactive learning contexts, careful use of groupings and audiences, the support of other pupils and the appropriate use of specialist support, such as signing. Children who are, for example, excessively shy or lack confidence, which can hold them back from full oral engagement, still need planned opportunities for talking and learning if they are not to become 'invisible children', actively opting for mediocrity when capable of more (Pye 1988). For many children, their ability to communicate orally outstrips their ability to read and write and these learners need to utilise their strengths in oracy to overcome or compensate for other difficulties.

'School Inspection', Raymond Wilson, from *Nine O'Clock Bell*, compiled by Raymond Wilson (Kestrel 1985) © Raymond Wilson 1985, reproduced by permission of Penguin Books Ltd.

We do not know how many people are frustrated in their lives by the inability ever to express themselves adequately, or how many never develop intellectually because they lack the words with which to think and reason.   (DES 1975)

Planned speaking and listening opportunities that offer increased access to learning across the curriculum therefore need to be profiled and integrated into current provision. However, although the planning and structuring of activities is important, the interactive climate for learning, the role of the teacher and the experience of collaboration are also significant (Corden 2000). As Figure 9 from the National Oracy Project shows, collaborative learning through talk is central.

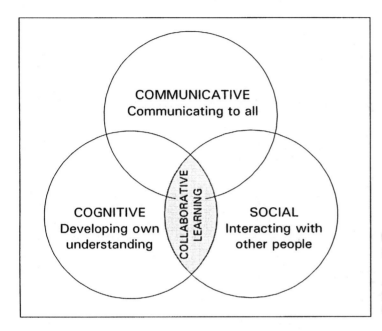

Figure 9 Speaking, listening and learning (From: Norman, K. (1990) *Teaching, Talking and Learning in Key Stages 1 and 2*. National Association of Teachers of English (NATE) and National Curriculum Council (NCC))

Learning through talk

- Talk enables us to think aloud, formulating our thoughts and opinions.

- Talk enables us to order and reorder our thinking.

- Talking and listening help us refine and develop our ideas and understanding.

- Talking and listening allow us to appreciate and discuss others' ideas and opinions.

- Talk enables us to relate new experience to previous experience and make meaning.

- Talk helps us value our ideas and our sense of self and identity.

- Talk motivates us to take more responsibility for our learning.

- Talk enables us to reflect on what we know.

Speaking and Listening in the National Curriculum

The National Curriculum (DfEE 1999a) focuses explicitly on effective speech in a range of contexts, and profiles the communicative and social aspects of oracy at the relative expense of the cognitive function. It is oriented towards educating children to speak well and listen carefully, at the expense of considering in more depth the speculative and exploratory talk that characterises much good learning (Doddington 1998).

> **Speaking and Listening: during Key Stage 1**
> Pupils learn to speak clearly, thinking about the needs of their listeners. They work in small groups and as a class, joining in discussions and making relevant points. They also learn to listen carefully to what other people are saying, so that they can remember the main points. They learn to use language in imaginative ways and express their ideas and feelings when working in role and in drama activities.
>
> **Speaking and Listening: during Key Stage 2**
> Pupils learn how to speak in a range of contexts, adapting what they say and how they say it to the purpose and the audience. Taking varied roles in groups gives them opportunities to contribute to situations with different demands. They also learn to respond appropriately to others, thinking about what has been said and the language used.
> National Curriculum (DfEE 1999a)

However, the useful QCA document *Teaching, Speaking and Listening in Key Stages 1 and 2* (1999b) does recognise the vital importance of AT1 in underpinning thinking and learning, although, in providing a framework for implementing speaking and listening requirements, it inevitably focuses on teaching objectives and not learning processes. In schools where oracy is 'a state of being' and Vygotskian principles about the social nature of learning are firmly held, the National Curriculum and the QCA framework will be welcomed and flexibly adapted, since it is quite possible to use the spoken word as a tool for enquiry, reflection and knowledge construction within the four National Curriculum (DfEE 1999a) strands: speaking; listening; group discussion and interaction; and drama activities. However, in schools where debate has focused on knowledge and skills at the expense of understanding, attitude and pedagogy, and where no teaching and learning policy exists, the requirements for AT1 may be perceived as an additional planning burden, constrained by time. In these contexts, the gap between the evident value of talk and the day-to-day reality that children encounter may continue to be marked. Even today some children are silenced by some forms of teaching.

Speaking and listening and the National Literacy Strategy

> Good oral work enhances pupils' understanding of language in both oral and written forms and of the way language can be used to communicate. It is also an important part of the process through which pupils read and compose texts.
> NLS (DfEE 1998)

Although within the NLSF there are no specific teaching objectives for oracy, the framework has the potential to promote interactive teaching and involve all the National Curriculum elements of AT1. However, as a result of the plethora of objectives at text, sentence and word level, the speed of implementation, time constraints and teacher confidence, the literacy hour has, in some schools, been delivered to children and not confidently developed by teachers (Frater 2000). The emphasis on literacy instruction and the need to cover the syllabus provided in the framework has led some teachers to inform, instruct, demonstrate and deliver knowledge, rather than develop children's understanding. Such a literal reading of what is required, if translated into practice, ignores how children learn, or at the very least what is known about the role of talk in learning. Opportunities certainly exist to integrate oral work into the literacy hour, to create interactive examinations of texts and to develop enquiry based learning, but the quantity of objectives and predominance of whole-class teaching can challenge and restrict practice.

Active involvement in their own literacy learning is the right of each child and through shared and guided work all children need to be prompted to engage, respond and interact. But without a deeper understanding of the role of talk in literacy learning and an appropriate interactive pedagogy to develop this, teacher talk can take centre stage and transmission teaching of the chalk-and-talk variety can be reaffirmed. Particular individuals, who are both confident of their views and able to articulate them, can easily dominate whole-class work. If this is sustained over time, it encourages passivity in the very individuals who most need interaction and engagement. The NLS does acknowledge the significance of engaging literacy teaching or, as they call it, 'literacy instruction'.

The most successful teaching is:

- **discursive**: characterised by high quality oral work

- **interactive**: pupils' contributions are encouraged, expected and extended

- **well paced**: there is a sense of urgency, driven by the need to make progress and succeed

- **confident**: teachers have a clear understanding of the objectives

- **ambitious**: there is optimism about and high expectations of success

NLS (DfEE 1998b)

However, to develop such practice, professionals need more than imposed teaching objectives and explicit class and school targets. Detailed knowledge of the children and their needs and interests is absolutely essential, as is considerable knowledge about how children learn and the social nature of learning. The pressure of league tables, measurable outcomes, accountability and increasing prescription is taking its toll, yet teachers need time to develop their pedagogical understanding and consider the influence of their teaching styles on children's access to learning.

Teaching styles and teacher talk

Although a rationale for the importance of talk is widely accepted in the profession, it is another matter to operate in line with this rationale on a daily basis, especially in an overcrowded timetable. Research suggests that many teachers implicitly constrain interaction to maintain control of both the content and outcome of discussions (Edwards and Furlong 1978; Mercer 1995). Driven by results and with the product, not the process, currently being foregrounded, teachers are likely to maintain or re-establish the dominant pattern of teacher-centred instruction in order to ensure curriculum coverage. Even teachers who seek to provide opportunities for collaboration and investigation are compromised, since they have to ensure that what their pupils learn conforms to the predetermined knowledge enshrined and tested by the curriculum (Edwards and Mercer 1987). However, teachers can modify their style of talk (Wood and Wood 1989) and the time devoted to whole-class work could well be harnessed to model genuinely exploratory talk about text and to demonstrate tentativeness and genuine interest in others' views as well as prompt collaboration (Barnes and Todd 1977). Informal conversations in pairs can enable all children to voice their thoughts to a friend, to think aloud and articulate their own understanding as well as hear someone else's perspective. Feedback to the whole class may then involve a wider than usual number of voices and increased participation is prompted. Likewise, investigative techniques can be a powerful tool for learning, since through problem-solving activities, children can develop independence and explore and discuss their own and others' ideas.

Teachers using hypothetical talk, and modelling a speculative and open stance, are also more likely to be employing open-ended questions (Cambourne 2000; Haworth 1992; Wood 1992), which create more cognitive demands and facilitate analytical thinking. Increasingly divergent and evaluative questions need to be woven into teachers' repertoires since predominantly open questions and questions that push learners to meta-textual levels of response have been found to contribute to effective literacy learning (Cambourne 2000). Constant recapping, demonstrating and summarising during teacher-led discussions are also noted as key features of effective practice. While teacher talk strategies such as questioning, modelling, scaffolding and reconstructing lie at the heart of good teaching, it must be remembered that these are closely related to the listening ear and observational skills of the teacher and frequently reflect the climate and ethos established in the classroom. Relationships are central to any learning encounter and mutual respect is needed to ensure that inclusive education is offered to all.

Teachers not only need to provide children with time to think through their responses, they also need to *reflect on their own talk*; monitoring their talk through, for example, taping a shared reading/ writing session and evaluating the ratio of adult:child talk, the kinds of questions or comments used and the nature of the children's contributions. There is a wide range of talk types that can be adopted:

- *mirror words or insights:* reflect what you've heard – 'so are you saying that ...?';
- *model speculation:* acknowledge your open stance – 'I'm never sure if ... I was wondering ...';
- *allow thinking time:* pause, let silence reign;
- *show you are interested:* praise specifically and authentically – 'you describe that book so well, I really want to read it ...';
- *clarify ideas:* highlight main ideas – 'we seem to have identified three issues';
- *encourage elaboration:* invite more detail – 'tell me more about ...';
- *suggest alternatives:* explain options – 'you could try ... or ... which do you think will be more useful to you ...?';
- *make personal connections:* share your own views – 'that reminds me of ...';
- *voice your affective responses:* declare your feelings – 'that story made me feel ...';
- *encourage tentativeness:* validate uncertainty, acknowledge alternatives – 'that's a possibility, I wonder';
- *deflect decision making:* hand back the responsibility – 'what do you ... think, feel, want to change?'

Reflecting on speaking and listening

Teachers need to help children reflect on their competence and confidence as talkers and listeners, to widen their knowledge of how spoken language is used in society and to develop their awareness of the role of talk in learning. By reflecting on talk, teachers can raise the profile and status of talking and listening in their classrooms and enable children to consider, review and evaluate their own spoken contributions as well as those of others. Much of this work will be embedded in purposeful contexts, which involve the children in making linguistic choices and gradually becoming more conscious of these choices. Through talking about talk, and sharing their perceptions of its value and through reflecting on the spoken word in various contexts, children can become more aware of its use and simultaneously make more effective use of it (Reid *et al.* 1982; Wegerif and Mercer 1996; Corden 2000). This will involve learners in various activities noted in Table 5 and in:

- reflecting on their own talk;
- reflecting on other's language use;
- reflecting on the construction of language.

As pupils learn how to work together, they need to be guided to develop strategies to keep on task, share the work and negotiate decisions. There is evidence that children who are aware of the purpose, nature and value of group discussion, benefit more from such discussion (Edwards and Mercer 1987; Sheeran and Barnes 1991). In reflecting on their own discussions children develop their understanding of the characteristic features of talk and how these contribute to discussion (Hardman and Beverton 1993).

An essential element of successful groupwork therefore is the development of children's meta-discoursal awareness: that is, their understanding of group interaction and their ability to monitor, control and reflect on their use of language.

(Corden 2000)

Table 5 Reflecting on spoken language (adapted from Norman, K. (1990) *Teaching, Talking and Learning in Key Stages 1 and 2*. National Association of Teachers of English (NATE) and National Curriculum Council (NCC))

Reflecting on their own talk	• confidence and competence in a range of contexts • choice and appropriateness • oral histories • using language to learn • targets for personal development
Reflecting on others' language use	• how people talk differently in different situations and social groups • how people use language for different purposes • how people use language to learn • languages, regional and social variations in accent and dialect • the use of Standard English
Reflecting on the construction of language	• different kinds of talk • differences between spoken and written language • the history of languages and language development

Ground rules for groupwork need to be identified and agreed on and a range of groupings used, such as friendship, interest, single gender, mixed gender. Cooperative groups (when pupils each have a separate but related task and work towards a joint outcome) can be particularly productive in terms of task-related talk (Bennet and Dunne 1992). Using a tape recorder for drafting can create a text for the children to reflect upon. Spoken language investigations can complement investigational work into the forms and features of written text and can include examinations into the wide variety of dialects, accents and languages used by the children, their families and the community. Such language awareness programmes can provoke reflection and consideration of oracy alongside literacy and can raise the profile of talk in the children's eyes.

Speaking and listening: Institutional self-review

- Does the school have a teaching and learning policy that acknowledges the role of talk in learning?

- How actively involved are all the children in the literacy hour?

- Is there a balance between oral and written activities in independent work?

- Is clear provision made for learning through drama?

- How is planning for speaking and listening recorded on medium-/short-term plans?

- Is progression in speaking and listening planned for, monitored and evaluated?

- How are the children's oral competencies assessed, recorded and reported upon?

- Are staff aware of the influence of their talk repertoire, in particular their questioning skills, and the need to model tentativeness and allow thinking time

- How are the children's and their parents' perceptions of talk strengthened?

- Does the profile of oracy need to be raised?

Speaking and listening: Ideas for action

Organisational strategies for group work

Options for grouping

- *Friendship groups:* children choose.

- *Randomly selected groups:* number the children 1–8 and regroup, or use book jigsaws made from a colour photocopy of the front cover (children to form groups of those holding pieces to the same jigsaw).

- *Teacher selected groups:* sort for a purpose in response to ability, age, relationships, and so on.

- *Personal interest groups:* children express interest in topic and groups are formed.

- *Physical proximity:* gather groups of children together quickly from the carpet or during a drama session.

- *Doubling pairs:* initially pairs work together and then join to make groups of four.

Group activities

- *Rainbows:* When a group has worked together, for example on predicting the end to a folk tale, each member of the group is given a colour and new groups are formed, in which each child can retell their group's ending scenario.

- *Snowballs:* Individuals note down two views/ideas on an issue, then pairs are formed and their views exchanged, pared down or rephrased as two statements. Groups of four then work together, again discussing the statements and agreeing two final statements. The snowball can be enlarged even further if desired.

- *Jigsaws:* The children in 'home' groups agree that each member will find out about one aspect of the topic and become an 'expert' in this. Groups of 'would be' experts join together for this work and later return from the 'expert' groups to their 'home' group to report on their findings.

- *Envoys:* One member of each group is sent to visit another group, to ask questions, to find out information/ideas, or to explain what their group has done.

- *Listening triads:* In groups of three, children take up the roles of talker, questioner and recorder. The talker talks about the chosen subject. The questioner seeks further detail and clarification. The recorder makes notes and reports back in the triad and perhaps to the class.

- *Think – Pair – Share:* Children consider an issue individually, then explain their ideas to a partner and discuss these. Pairs then report back to the main group/class.

- *Reviewing partners:* At the end of a session, children pair up with a child from another group who has not been engaged in the same activity, they describe what they've done, how they did it, what has been achieved and what they have learnt.

- *Gallery walks:* After groups have worked on a common task and produced a piece of writing – for example a concept map, a list of key issues, or a brainstorm – each group tours the others' work, moving as a group and discussing alternative responses, ideas and so on. On returning to their work, the group add ideas to their work if they wish.

Speaking to different audiences

Such audiences might include: their peer group; members of another class or key stage; staff; LSAs; dinner supervisors; parents; visitors (e.g. police, authors, Theatre in Education (TIE) groups); and governors. Many of these opportunities will be informal and spontaneous, while others will be planned and involve the children in preparation and rehearsal prior to an event. A number of activities are highlighted in this section, based on the QCA (DfEE 1999b) document. Alongside circle time (serving as it does a range of social and emotional purposes), these provide opportunities for children to engage, interact and become involved.

Oral storytelling

Storytelling enables children to develop their confidence and sense of self and identity. It can lead towards a storytelling event and undoubtedly enriches story writing as well as AT1 (Grainger 1997).

- Personal anecdotes, memories and events are told in pairs. These may be given titles, which are displayed, and the stories are retold in other contexts.

- Create a 'lucky dip' of traditional tale titles from the class's repertoire. One child from a pair dips in to remove a title and the pair work on a joint oral retelling.

- Divide the class into two groups, and tell or read a different tale to each group. Provide support and practice time and later pair up children from the two groups to exchange their stories.

- Create a whole-class story circle and use a symbolic token (related to the tale) to pass around. Whoever holds the symbol tells the next part of the tale.

- Groups retell a tale with the use of stick, glove or finger puppets. They sequence the tale and use expressive voices and repetitive story language.

- Create a storytelling bazaar. Groups, pairs or individuals prepare to tell their tales to others (avoid well-known tales). Set up the room with storytellers' chairs or make dens, using drapes and cloths. Invite younger or parallel classes and adults.

Read aloud and performance

In reading poetry, stories, playscripts, informative texts or their own work aloud, children learn to bring the text to life and tailor their reading or performance to the audience and purpose of the occasion. Use assemblies, open afternoons, school shows and brief performances or in other classrooms.

- Groups read a story together on tape, each taking parts or reading the narrator's lines. This could involve a rereading of a class literacy text, with considerable expression and intonation.

- Create story tapes for a younger audience with musical denotation of the page turning and a number of very well told texts performed on the tape.

- Run a Book 'Wander, Wave, Stop, Swap and Tell' (A Book WWSST). Each child takes a favourite book and walks about the room, holding it up and looking at others' books. The teacher halts the action and the children swap books with the nearest child and tell each other briefly about their book. The Book WWSST then resumes.

- Perform a class poem (preferably with a choral refrain) to others, with groups interpreting verses, adding ostinatos and the whole class joining in with the chorus.

- Groups create a choral performance of a poem together, adding percussion and movement, and using different voices for different parts.

- Perform conversational poetry in pairs or groups using the poem as a playscript and adopting the persona and voice of the character. Such poems can be found in the work of, for example, A. Alhberg, K. Wright, M. Rosen, R. Brown and T. Millum.

Giving talks/presenting arguments

Talks can be planned, rehearsed and presented individually, in pairs or small groups. Oral drafting on tape is useful to allow children to reflect on their talk, the organisation of their material and the presentation of the views expressed. Awareness of the use of gesture, volume, humour, repetition, coherent argument and resources can be heightened through such work.

- Set up individual or small group talks about chosen areas of interest, contemporary crazes, aspects of popular culture or a hobby. Visual aids can be used to interest listeners.

- Introduce 'video shorts' when individuals select a 2–3-minute extract and share these with the class, explaining their choice and stating their view of the film.

- Play the 'Sentence Game' (Chambers 1993). Groups read, discuss and reflect on a chosen picture book, and each child offers a sentence about the text that they want to tell others. Each group sorts these into a paragraph and reads this to the class, sharing favourite visuals also. The rest of the class ask questions about the text and vote to indicate whether the presentation has tempted them to read it.

- Groups present an argument with logically sequenced points and clear views on a moral issue (e.g. bullying, injustice) or a local issue of concern (e.g. an environmental issue in the community or a school concern).

- In the manner of a TV documentary or debate, focus on an issue and chair a programme as the television presenter, introducing small group presentations that offer different perspectives and alternatives.

Listening and responding

To stories or poems

- After a storytelling or reading children divide the story into three seeds, reflecting the beginning, middle and end of the tale, and draw key elements on three differently sized seed shapes. Groups of three children retell the story, watering the seeds with their words and telling part of the tale each.

- Having created their own story retelling on tape, groups listen to each other's and discuss the stories and the effects of voice, sound and music on retelling.

- In response partnerships, children listen and respond to each other's writing, commenting constructively on the strengths of their partner's work, as well as on areas that need development.

- Groups watch other groups' poetry performances or improvisations in drama and comment evaluatively, identifying and recalling main points and ideas.

- Invite a professional poet or storyteller to perform for the class and encourage the children to join in, ask questions and discuss the text's evocation.

To an adult or expert

- Each child prepares a talk on a subject of their choice, for example Pokémon, pop music, football. As experts on this subject, they respond to questions from the class or group.

- In drama, give the children expert roles, for example knowledgeable health specialists setting up a new sports centre. Throughout the drama, defer to their expertise and ask for their learned views.

- Invite a visiting expert to present information in assembly or class. The children respond to this by asking questions identifying the main points, and summarising what they have learnt.

- Listen to a radio broadcast that includes different views, and discuss and record the pros and cons expressed, or summarise and compare views shared in a drama session.

- Groups prepare to interview an adult and tape the interview, generating a list of questions and presenting the information to others.

To video or television

- Watch the title sequences of two contrasting television programmes. Respond to these, noting how the music, words and visuals shape the content, style and mood for particular audiences.

- Watch a trio of adverts and discuss the different presentation styles, presence or absence of music, characters, appeals to listener, repetition, and so on.

- Create adverts in groups and if possible video these and respond to each other's.

- Improvise short documentary style television programmes or news broadcasts, which report on an issue under investigation. Watch each group and comment on and evaluate these together.

- Watch a video or television broadcast and identify the main points shown, the key presentation features and the children's responses to it.

Discussion and group interaction

Investigating, selecting and sorting

- Teach the 'Aim – Review – Question' (ARQ) technique to monitor progress and keep on task (Hawke 1989). Any member of the group can request an ARQ if they feel uncertain of where the group is heading and wish to recap or refocus and move forward together.

- Pairs generate a list of questions about a picture book, then sort these into open and closed questions and select several for another group to answer, 'marking' their work afterwards.

- Groups identify the resources needed for a task and select and sort these appropriately.

- At the close of an activity (e.g. a maths investigation) the contributions made by group members are identified and the need to pool ideas, allocate tasks, and make decisions are discussed.

Planning, predicting and exploring

- Create a class poster with ground rules for working in groups. Highlight particular elements in different group tasks.

- Plan, discuss, try out and evaluate different ways of ensuring that everyone in the group has a turn to speak.

- Groups devise a plan for a group presentation, which might include research, writing timescales, craft or visual work to be completed, work review dates and a final rehearsal stage.

- Groups decide on roles for group members, such as leader, reporter, scribe. Review these following a given task.

- Pairs make an action plan to undertake an activity and mark off each stage when completed, seeking to meet the deadline set.

Explaining, reporting and evaluating

- Individuals take it in turns to be a 'talk detective' and listen to the group at work, making notes and commenting on their interaction afterwards.

- Individuals take it in turns to report back following small group work, discussing with the group afterwards if it was a fair summary.

- Groups listen to a taped extract of their work and comment on the contributions of group members.

- The class identifies the characteristics of good talkers and listeners and creates posters of these for classroom reference and use.

- Through improvisational drama, explore the language of disagreement and persuasive argument. Using forum theatre, note the key features and phrases used and discuss how conflicts are expressed and resolved.

Drama activities

Improvisation and role play

- Use a picture book to guide a drama, alternately reading then creating new insights through drama. Avoid re-enactment but explore the language of the unsaid.

- With the teacher in role as a local police officer, quiz the class on an allegedly missing child. Build up a sense of this child through flashbacks, hot seating and thought tracking.

- Use newspaper titles to generate ideas for classroom drama. Groups create freeze frames around the titles and then select one to investigate further.

- Receive a letter from a business manager inviting the class, as adult experts in leisure facilities, to help design a new local park. Create the park and then suffer vandalism.

- Create the next chapter in a class novel through drama, building on their knowledge of the characters, title of the chapter and the story so far. Use a range of drama conventions to dig beneath the surface of the co-authored text to make meanings and shape understanding.

Writing and performing

- During drama, pairs and groups share snippets of their improvisations with the class.

- Write in role within a drama as one of the characters; for example letters or diaries, police notes from an interview, or maps of the scene of a crime.

- Following a drama, write alongside a role from a distance; for example a magazine article, a television documentary on the issue, or a newspaper report about an incident.

- Groups script the scene they have improvised, adding stage directions and props if desired. This can be performed by another group.

- Develop forum theatre as a class, with one group improvising a difficult encounter. This is watched, interrupted and commented on by the rest of the class and then the scene is revisited using the ideas offered.

Responding to drama

- In reflective discussions throughout classroom drama, encourage the class to offer feedback, praise and suggestions to each other.

- Create group sculptures that respond to the class's drama and reflect the themes examined in it. Discuss the alternative interpretations.

- Consider characters in the drama and use different conventions to find out more about them. Discuss how hot seating, interior monologues and decision alley create new insights.

- In reflecting on a drama session discuss the drama conventions employed, such as ritual or flashback. Discuss how these created a deeper understanding of the narrative.

- Discuss live or recorded performances and identify features of the work that contributed to its effectiveness, the mood created and so on.

Reading – shared, guided and independent: Principles

The Colour of my Dreams, by Peter Dixon

I'm a really rotten reader
the worst in all the class,
the sort of rotten reader
that makes you want to laugh.

I'm last in all the readin' tests,
my score's not on the page
and when I read to teacher
she gets in such a rage.

She says I cannot form my words
she says I can't build up
and that I don't know phonics
– and don't know c-a-t from k-u-p.

They say that I'm dyxlectic
(that's a word they've just found out)
but when I get some plasticine
I know what that's about.

I make these scary monsters,
I draw these secret lands
and get my hair all sticky
and paint on all me hands.

I make these super models,
I build these smashing towers
that reach up to the ceiling
– and take me hours and hours.

I paint these lovely pictures
in thick green drippy paint
that gets all on the carpet –
and makes the cleaners faint.

I build great magic forests
weave bushes out of string
and paint pink panderellos
and birds that really sing.

I play my world of real believe
I play it every day
and teachers stand and watch me
but don't know what to say.

They give me diagnostic tests,
they try out reading schemes,
but none of them will ever know
the colour of my dreams.

As the poet Peter Dixon suggests, the uniqueness of each child needs to be acknowledged, their talents and interests identified, their reading skills and strategies assessed, and their attitude to reading and range and preferences recorded. In most cases schools do review their planned provision for readers who struggle, but targeting specific support through IEPs should not involve a narrowing of the curriculum, a reduction in the range of opportunities experienced or a diet of impoverished texts. On the contrary, a rich engaging reading curriculum is every child's entitlement, a prerequisite for developing readers who can and do choose to read independently. It is therefore encouraging that the National Curriculum requirements for reading highlight interest, enthusiasm and independence.

During Key Stage 1, pupils' *interest and pleasure in reading is developed* as they learn to read confidently and independently. They focus on words and sentences and how they fit into whole texts. They work out the meaning of straightforward texts and say why they like them or do not like them.

During Key Stage 2, pupils *read enthusiastically* a range of materials and use their knowledge of words, sentences and texts to understand and respond to the meaning. They increase their ability to read challenging and lengthy texts independently. They reflect on the meaning of texts, analysing and discussing them with others. (DfEE 1999a)

'The Colour of my Dreams', Peter Dixon, from *Lost Property Box* (Macmillan 1988), reproduced by permission of the author.

In both these National Curriculum statements, children's interest and pleasure in reading is appropriately foregrounded, for without such pleasure and enjoyment, children will not develop as readers. Books need to be read *to* children, *with* children and *by* children in order for them to make meaning and develop independence (Clay 1991a), as the NLSF acknowledges in requiring read aloud time (*to*), the literacy hour (*with*) and independent reading time (*by themselves*) (Figure 10).

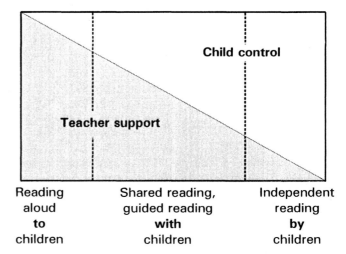

Figure 10 The relationship between teacher support and child control (adapted from Norman, K. (1990) *Teaching, Talking and Learning in Key Stages 1 and 2.* National Association of Teachers of English (NATE) and National Curriculum Council (NCC))

The planned reading curriculum needs to be predicated on interest and motivation since children need to learn what reading can do for them. A rich diet of 'involved read aloud', interactive shared reading, supported guided reading discussions and a plethora of independent reading activities must be enthusiastically offered to all readers. The experience of learning to read, and the satisfaction and rewards offered by reading, motivate learners to apply the skills they have been taught and extend their reflective reading, confidence, competence and pleasure. However there are challenges.

There is a clear danger that, in some classrooms, the important pleasures and understandings, which gradually evolve through the experience of reading could be lost if the 'penalty' for reading together is too much close textual analysis. It takes great skill and sensitivity by teachers to achieve an acceptable balance between the macro-and micro-features of particular texts.

(Furlong 1998)

It also takes great skill to teach the reading strategies and skills in an interactive manner that involves the integration of reading, writing, speaking and listening and ensures that practice is not reduced to discrete tasks that mostly relate to sentence/word level work (Frater 2000). As research into effective literacy teachers has shown, these teachers continually and explicitly make connections for their pupils between text, sentence and word level features (Medwell *et al.* 1998). A balance between these features needs to be maintained, while bearing in mind two key concerns in English teaching: the exploration of meaning and the evaluation of quality.

Text, sentence and word level work

At text level, the focus is on comprehension: response to text. This will involve both the personal responses of readers, and critical reflection on those responses in order to understand why and how the text provoked that response. Children need to examine the text closely to support and justify their response, so that 'the parts played by both the text and the reader are recognised and given status in the classroom' (Martin 1999). Understanding the purpose, audience and form of the text will contribute to this comprehension, as will sentence and word level knowledge and a range of reading strategies. If comprehension is viewed as an active, informed and reflective engagement with texts then the involvement of the children and the quality of the text are critical. Comprehension activities are essentially interactive and discursive, since through this interaction the reader uses both themselves (their life experience, personality, thoughts, interests and values), and their developing knowledge of how the text is crafted (and its conventions) to make meaning.

The organisational and structural features of text, content, themes and language, all need to be explored, attended to and understood for children to develop conscious and justified preferences and a deeper understanding of the craft of writing. A range of fiction, poetry and non-fiction must be shared, enjoyed and actively examined. A range of comprehension activities can be employed including, for example, drama, role play, performance, discussion, retelling, re-enactment with puppets, questioning and a variety of written responses. These will draw on the text as a model and illuminate its meanings and its construction. They may also seek to represent it in another genre or use it as a basis for creating an imaginative alternative or parody.

At sentence level, the focus is on the grammatical features and punctuation used and how these contribute to the meaning of the text. Work highlighting these aspects will mostly be embedded in the text itself and will involve the teacher and pupils identifying, discussing and interpreting the specific use of grammar and punctuation in different genres. While much grammatical knowledge will remain unconscious, it is important that readers can call on some explicit knowledge of grammar and punctuation when they meet a difficulty in their comprehension. Rereading to check for sense, reading on to the end of the sentence and so on, are some of the many self-correction strategies that readers need to learn. Active participation and involvement is essential to make reading–writing connections explicit (Corden 2000). Through these activities children can learn more about the linguistic features and this understanding can be transferred to their own writing. In attending closely to a shared text and noticing, say, exclamation marks and discussing how they are used, children can identify these in other texts (particularly their own reading book), and try them out in writing. As with all language skills, however, it is likely that young or inexperienced readers' appreciation of punctuation will precede production, but with contextualised teaching that encourages discovery, discussion, participation and investigation in shared, guided and independent contexts, their appropriate use of it will grow. Children receive mixed messages from printed matter around them. For example, Oxford Reading Tree uses single quotation marks but many schools teach the use of double quotation marks; 'sixty-six and ninety-nine' (Scott 1997). In one book sample, 74 per cent of the children's texts studied had sentences that ended at the end of a line (Robinson and Hall 1996). Such issues need to be attended to in selecting texts for shared work.

At word level, the focus is on the teaching of phonics; sounds and spelling. Grapho-phonic decoding skills will be taught, practised and applied in shared and guided reading, and in time set aside for this purpose. This involves the explicit teaching of phonic skills, word recognition, graphic knowledge and vocabulary at KS1, and spelling and vocabulary work at KS2. Again, empty mechanical exercises are to be avoided and engaging focused activities are recommended. Some of this work will be drawn out of shared texts, and some will be undertaken separately using investigations, explorations and language play in quick 'game' based learning encounters. A high profile structured approach to phonics teaching is articulated in the NLSF, which builds on the work of Adams (1990), who concluded that successful teaching approaches include both systematic code instruction and the reading and writing of meaningful text. The need for grapho-phonic teaching is clear (e.g. Beard 1993; Dombey 1998a) and an inclusive approach is argued for (Bielby 1998; Dombey 1999). This would include onset and rime and chunking (e.g. Goswami and Bryant 1991; Goswami 1999), one-to-one relationships (e.g. Watson and Johnson 1998; McGuiness 1998) and the study of morphemes. A useful conceptual framework for phonics learning is provided by Frith (1985), who argues that there are three stages in children's progress in reading and spelling:

- the logographic phase – whole word recognition, and more attention to the letters that words are composed of, but not yet associated with the speech sound;

- the alphabetic phase – of onset learn about the alphabet letters and correspondence, awareness and rime, and learning by analogy;

- the orthographic phase – no longer process new words bit by bit, the major spelling patterns are internalised.

Frith (1985)

From this framework explicit whole-to-part phonics instruction has grown, teaching parts of the words after a story has been read to, with and by children, rather than before the story is read (Moustafa 1999). Children must receive balanced phonics instruction and need to be encouraged to see patterns, draw inferences and make inductions and analogies for themselves, so they will be equipped with a systematic but flexible grapho-phonic approach to word identification, which enables them to take an active role in their own learning. As the NLS argues:

> Phonics can and should be taught in interesting and active ways that engage young children's attention, are relevant to their interests and build on their experiences.   NLS (DfEE 1998b)

All word level work should be relevant to learning needs, involve explicit teaching and demonstration, investigation and enquiry, a synthesis of understanding and practice and consolidation. In learning to spell, for example, children need to be encouraged to investigate words, to discover rules and definitions for themselves through problem solving and to accept responsibility for their own learning. In studying words in shared reading, spelling patterns and meanings of word structures become more explicit, and children can develop a stronger word consciousness, which builds on their use of a range of reading and spelling strategies.

The reading environment and the texts

The reading environment and the texts made available to children make a substantive difference to their reading development. However, teachers must not confuse the provision of a wealth of quality texts in a print rich environment with the teaching of reading, for books are a medium, not a method. But without motivating materials and a physical as well as social profile for reading, readers are not easily tempted into persisting in the enterprise. Recent TTA commissioned research showed that three main features characterise quality literacy environments: presence, function and use by the children (Medwell *et al.* 1998). In the effective teachers' classrooms, the physical presence and variety of resources was marked (e.g. listening centres, literate role play areas and displays of books, word games, labels, posters of instruction and support); these had clear functions and were constantly in use by both teachers and children. Such reading environments fostered independence and prompted children to use the resources available, while also carrying a clear message about the significance of literacy and the pleasure available in both fiction and non-fiction.

The role of the text itself in the reading process has been highlighted in the work of Meek (1988), who argues that texts can teach children about layers of meaning, offering untaught lessons about inference, deduction, irony and viewpoint. Such early reading lessons lay strong foundations for later reading. The nature of the texts offered to children has historically profiled theories of reading development, theories that have mostly reflected either the salience of low-level information, the 'small shapes' in reading, and/or high-level information, the 'big shapes' in reading (Rumelhart 1976). However, as a consequence of the NLS and additional funding, schools can now draw on a wider range of texts for reading aloud and shared, guided and independent reading, choosing texts that reflect their children's cultures, languages and interests. What is clear is that children need to meet meaningful, memorable and enjoyable texts that prompt them to join in the reading, tempt them to reread, and support and reward their endeavours. Teachers undoubtedly need an extensive knowledge of children's literature in order to select powerful texts for teaching reading and learning about literature and life.

For EAL learners, who are both learning to read and learning English, and for less experienced readers, the supportive nature of the text and its interest level are very important. Personal response to text is at the heart of all reading, so these children in particular need texts that stimulate their engagement, reward their labours and extend their understanding. Authors such as Allan Ahlberg, Jez Alborough, Sarah Hayes, Jeanne Willis and Jonathon Long deserve to be read widely for their strongly rhythmic and engagingly illustrated texts. Likewise, the work of Michael Morpurgo, Dick King Smith, Anne Fine, Jacqueline Wilson, Laurence Anholt, and Berlie Doherty, to mention but a few other contemporary writers, need to be shared with readers for their emotionally powerful, sensitive and sometimes humorous writing. In recent years, the work of Fox (1996), Doonan (1993) and Cliff-Hodges *et al.* (2000) has shown how quality picture books can specifically contribute to the reading experience of older readers. Examples might include *The Green Children* by Kevin Crossley Holland, *Way Home* by Libby Hawthorne, *The Dog that Dug* by Jonathon Long or *Voices in the Dark* by Anthony Browne. Some books that overtly play with particular features of grammar and punctuation are extremely useful if they are powerful enough to withstand scrutiny and still offer delight. Examples include *Tell us a Story* by Allan Ahlberg, *Knock Knock Who's There?* by Anthony Browne and *What's the Time, Mr Wolf* by Colin and Jacqui Hawkins. The *Core Book List* is recommended since it provides a list of poetry, non-fiction, short stories and novels, all of which have been specifically chosen to support children who are still inexperienced KS2 readers or who are having some difficulty (Centre for Language in Primary Education (CLPE) 2000). Teachers know from experience that the books they choose to share make a difference to the children's engagement, motivation, satisfaction, and involvement, and the success of the planned reading curriculum depends to some extent on the resources upon which the teaching is based.

The Reading Curriculum

All children need:	*So teachers need to offer:*
1. To hear texts read well aloud and experience their rhythms, tunes and sentence structures.	An engaging read aloud programme.
2. To experience targeted opportunities to progress as readers.	Formative assessment of reading strategies, range, response, attitude and tailored teaching.
3. To develop reading strategies at text, sentence and word level.	Teaching with clear teaching objectives (read aloud, shared, guided and independent).
4. To make use of their reading experience in written work.	An integrated reading/writing curriculum.
5. To practise reading and responding in supportive contexts.	Regular reading opportunities of a diverse nature.
6. Access to a variety of high quality, motivating and memorable texts.	Quality text provision from a wide range of genre.
7. To browse and choose, developing preferences and reflecting on their development.	Explicit support for book selection, promotion and reflection on reading.
8. Time, support and encouragement at home.	Parental involvement and effective partnerships.
9. Clear environmental messages about the significance and purpose of reading/writing.	Print-rich classrooms, which are used to profile and develop literacy in action.

Reading aloud: Principles

To stop reading to children is to deny them one of the most basic and continuing motivations to literacy.

(Holdaway 1979)

Reading aloud *to* children is the foundation stone of teaching reading, since children's pleasure and involvement precedes their full understanding of the text read. Provision of regular reading aloud widens children's repertoire of stories, poetry and non-fiction, reaffirms their knowledge and engagement in known or familiar texts and motivates them as readers (Campbell 1990). There is strong evidence to indicate that being read to is a critical experience in learning to read (Durkin 1966; Clarke 1976; Wells 1986) and it remains an important activity throughout the primary years. With the current pressures on the timetable and the emphasis on curriculum coverage, however, reading aloud provision is somewhat vulnerable, and there is evidence to suggest that teachers are reducing the amount of whole-text reading, choosing extracts instead – not for their pleasure or value as literature, but for their grammatical or language features (Frater 2000).

Reading aloud is sometimes viewed as an extra, a 'treat' in a skills focused curriculum. Yet it is far more fundamental than this, for as teachers read aloud to children they are opening doors on all the possible worlds of literary experience and encouraging the children to step inside. Vicariously, literature offers children the chance to share in and evaluate others' experience and to learn in the process (Hughes 1970; Britton 1982). In addition, if texts are well chosen and reread, then the tunes and patterns and other formal properties of language are repeatedly exposed and reinforced (Taylor 1994). Others also argue that through reading and listening to stories, children learn about language features and organisational aspects of texts (Perera 1984; Hansen 1987). Carefully chosen children's books read aloud to a class can serve a number of significant functions: scaffolding the young reader; supporting predictability and memorability; prompting active participation; and offering a range of discourse structures (Holdaway 1979; Barton 1986; Wells 1986; Dombey 1988; Ellis and Barrs 1996).

Some advantages of reading aloud

Children develop their knowledge of:

- the pleasure and involvement that texts offer;
- the language of texts;
- the tunes and patterns of written language;
- a range of different kinds of text and text structures;
- imaginary worlds and characters;
- particular authors, poets and illustrators;
- others' experiences and through this, their own.

Reading aloud may be to the whole class, to a group or a one-to-one experience, and can help children to reread the same texts independently. Regular rereading of a text by the teacher facilitates this process of becoming acquainted with the text and may involve shared reading in line with Don Holdaway's (1979) bedtime story model. Holdaway highlights that reading aloud and exploration of books through rereading offer the child independent practice of the familiar text. He recommends that in reading aloud in the classroom it is useful to reread a well-known text, revisit not such a familiar one and introduce a new one regularly, thus building up the children's repertoire of familiar texts. Older children, indeed all children, benefit from hearing challenging and demanding texts that they might not be able to manage alone. The teacher mediates the text enabling children to gain access to the layers of understanding offered. The fluency of sustained reading aloud can, over time, make a significant contribution to the children's meaning making and their tacit knowledge of coherence in the text, as well as keep alive the desire to read. There is a close relationship between reading aloud and storytelling, as Barton (1986) observed. Both are social and interactive events that can help to build a sense of community in the classroom (Zipes 1996). Reading aloud plays a particularly important role in supporting children with reading difficulties, and the choice of text is crucial in helping older inexperienced readers. Such texts need to 'lend themselves to discussion, reflective reading and creative interpretation' (Ellis and Barrs 1996). Various kinds of response to text activities need to be woven into reading aloud so provision is varied, with plenty of opportunities to debate and discuss the text, the use of drama conventions, story props and puppets to enliven and investigate the text, as well as other opportunities to hear it performed without interruption.

'Performance read aloud'

It is only through listening to words in print being spoken, does one discover their colour, their life, their movement and drama.   (Chambers 1993)

Teachers need to read aloud well, with marked emphasis, appropriate intonation and energy, lifting the words off the page and providing a quality model of expressive and engaging read aloud. If book readings are turned into skilled performances and are given profile and priority, children can be enticed into the text by the dramatic presentation or rhythmic regeneration of it that highlights its meaning. Recent research has shown that inexperienced KS2 readers (and in particular boys), became keen to take part in what L. Graham (1999) came to call 'performance read aloud' when this had been modelled by their teacher. They reread the texts performed for them and were found to imitate the intonation and expression used by their teachers. The opportunity to engage in pleasurable rereading and performance of texts tempted these inexperienced readers to reread them, perform them and feel part of the class community of readers. In so doing these readers were engaging with Harding's (1977) most basic level of response to written text: an appreciation of rhythm and pattern. Young readers need to respond to the pattern of sound in text and feel the rhythmic structure of repetitive texts through their rereading and performance. Perhaps, as L. Graham (1999) suggests, less experienced KS2 readers have missed out on early chanting, reading, rereading and joining in with highly structured repetitive texts. Knowledge of nursery rhymes for example, has been shown to be a good predictor of early reading success (Bryant and Bradley 1985). In offering groups of children the chance to read aloud to the class and perform, say, poetry or a dialogue from a story, they develop their own style, fluency, confidence and intonation, all of which will support them as readers (Bromley 1996). Perhaps more significantly however, such groups will be discussing the text and networking as readers in preparation for their performance.

Choosing texts and book promotion

A wide range of reading material including literature, poetry, non-fiction texts, texts related to children's interests and popular culture, televisual texts, pamphlets and newspapers need to be read aloud. Inexperienced readers need a richer diet of reading aloud, since as Wells's (1986) research showed, 'being read to' was the most significant indicator of achievement in literacy at both 7 and 11 years old. Taped stories (especially for home loan), classroom assistants and parent helpers can be used to enrich provision for these learners. For EAL learners repetitive structured texts, read aloud by the teacher and revisited by the class, play an important part in not only learning to read, but also in their learning of English. Such high quality texts with overt story structures, quality illustrations and repetitive rhythmic language are also valuable as resources for shared reading since they encourage joining in, and are memorable and rich with meaning. Story props, magnet boards and puppets can also be useful in reading aloud as concrete referents and visual support.

While some of the literature read will relate to the genre, focus or text type currently being explored in the literacy hour, the NLSF range suggestions should not drive all choices. If a novel is being read aloud it is likely that one or two of its chapters, or extracts from it will be focused on in the literacy hour. This enables the children to discuss the selected extract in the context of the whole story and therefore make more meaning through drawing on their wider understanding of the narrative being read. Read aloud provision can also offer children parodies of the genre, which, while they are not studied, will be read, predicted, discussed, joined in with, heard and enjoyed. However, reading aloud time also needs to incorporate children's choices, revisiting favourites as well as explicitly introducing unfamiliar authors, poets and the different tunes of non-fiction texts.

Read aloud is major way in which children will meet new books and writers. Reading exciting snippets from novels, sharing only the first chapter (leaving on a cliff-hanger), performing a selection of humorous poems from an anthology, or showing and discussing one or two illustrations from a picture book or non-fiction text can all act as effective text introductions. Such brief reading aloud recommendations are essential to help children make their own choices for independent reading and to profile pleasure and enjoyment. These important book promotion activities need to be shared with the children, and time should be made available for children to introduce books to each other. Children's own reading interests and the texts they read at home also need to be explicitly valued and profiled in the read aloud and recommendation programme.

Reading aloud: Institutional self-review

- How is the regularity and quality of read aloud monitored?
- How is staff knowledge of high quality literature and non-fiction updated and shared?
- To what extent does the read aloud programme complement and feed into literacy hour work?
- Are books/authors/poets regularly promoted by each member of staff?
- How are the children involved in read aloud provision?
- What support is available for staff who are less than comfortable/confident in bringing texts to life?
- Is the school policy on read aloud underpinned by an understanding of the benefits of quality read aloud provision?

Reading aloud: Ideas for action

Teachers reading to children

- *Establish interactive reading aloud sessions:* Pause to discuss, predict, role play, become involved.

- *Offer some texts untouched:* Occasionally offer some poems, chapters, etc. without reflective discussion or analysis unless the children initiate this.

- *Plan to enrich reading aloud provision:* Focus on a chosen genre and over a half term or unit of work immerse the children in examples.

- *Increase access to audiotapes:* Make available more poetry and fiction on tape, for use in independent work or for home loan.

- *Increase storytelling opportunities:* Widen your repertoire of retold tales, to capture your audience with strong narratives, rich intonation and expression.

- *Let children choose:* Establish a regular session when the children choose, request repeats, make suggestions and perform their 'read aloud' performances.

- *Plan weekly book promotions:* Allow a few minutes for you or the children to sell books, tempt others to read them and read the blurb or extracts, and highlight their response. Focus on new authors, revisiting genres and sharing enthusiasm and enjoyment.

- *Experiment with a range of voices:* Explore the range of your own voice; play with different intonation, accents, volume and pace to bring the text to life.

Children reading to one another

- *Create reading partnerships:* Arrange regular visits across year groups (e.g. Year 4–Year 2) for reading aloud and discussion.

- *Select and share extracts:* Following quiet reading, pairs select a favourite passage or sentence and read it aloud to one another, explaining why they like it.

- *Profile storytelling:* Encourage fluency, intonation and expression through retelling tales to small groups.

- *Establish readers of the week:* Invite parents to join the class to hear 2–4 children talk about their reading, their preferences and recommendations, read aloud an extract. Discussion and questions can be generated.

- *'Performance read aloud' sessions:* Allow groups to prepare a passage, playscript or poem for a 'performance read aloud' session when the group perform the piece.

Shared reading: Principles

Aside from the literacy learning involved, another value of shared reading is the role it can play in creating a community of readers who enjoy participating together in literacy events.

(Fountas and Pinnell 1996)

Shared reading involves the teacher and the children reading together from a large format text and making a shared reading of it. The arguments for shared reading are extensive and seek to reproduce in the classroom the conditions for successful home learning, which are essentially pleasurable and collaborative (Holdaway 1979, 1982). Drawing on the work of Clay (1972) and Clark (1976), Holdaway (1979) sought to mirror the visual intimacy with print and meaning making that characterise preschool book experiences of children at home and so he developed shared reading. In demonstrating the reading process with the class or group, the teacher explicitly models reading and focuses on making sense of the text and the rewards to be gained from reading, as well as teaching specific word, sentence or text level objectives. In this shared reading interaction the supportive context fosters confidence and enables the children to read together like fluent readers (Sulzby 1985; Rowe 1987; Button and Johnson 1997). The children's comprehension of story is also developed through deconstruction activities in shared reading, which seek to help them understand story grammars (Mandler and Johnson 1977; Whaley 1981) or the structure of non-fiction or poetic texts. This knowledge will support both their reading and their writing. Through their active involvement and motivated examination of the text, children can internalise the structures of written texts as a precursor to constructing further texts using the same features (Derewianka 1990; Wing Jan 1991; Lewis and Wray 1995).

The advantages of shared reading

- It offers active involvement, participation and enjoyment.
- It provides opportunities for teaching phonic, syntactic and semantic strategies.
- It provides explicit demonstrations of the reading process and response.
- It encourages rereading and provides the opportunity to behave like a reader.
- It helps children become well acquainted with texts that they can use as resources for reading and writing.
- It provides regular supported reading practice.

Texts for shared reading

Texts chosen need to be very high quality and capable of capturing the children's interest and imagination. A wide range of texts will be read over time, often selected in response to the literary genres or non-fiction text types suggested by the NLSF. Commercially produced big books, home-made versions of well-known tales, or class books and charts made in shared writing, poetry posters, colour or black and white overhead transparencies and enlarged extracts can all be used. A variety of formats is helpful and choose print to ensure easy visibility for all. Texts should be within children's comprehension but above the independent reading level of the majority of the class, as this provides some challenge and extension of the children's skills (Strickland and Morrow 1990; Swindal 1993). Since the text chosen is revisited over the week, reread regularly (in the early years) and may be the basis of much independent activity and writing, it needs to be relevant, motivating and capable of triggering further work. J. Graham (1999) suggests that texts where the writer draws attention to his or her language in an overt manner are the most useful, since shared reading texts need to be able to bear examination and discussion and not lose their pleasure and impact. HLiterary texts need to be chosen for their quality, meaning, relevance and ability to entice children into their world of fiction, not because they exemplify a particular word or sentence level objective! As the work of Meek (1988, 1991), Graham (2000), Doonan (1993) and others has shown, high quality challenging texts make a significant difference to the reading experience, and this needs to be recognised in all textual encounters, not least in shared reading. Much high quality literature for early readers is patterned, repetitive and rhythmic and should prompt joining in, singing or chanting. However, over time a variety of texts will be read together. Teacher selection needs to take into account quality, the author or illustrator and genre appropriacy for the class as well as the range and format of the texts to be read during that half term. The reading aloud programme should complement the shared reading plan by, for example, providing further examples in the same genre or introductions to other books by the same author.

For fiction, picture books and short stories are highly recommended since it is possible to read these over a week and enjoy the whole text through reading aloud sessions and shared reading. Extracts studied will be in the context of the whole text and a coherent understanding of the characters and the narrative. If extracts from a novel are used it is extremely important that the novel itself is being read aloud to the class outside the literacy hour. Selecting extracts from a story to read, study, discuss and learn from, without honouring the children or the texts by reading the whole story is not recommended. This fails to introduce new texts or authors in sufficient depth to prompt independent reading and reduces the children's ability to understand and respond to the extract. It also mutilates the story and prevents literature spinning its motivating web around the readers. Such practice makes reading harder and drier, particularly for less experienced readers at KS2 who need to hear *more* whole texts (while studying part of them), rather than less. In the early years, story props, a variety of puppets, soft toys, magnetic and duplo figures are a useful resource for shared reading. They can help the story come to life, can be used for role play or retelling and support an understanding of structure and character. Such symbols and props can be particularly helpful to bilingual learners whose first language is not English, and can foster small group re-enactment of the tale in independent work.

The practice of shared reading

Shared reading provides a multitude of teaching opportunities while reading and enjoying the story, poetry or information text. These involve explicitly teaching and practising skills and strategies as well as interactively engaging in the reading process.

Shared reading involves interactive teaching of:		
Reading processes	• Predicting • Picturing • Connecting	• Questioning • Engaging • Evaluating
Reading strategies and skills	• Semantic: text level skills • Syntactic: sentence level skills • Grapho-phonic: word level skills • Monitoring and self-correction • Fluency and expression	
Developing response	• Inference and deduction • Awareness of language • Understanding of text construction • Use of text knowledge	

Teaching the reading processes

As readers engage in the process of making meaning from black marks on a page, they are actively involved in a number of cognitive activities. Good readers tend to generate questions while they read and translate what they read into mental images, while less able readers tend to view reading as a passive act of translating into sound and often lack a clear picture of the purpose of reading. In shared reading there are opportunities to prompt and engage children in developing the reading processes of predicting, picturing, questioning, connecting and engaging with the text and evaluating it (Benton and Fox 1985). Prediction is acknowledged as playing a significant role in reading (Smith 1978; Martin and Leather 1994) and through shared reading teachers need to support children in creating hypotheses about the text and suggesting future scenarios or flashbacks that may illuminate it. To prompt children to visualise pictures in their heads as they read, use of a wide range of high quality picture fiction, different versions of the same text and work on picturing unseen characters or settings can be helpful. Relating their images to the author's words can help readers see how writers create their effects and evoke mood and characterisation. As Fry (1985) observes 'picturing is a fundamental act of imagining' and absolutely necessary to make sense of text. Readers also ask questions of printed texts, which drive them forwards into the text or cause them to pause and reflect on the text. Modelling questioning and practising pondering on a text can be undertaken in shared reading, and enable children to read with greater comprehension and enjoyment.

> The smartest readers ask of themselves the most effective questions for reducing the uncertainty, the poorer readers bumble around with trivial questions and waste their opportunities to reduce uncertainty. They do not put the information seeking process into effective sequences.
>
> (Clay 1991a)

Reading also involves making connections to the text, by bringing what is known about a subject, author and theme to the surface and making connections to other texts – television, film, books and life experience – in order to make sense of it (Martin and Leather 1994). Making these 'life to text' and 'text to life' moves (Meek 1991) enables the reader to connect emotionally to the text and learn about literature in the process. Emotionally engaging with the text, empathising with the characters and sharing an affective response to text is significant for all readers and needs to be built into shared reading and responding. In sharing their personal affective responses in shared reading teachers need to encourage others to do so, and demonstrate that there is not one accepted view, for each reader's experience of a text is unique, so uniformity is not required. Readers also engage in reflection and evaluation of texts, developing their views about it personally as a piece of writing. By demonstrating these processes in shared reading, teachers enable children to take an active role in constructing meaning from the text and help them recognise the kinds of thinking processes involved. Such processes are closely related to developing their comprehension and response to the text.

Teaching reading strategies and skills

Readers use a range of different strategies and skills as they read, in order to make meaning from text. Such strategies enable the reader to apply, use, transform, interpret and reinterpret information. In broad terms there are three general categories of such strategies that interrelate; strategies for problem solving new words; strategies that maintain fluency; and strategies that monitor and self-correct (Clay 1991a). In shared reading these strategies are modelled, explained, practised and revisited constantly and explicitly. Good readers search for cues, check sources of information, correct errors and problem solve new words by using a wide variety of information, so all readers need to employ a range of strategies to make sense of what they read. Good readers also read for meaning, but as they do so their attention is divided between focusing on the meaning, while at the same time paying attention to visual information and using grapho-phonic knowledge of sentence structure and punctuation. Effective teaching of shared reading demonstrates the range of cueing systems that readers simultaneously employ, and teaches children to use strategies for themselves (Goodman and Burke 1972;

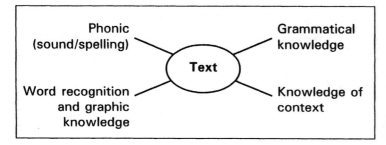

Figure 11   Searchlights for reading
(NLS 1998b)

Weaver 1980). Such strategies are taught in the context of shared reading and in planned grapho-phonic and syntactic (sentence level) teaching sessions, which extend their knowledge.

Readers draw on these searchlights (Figure 11) continuously, oscillating between high semantic and syntactic levels to lower levels of information such as knowledge about word and letter features (Rumelhart 1976). Effective shared reading sessions need to acknowledge the complexity of reading, and teach strategies to enable this orchestration to take place (Holdaway 1982; Park 1982), enabling learners to solve new words, maintain fluency and monitor accuracy.

Problem solving new words

Shared reading provides a motivating context to teach and apply a range of strategies for working out new words. Children need to know what to do when they come to a word they don't recognise and avoid becoming over-reliant on any of the cueing systems, so balance and breadth is essential. Children's ability to employ the strategies available to them is critical to support them in the meaning-making process (Campbell 1988). The teaching and application of phonics and word recognition strategies are essential in shared reading in the early years and for less experienced learners whose phonic knowledge is poor. Separate or related word level work focusing on phonics and spelling will complement this contextualised work. Extensive use of highly patterned texts (which exemplify particular phonemic structures) enables such work to build on research findings indicating that awareness of onset and rime is positively associated with learning to read (Bradley and Bryant 1983; Treiman 1985; Goswami and Bryant 1990). However, a balanced approach to teaching phonic strategies is required; synthetic phonics approaches need to be employed alongside analytic methods. This will involve demonstrating different ways of problem solving a word grapho-phonically, building on children's knowledge of sound/symbol relationships and helping them perceive sound and spelling patterns and build analogies for themselves. Children who are learning to read often begin by paying particular attention to the shapes of words and recognising familiar letters, words within words or parts of their names in words (Tuxford and Washtell 1990). They can also use their growing grapho-phonic knowledge if attention is given to sound symbol relationships, to word endings and to prediction based on graphonic cues. Expanding and reinforcing children's sight vocabulary of high frequency words and graphic features of words is also important in this context, as well as in word level work.

Demonstrating syntactic strategies will involve the teacher in drawing the children's attention to the use of punctuation and to sense and sentence structure. In identifying these and exploring how they influence the reader's expression, intonation and sense making, teachers are helping children draw on and develop their syntactic knowledge, for it is clear that the 'tune on the page' plays a significant part in supporting the reading of unknown word (Barrs and Thomas 1991). Young readers who are being read to will already be developing an ear for rhythm, rhyme, tune and textual structures and will learn to apply this to written language through shared reading. By using their tacit knowledge of language and its structure, and through direct instruction, young children are helped to predict what will come next in a text and learn to recognise whether a sentence 'sounds' right.

Modelling contextual/semantic strategies will involve the teacher in helping the children draw on their prior knowledge of the subject, the author and the genre in order to make predictions. It will also involve teaching close reading of the illustrations or diagrams offered in order to problem solve new words. Bussis *et al.* (1985) have shown that children make fewer miscues when they are reading the second half of the book, since they have much more information to go on in respect of the overall meaning of the text. Much teacher demonstration of word, sentence and text level strategies is involved in shared reading, although none of these strategies will operate in isolation because multiple sources of knowledge are orchestrated to construct meaning.

Fluency and expression

Fluency is an important factor in reading comprehension (Arnold 1982; Pinnell *et al.* 1995). It is closely related to the child's syntactic knowledge of the way written language sounds, is organised and is punctuated, as well as to the child's contextual knowledge, and their knowledge of different narrative and non-narrative structures. It is also supported by their ability to recognise words or parts of words quickly enough, problem solve them and maintain a meaningful flow of text. So once again text, sentence and word level strategies are essential. Wide experience of text – read with marked intonation, phrasing and fluency – provides strong support for developing fluency in readers. Children use their oral language as a cue to maintain fluency, so it helps younger or poorer readers if the texts they read resemble their oral language, or are rich in repeated language patterns and lively dialogue. If the shared reading prompts joining in and rereading and it seeks to create a richly textured reading, with exaggerated emphasis and intonation, then support for fluency is offered. Work on character, dialogue, drama and storytelling in shared reading can also extend children's confidence and experience of voice flavour and tenor. Quality reading aloud by the teacher also provides experience of the tunes and grammatical patterns in text and shows how phrasing and fluency can affect meaning. However, if children read unseen text aloud, preparation time is essential if fluency is desired, since word accuracy can dominate and concentration may remain at word level (Smith 1978). The re-reading and joint endeavour involved in shared reading are very supportive for developing and maintaining fluency.

Monitoring and self-correction

Readers use information from a range of sources to check their own reading as they read. This self-monitoring may take many forms and indicates that the reader is beginning to control the reading process. By employing grapho-phonic, syntactic or semantic strategies the reader may be able to search for an alternative word and self-correct. Clay (1991a) calls this cross-checking and again it depends on the reader's knowledge of word, sentence and text level features of language. In shared reading the use of these reading strategies in this process of self-monitoring, searching for and confirming alternatives needs to be highlighted, demonstrated and discussed explicitly. Some younger children and less experienced readers seem not to notice when they don't understand, so teaching the skill of monitoring, reflecting and checking comprehension is very important. Through explicit teaching of word, sentence and text level strategies in shared reading, children become more confident in using these overtly in the whole-class context and begin to consciously and unconsciously adopt and practice appropriate strategies that help them read independently in other contexts.

Developing response

By responding to reading children come to understand the very nature of reading, so developing children's responses throughout the primary years is essential. Readers respond to the same text in different ways at different times, making connections and analogies between their own lives and those represented in texts (Iser 1978; Rosenblatt 1978). So in shared reading teachers need to begin by validating and exploring the different readings that children produce. What must be avoided is presenting the class with a passage in shared reading and then bombarding them with a battery of questions to check their comprehension of teacher-selected features of the text. This kind of oral comprehension is profiled in many commercial schemes for the literacy hour, which often fail to offer a variety of activities to develop response. Helping children reflect on what they have read through response work is more complex than merely assessing their apparent comprehension in a question and answer format, although *genuine* questions offered as prompts for pairs to discuss can have a role to play, providing diversity is acknowledged. Involvement and affective engagement are sought and the children's own questions about the text are honoured. Questions, when used, need to be differentiated appropriately to stretch less able as well as more able readers. Imaginative response activities, by contrast, may involve more collaboration, discussion and full pupil participation. As their response deepens and the text is revisited, the children can come to appreciate how the language used by the writer evoked this response. In shared reading, teachers are likely to be combining elements of both traditional literature teaching and reader response.

Traditional literature teaching	Reader response teaching
• The primary emphasis is on the text	• The primary emphasis is on children's oral or written response – the text takes second place
• Guided by the teacher, the 'correct' meaning must be found	• Guided by the teacher, personal meanings are made and shared
• Specific comprehension questions about the literary text are set (e.g. questions about setting, character or plot)	• In responding to activities or questions, children use their knowledge of literary conventions to support their interpretation
• Children's views are validated (or otherwise) by their teacher alone	• Children's views are shaped and extended by others' views (including their teacher's)

The National Curriculum (DfEE 1999a) states that to develop understanding and appreciation of literary texts, pupils at KS2 should be taught about characters, settings, plots, authors, poets and sentence construction. Active open-ended approaches are needed in shared reading, which allow a genuinely shared reading of the text to be made that, while it informs and widens understanding, does not mutilate the literature in the process. It is clear that to include *all* children in shared reading (particularly those who lack confidence and experience as readers) priority needs to be given to reader response and the affective nature of reading (Rosenblatt 1978; Meek 1991; Martin and Leather 1994; L. Graham 1999). Children's intuitive perceptions as well as their feelings and memories triggered by the text need to be honoured if children are to develop as thoughtful and involved readers, who understand what they read and retain a positive and motivated attitude.

> The great danger is that we forget the affective in our misguided orientation towards a watered down version of literacy criticism.
> (Martin and Leather 1994)

Older inexperienced readers often need more experience of response through interactive shared reading opportunities. Imaginative response to text may involve the physical experience of recreating the text in performance, investigating it through improvisation, or shaping it through retelling in order to create a richer understanding. It will also involve the text-to-life and life-to-text engagement of readers, so that new insights about the text are gained in the process. Such responses to text will take place to different degrees in reading aloud sessions, shared, guided, and independent reading, but in shared reading it is particularly important to involve all the class and tackle the text level objectives within the NLSF. By making an interactive shared class reading of the text, a knowledge and understanding of the text can be achieved that far outweighs what any member of the class could have achieved on their own. In creating insights and sharing their views, the class operate as a community of readers and learn to make meaning together.

Shared reading:
Institutional self-review

- How interactive is shared reading and are *all* the children actively involved in shared reading?
- Is phonic, graphic and syntactic knowledge taught explicitly and in an engaging and effective manner?
- Are the reading processes and strategies taught and children's response to text developed?
- Are whole texts explored over a week or within coherent units of work on a genre or text type?
- How visually stimulating is the textual material used?
- Does the text level work regularly provide a coherent context for the sentence/word level work?

Shared reading: Ideas for action

General: text level

Much word and sentence level work will develop from the shared text and, where appropriate, related ideas have been noted. However, a number of other generic grapho-phonic and syntactic teaching activities are also noted. Further related ideas are found in the shared writing section.

- *Create a class reading journal*: Read and respond to a text, stopping to record ideas, reflections, connections, predictions or questions in a class reading journal. Work on, say, collecting quotes and explaining their choice; initial these to highlight the diversity.

- *Prompt discussion and response*: In pairs or groups discuss any of the following questions and the reasons for their views. The children's responses can then be shared in a whole-class discussion; stress the active thinking processes involved:

  - prediction: what might happen next?

  - picturing: what pictures do you see in your heads?

  - connecting: what other stories or films or life experience does this remind you of?

  - questioning: what questions do you have or I wonder why/what/whether …?

  - hypothesising: what if a character did … or what if the setting or time was altered to …?

  - emotionally engaging: what do you want to happen or what do you feel about characters?

- *Like, dislike, puzzle, pattern:* In pairs, the children discuss or make notes of their, likes and dislikes and the elements that puzzle them and the patterns they can observe (Chambers 1994). These are then shared and discussed. Diversity of response is affirmed, and focused explanations are sought.

- *Undertake a class bookzip*: Explain that the unknown text has an imaginary magical bookzip and cannot be opened. Based on the cover information, predict the narrative, the genre and theme. Or focus on a character pictured, name them and suggest their role and behaviour in the tale. Probable vocabulary can also be listed and shared writing could result.

- *Cover over words:* Create missing words to help children problem solve unknown words. Teach strategies to read these and articulate the options clearly. Be careful to delete or cover words (or pairs of words) that can be predicted using contextual, syntactic or grapho-phonic knowledge. List suggestions and evaluate their appropriacy together.

Text level: fiction

Story structure

- *Make a physical storyboard:* Create a series of class or group freeze frames depicting the main events in the story. The text can then be reread, or told and divided into sections.

- *Draw Willow Pattern plates:* Tell the story and show a Willow Pattern plate. Use pictures or symbols to summarise another story, highlighting the structure visually on the design.

- *Improvise a flash forward:* Create small group improvisations of the consequences of events and a character's actions, which also reflect the underlying themes in the narrative.

- *Examine story grammar:* Collect several texts with similar story grammars: i.e. similar story structures or schemas. Summarise these in a grid. In shared writing plan another tale with a similar structure (e.g. cumulative, journey, days of the week, problem resolution stories).

Story structure: problem resolution				
Title	The Three Billy Goats Gruff	The Three Little Pigs	Snow White	Cinderella
Problem				
Setting				
Good characters				
Bad characters				
Events 1				
2				
3				
Resolution				

Character

- *Create emotion graphs:* Examine a character's changing emotions by listing the significant events in the tale and place these on the graph in relation to the character's feelings at that moment. Name the feeling as well as the narrative moment. Work on synonyms for the emotions, and retell the tale or part of it from that character's point of view (Grainger 1997).

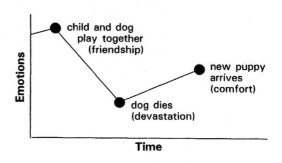

- *Replay dialogue:* Transcribe a small section of significant dialogue from a well-known children's film. Use this to read and recreate expressively in pairs. Watch the video extract, and discuss expression, gesture and intonation. Work on extending the dialogue, or turning the script into prose in a narrative.

- *Develop a role on the wall:* During several shared reading sessions, each child records a particular character's feelings inside a lifesize outline and notes other characters' views and attitudes towards this individual at different points in the tale. Quotes from the text can also be used.

- *Explore behaviour, appearance, speech and emotions:* Reread a passage, underlining in different colours words that describe what a character does, says, looks like and feels. These can be presented as a character web, synonyms can be sought and parts of the passage rewritten.

Text level: non-fiction

- *Mask the title and predict:* Using only the remaining visual or written information on the covers, predict the subject matter, contents, type of text, glossary and publication date.

- *Model a book sort:* Collect fiction and non-fiction on a subject and discuss how and whether it is possible to decide which are factual texts if only the cover is examined. (Acknowledge the reality that fiction may well contain facts.) Classify the texts and agree criteria.

- *Change the presentation:* Reading, say, a piece of prose on butterflies, represent this in another form, as a flow chart, diagram, pie chart or whatever is appropriate. Discuss purpose in presentation.

- *Prompt discussion through questioning:* Pose questions for pairs to discuss prior to a whole-class discussion. Use everyday publications (menus, brochures, junk mail) as well as books:
  - What purpose does this text serve?
  - Who produced it (all those involved) and who is speaking?
  - Who is it speaking to or aimed at?
  - How could we check for information on …?
  - Why do you think the authors included … (e.g. map, phone number, website, photograph)?
  - What message or effect do you think it is trying to convey or achieve?
  - How successful is it at doing this?
  - Is there any way of distinguishing the facts and opinions in it?
  - What type/s of writing is/are evident in it?

- *Use everyday publications:* In addition to non-fiction books, use a wide range of everyday publications. These provide real-life examples of different text types.

- *Create a book matrix:* Identify with the class what they think they know about a topic and what they want to know. Collect several books about the general area and check together which has relevant information by using the contents page and the index. Record this as a book matrix.

- *Model recording main points from reading in different ways:* This ensures that children are taught how to make, say, lists, charts, diagrams, mindmaps and webs to aid memory retention.

- *Collect comics to read and analyse:* Comics contain a wide range of text types (e.g. adverts, instructions, cartoon stories, competitions, letters). Classify the contents and create a poster with examples of one type. Use this to annotate, analyse and understand.

- *Read and sort food labels:* Look at a range of packaging and labels. What kind of information is offered and for what purpose? Classify the information and create posters with annotated examples.

Text level: poetry

Poetry must be experienced before it can be analysed. Joint readings, performances and explorations are essential to bring it to life before focused discussion of language features. Access to understanding and comprehending poetry comes through this experience and discussion of the linguistic features (felt and noticed in the engagement) should follow. Direct teaching can then extend these insights still further.

- *Create a musical interpretation:* Read a poem and decide on instruments and body percussion that suit the style and theme of the text. Bring it to life corporately in some form of choral recitation enhanced by percussion and perhaps an ostinato throughout. Discuss how this interpretation helps to shape the readers' understanding.

- *Physically interpret it:* Perform the poem together. This may involve miming the narrative (e.g. *We're Going on a Bear Hunt* by Michael Rosen), or making a less literal, more symbolic representation involving movement and dance (e.g. *Sea Timeless* by Grace Nicholls).

- *Do some vocal jazz:* Play with a poem, adding sounds, pauses, repeating words, chanting phrases and changing volume and speed. This creates an impressionistic interpretation of its tunes, rhythms and patterns. This activity suits oral and performance poetry best, or just explore a chorus in this manner.

- *Play the puzzle–possibility game:* Each pair identifies one or two puzzles in the text. These are offered to the class for a possible response. There are no questions and answers; only puzzles and possibilities. This encourages and values diverse views.

- *Interpret the theme through group sculpture:* Groups create a freeze frame that represents the key theme or message of the poem. This is distilled into a few words by each group, who title their piece of sculpture. These act as summaries of the poem's theme and can be used to generate shared prose writing in another genre on the same theme.

- *Focus on point of view:* Compare and contrast several poems about the same subject and discuss each poet's point of view. Find evidence in the verses to support the point of view. If this view was reversed, what changes would need to be made?

- *Use poetry as a playscript*: Many poems involve conversations, while others have been explicitly written for four or more voices (e.g. *My Dad, Your Dad* by Kit Wright or Richard Brown's collection *The Midnight Party*). Groups of children can read 'a voice', combining together to create a shared poetry reading with speaking parts.

Sentence level

- *Connect to the children's reading material*: Having worked on, say, punctuating dialogue or speech verbs, children examine their current reading book and identify relevant examples. Brief examples can be quoted and annotated.

- *It doesn't make sense*: Tell the class you are deliberately going to make errors as you read, and they should call out 'It doesn't make sense' when you do. Then read, creating occasional grammatical errors. If appropriate, discuss the nature of the error.

- *Taking parts:* Develop fluency, use of punctuation and intonation by grouping the class as characters or narrators. All the class take part in bringing the text to life.

- *Underlining and highlighting:* On laminated texts or A3 acetates, encourage children to underline particular grammatical features, or circle punctuation marks. Offer more complex examples to challenge learners.

- *Perform punctuation 'plays':* The class or group list the punctuation used in a passage, then make up a sound for each punctuation mark. The text is then read aloud with the appropriate sounds. Discuss their use and reflection in the reader's voice.

- *Sequence and sort a text:* Cut up a text with punctuation in mind (e.g. separating dialogue from its punctuation, or cutting the text just after a connective to examine complex sentences).

- *Predicting from limited information:* Select examples of parts of speech from the class text, preferably from an unread section. Predict what is going on from these, and then read the passage together, once to compare to their hypotheses and once to underline the part of speech noted early. Work on altering some of these.

- *Sentence completion:* Retell an oral story, pausing occasionally for the class to suggest the end of various sentences. This works well at cliffhangers and can be used to explore sentence construction and connectives if some sentences are recorded and analysed.

- *Play 'the unnamed object':* Pairs cut out a picture of an object advertised in a magazine and generate words, phrases or a paragraph to describe it using as many adjectives as possible. The class try to guess the object.

- *Explore characters' names:* Record characters' names from the shared text, creating a list of others whose names signify particular attributes (e.g. the Big Bad Wolf, Veronica Beauregarde, Plop, the Barn Owl, Aunt Spiker, Mr Snape).

Word level

- *Physical word sorts:* Every child is given one word from the text on card. In an *open sort* they move around, trying to create connections with others, and justify their criteria to the class. In a *closed sort* the teacher provides the frame (e.g. find others with the same number of syllables, same root, same suffix, same letter string).

- *Play high frequency word Bingo.* Create a large baseboard with high frequency words and in rereading the book play Bingo, seeking a full house.

- *Find words hiding in place names:* On a school trip collect local place names, and hunt for words within words (e.g. in Sidcup, Blackwall Tunnel, Lewisham, Waterloo, London Eye).

- *Find prefix partners:* Having hunted for and collected words with prefixes, display some without their prefix partner and decide together which can be foined.

- *The one/two/three beat team:* Sort words from the text into teams according to their syllabic beats. Create lists for each team.

- *Play 'I'm thinking with my brain clinking':* Create rhyming lists from a variation on I Spy: 'I'm thinking with my brain clinking of something that rhymes with …'

- *Act out antonyms:* Produce a list of antonyms that can be demonstrated through mime. Children mime one and the class guess (e.g. happy, sad, above, below, hot, cold, full, empty).

- *Make an onset and rime flick book:* Starting with a word from the text generate a list of rhyming words, sort them into lists and create a large flick book to model the structure. The back strip has the rime in large letters, and earlier pages show a picture with the onset.

- *Model sequencing a rhyming poem:* Sort the poem's order and underline any words with common letter strings.

- *Create story base boards:* These can be used for a form of Bingo using single words or repetitive phrases from the text. In reading the book together model the use of the illustrated base board.

- *Create character webs:* Read a passage and highlight words and phrases that relate to a character's actions, speech, feelings or appearance. Categorise these and present them as a web. Find a synonym for each one.

Guided reading: Principles

Guided reading takes the place of an individual reading programme and should be a fundamental part of each school's literacy programme. As a carefully structured group activity, it significantly increases time for sustained teaching.   NLS (DfEE 1998b)

Introduction

In essence, guided reading involves the teacher in working with a small group of children who have similar reading abilities. It is designed to bridge the gap between whole-class shared reading and private, undirected reading. The teacher selects and introduces an appropriate text and supports the children in reading the text to themselves. Following the reading, the group respond to and discuss the reading strategies they employed and/or the layers of meaning in the text. The goal of guided reading is to enable children to read independently, be able to introduce books to themselves and reflect on and respond to what they read. To achieve this each group works 'interdependently' with the teacher in the session, who scaffolds their learning and helps them consciously apply reading strategies (grapho-phonic, syntactic, semantic and bibliographic) and reading processes (prediction, connection, imaging, engaging and questioning) for themselves. The strategies and processes will have been taught in shared reading, and in the context of guided reading they are practised and reinforced in the small group situation with the teacher's support.

The focus in the early stages is on each individual reader's processing system, and children learning to self-correct and develop the problem-solving skills of reading (Fountas and Pinnell 1996). In the later years the focus is more oriented to comprehension and response. However, all teachers need to ensure a balance in guided reading between providing time for the development of encoding/processing skills and time for developing children's inferential understanding, response and critical faculties. Active participation and discussion are essential in order to support the literary value of group reading (Wells *et al.* 1990; McMahon and Goatley 1995; Ewing and Kennedy 1996). Guided group reading has several advantages over hearing children read on an individual basis. Since the needs of the group are similar, appropriate support is efficiently provided, it increases the time spent reading and can create a supportive social context in which learning can be developed. For children with particular difficulties, one-to-one support may still be necessary, but should be seen as additional support; guided group reading should be offered to all pupils. The time to respond in this supported context helps such children value and develop their ideas and extend their involvement in actively making meaning. It is a particularly helpful approach in developing increasing independence and in establishing small groups of readers who can, if encouraged appropriately, begin to talk about texts more freely and take a fuller part in the 'literacy club' (Smith 1988).

Some advantages of guided reading

- The text selection, introduction and guidance are tailored to the group's needs.
- Children are given the opportunity to practise reading strategies in a supported group context.
- The social context facilitates response to text and highlights the meaning and purpose of reading.
- Independent reading is supported and encouraged.
- Teachers can observe, support and assess readers.

Guided reading is not intended to involve reading around the group, since in this context children frequently pay little attention to the piece being read (in order to read ahead and prepare their paragraph), and often jump in quickly to offer a word to a peer (thus preventing the child from working it out for themselves and developing their own reading skills). If silent independent reading is practised in small group contexts, individuals are more attentive and able to contribute more to the group discussion about the text (Wilkinson and Anderson 1995). However, the nature of the text will sometimes suggest that oral reading is more appropriate (e.g. to reveal the rhythm and pattern in a poem, or to enable the playscript to come to life). So, the session will differ according to the age and ability of the children, the actual text involved and the objectives set. The teacher's role will involve the following elements to enable children to 'fly solo under supervision' (Mooney 1994).

The teacher's role

- Assess for needs based grouping.
- Identify appropriate teaching objective/s.
- Select an appropriate text.
- Introduce the text and offer guidance.
- Support children's independent use of cues and strategies.
- Listen, and prompt discussion and response.

Assessment to establish grouping

It is clear that schools make use of a wide range of information to sort children into guided reading groups, including: baseline assessment scores; SAT results; optional SAT papers; NFER scores; reading ages; the children's stage on the school reading scheme; reading conferences; previous teacher's reports; observation; informed intuition; reading questionnaires; school reading records; formative assessment frameworks; miscue analyses and running records.

> Needs based grouping for guided reading is recommended. It is based on ongoing, systematic observation for the purpose of gathering small groups of children who are similar in their reading development. (Fountas and Pinnell 1996)

The most appropriate forms of assessment are those that enable teachers to finely assess the knowledge, skills, attitude, self-assessment and range of each child's reading. So, in the context of grouping for guided reading – especially grouping less experienced readers – an essential assessment tool will be a running record or a miscue analysis. Dealt with in more detail in the assessment and target-setting section (pp. 26–43), this enables the teacher to ascertain the cueing systems that the child needs to develop further to achieve a balanced orchestration of reading cues and strategies. Their accuracy, fluency and understanding as readers is also recorded with this method. While very appropriate for younger and inexperienced readers or readers who are having some difficulty at KS2, a reading conference and information on the child's attitude to reading provides a sound alternative to this assessment with more independent readers. Guided groups may also be constructed around interest, text content and range issues if these are areas of concern. So children with common reading needs are grouped together. For example, one group may be drawn together because they all need to extend their use of syntactic strategies when meeting unfamiliar words, while another group may all be average readers for their age, but demonstrate negative attitudes and poor concentration in tackling longer texts. One or two weeks at the start of each term need to be spent assessing the children as readers, so relevant reading targets and needs based guided group work can be planned. Children's needs change however, and guided reading groups should not remain static for organisational convenience. Regrouping for specific new teaching purposes also enables the children to adopt different roles in group work and work on new and appropriate group reading targets.

Selecting appropriate texts

The choice of text is a critical issue. The material needs to be matched to the ability of the group with some degree of challenge and should capture the reader's desire to read. The children need to be able to read approximately 90 per cent of the text accurately and independently after the teacher's introduction and with the teacher's support. Publishers have produced a plethora of guided reading resources, but as always the interest level, subject matter and quality of the text will have a marked influence on each learner's engagement and motivation (Ellis and Barrs 1996). The Reading Recovery National Network has produced a valuable guide to help schools structure their resources, called *Book Bands for Guided Reading: Organising Key Stage One Texts for the Literacy Hour* (1998), available from the Institute of Education. It is not a list of recommended texts, but categorises 3,000 books according to their gradient of difficulty and is a useful resource, providing a resumé of texts and the textual features appropriate for children working within National Curriculum Levels.

However, books (literature, poetry and non-fiction) are not the only resource material suitable for guided reading. A wide range of pamphlets, magazines, fliers and environmental text can usefully be employed, so real-world print is introduced, read and discussed. The wide range of genre introduced in both reading aloud and shared reading needs to be revisited and read semi-independently, with teacher guidance and group discussion. Poems, articles, picture books, letters and short stories at KS2 lend themselves to reading at one sitting and are more useful than reading a novel chapter by chapter over several months. However, a chapter of the class novel might be used for an able group. Depending on the material, the teaching objective and the group, the length of the text read will vary: several pages, a chapter, a few paragraphs or columns or the whole text may be read at one sitting. Alternatively, teachers may challenge more able readers to read the next chapter at home, before returning to discuss it in the next session. The teacher needs to choose the text carefully and finely tune the activity according to the teaching objective and the group's particular needs.

The session introduction

> As a child approaches a new text he is entitled to an introduction so that when he reads, the gist of the whole or partly revealed story can provide some guide for a fluent reading.
>
> (Clay 1991a)

Instead of constantly expecting children to find their way into a text alone, the teacher introduces the text, providing different levels of support according to the group and the difficulty of the text (Mooney 1995). Knowing the text is essential since this preview is not merely meant to motivate and interest the children, but to mediate *this* text for *this* group of children. In effect, the teacher, by activating their prior knowledge and highlighting a structural feature of the text (e.g. repetition of narrative action), opens up the text and provides useful footholds to enable the children to more securely begin the process of problem solving the text for themselves. The guided reading introduction will also relate to the explicit teaching objective identified for the group, determined by their needs. As children develop their skills the focus will change, moving away from reading strategies and cues towards an emphasis on text understanding and appreciation (Plant 1999). As well as connecting the book to the children's experience or knowledge, this introduction might involve highlighting any of the features in Figure 12 or others that help the children read the text more successfully.

Preparation pays dividends. The introduction needs to be carefully planned and *involve* all the children. The conversation might required them to predict the content from the title, connect to the subject or author, hypothesise the content from the illustrations or discuss which elements of the text catch the reader's eye. This learning-focused introduction should not give too much of the text away and will vary according to the teacher's knowledge of the group, and the characteristics and challenge of the text. More challenging texts will involve richer introductions to increase accessibility.

Having engaged the children, aroused their interest and provided support for reading the text, the teacher might remind the group of the teaching objective (e.g. of strategies to employ for an unknown word), or may leave the children with one or two questions to take on the reading journey.

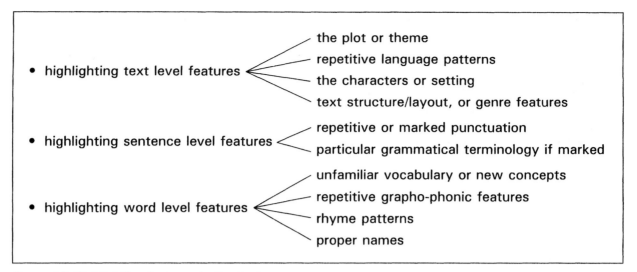

Figure 12 Highlighting features in the text

Independent reading

After the introduction, the children silently read the agreed passage or section of the text and try to use the cues and strategies they were taught in shared reading to make meaning. Having read the agreed piece of text they then discuss it in the group. However, overfragmenting a text can make the text more difficult and readers may lose the overall meaning, so with early readers, if time is tight, the teacher may need to read the remainder of the book to the group to make the experience a satisfying one. With non-fiction texts brief tasks may be set to develop independent research skills. During this independent reading time the teacher observes and selectively interacts with different children to provide support if meaning breaks down and to prompt, reinforce, confirm and draw attention to the strategies they are using. The teacher may also sit alongside one child and ask them to read aloud quietly to monitor the strategies being employed. If the reader needs support, the teacher helps them search for and identify appropriate strategies. With more fluent readers, use of reading logs, journals or Post-its can be incorporated at this stage, with children noting down their predictions and responses in anticipation of the discussion.

Response and discussion

Children need to be helped to talk about books, to try to make sense of them, to make explicit the processes they engage in when reading and discover how texts are constructed. In other words, they need to become active members of a community of readers.   (Robinson and King 1995)

In this part of the process, the teacher discusses the challenges encountered and the strategies employed or the questions set, as well as the meanings in the text and the children's responses to them. The teacher may also give feedback and praise for the reading behaviours observed. This involves revisiting the teaching objectives and taking the conversation wider, exploring the children's predictions, connections, points of view, particular features of the genre, information found and so on, always referring to the text itself to support their comments with evidence. This informal discussion, triggered perhaps by a teacher enquiry, should enable everyone to share their views, voice their understanding and reflect on the meaning of the text as well as the reading process itself. The teacher's role is critical, and genuine listening and authentic personal responses need to be shared. Initially holding back from offering a view can be helpful in prompting the children to share their thinking. Regular discussion and debate about texts in guided reading can substantially influence the children's involvement in the text and their appreciation of and pleasure in reading. The interpersonal dialogic nature of talk about texts becomes internalised and part of each individual's independent thinking about their own reading. The teacher's role at this point needs to evolve sensitively from the children's own concerns and interests, and, significantly, the tentative hypothetical nature of text related talk needs to be valued. This should ensure that the children feel confident to voice their partial understandings and share their questions and thoughts. A further examination of response to text is found in 'Shared reading: Principles' (pp. 64–69): it is a critical aspect of guided reading that must not be cut short. After reading and responding children may be given a small follow-up activity (e.g. hunting for poems by the same poet). Such focused activities emerging from a guided reading experience may be particularly useful support for inexperienced or struggling readers.

Keeping records

Brief anecdotal notes, using children's initials, can be valuable in recording the strategies employed or their response and understanding. The group's ability to tackle the text can also identify areas for further development. Over time, comments on the whole group will be noted in relation to their reading skills, strategies and response. A group record sheet also serves as a reminder of the group's overall learning needs and the half-termly teaching focus within which particular teaching objectives can be set for each session. Some record or statement also needs to be noted in home/school contact books.

Guided reading: Institutional self-review

- Are guided groups gathered on the basis of reading need and reviewed regularly?

- Is time in guided reading balanced between text introduction, reading, reflection and response?

- Do guided reading sessions retain an explicit teaching objective, tailored by the teacher in response to group need?

- Does the range of guided reading materials reflect the range in the NC/NLSF?

- How well do staff know the guided reading materials; is support needed to work with these?

Guided reading: Ideas for action

- *Set aside time for assessment/grouping:* Suspend guided reading at the beginning of the year until needs based assessment has been undertaken. In the spring only those about whom there are particular concerns need to be reassessed and regrouped if appropriate.

- *Increase the variety of everyday publications available*: Create, for example, sets of magazines, catalogues, local newspapers, menus, show programmes, maps, fliers for tourist attractions, or information leaflets about sports centres.

- *Respond to the text flexibly*: Read aloud a playscript, for example, or explore alternative readings of a poem, noting how presentation and intonation, rhythms and patterns affect the meaning.

- *Organise occasional literature circles*: Draw groups of children together who have all read different books by a particular author or the same book. Guide the group in responding and discussing the text.

- *Produce prepared guidance sheets for guided reading resources*: These can be placed with the set of books, or stuck inside the front cover of the teacher's copy. Teachers can select from the key features noted in response to group targets and teaching objectives.

Guidance sheet for guided reading

Book/text: _____

Author: _____ Year: _____

1. Key features to introduce to the children before reading the text:
   - Text level features: _____
   - Sentence level features: _____
   - Word level features: _____

2. Questions/issues for the children to focus on as they read the text *(choose from content questions, use of cueing systems, text, sentence, word level issues as appropriate)*:
   - _____
   - _____
   - _____
   - _____

3. Questions/issues to focus on during response and group discussion *(discuss some of these issues according to the text and the children's needs, exploring the evidence for their responses)*:
   - _____
   - _____
   - _____
   - _____

Independent reading: Principles

The aim of teaching children to read is not just to produce children who can read, but also children who want to read, and who do read for their own purposes and who can learn from and evaluate what they read …

(Browne 1996)

To develop independent, reflective readers who read *by* themselves, the practices of reading *to* children and *with* children in shared and guided reading contexts are important. Independent reading involves children not only in reading, but in choosing to read different written materials in school and at home for their own purposes (Hall and Coles 1995). It can take many forms, including a multitude of reading activities that may take place within the literacy hour or in a reading workshop, as well as sessions of sustained quiet reading in the classroom. Reading across the curriculum will also take place independently of overt teacher support and guidance, as will reading at home. In these contexts, children use their skills, strategies and growing knowledge about literary genres and non-fiction texts to read for information and pleasure. A balance between offering supported social contexts to develop independence and quiet reading sessions that develop stamina and concentration is helpful. Even the latter however, may prompt interaction with others in order to achieve increased comprehension and insight.

In the context of silent independent reading at school or at home, children need to be helped to choose what they want to read, to make recommendations to others, and to develop their own preferences and views. Imposing texts on learners, especially less experienced readers, does not develop independence or increase the reader's control or motivation. Choice is critical for independent reading and should be fostered from the start, so if a reading scheme is used each child needs to be regularly offered an additional text of their own guided choice. Children have rights in relation to reading and these need to be acknowledged and respected in relation to their independent reading choices, just as adult readers exercise their rights.

The reader's bill of rights, by Daniel Pennac

The right to not read
The right to skip pages
The right to not finish
The right to reread
The right to read anything
The right to escapism
The right to read anywhere
The right to browse
The right to read out aloud
The right to not defend your tastes

Surveys that record voluntary reading outside school have tended to suggest that a higher proportion of boys than girls choose not to read (Whitehead 1977; Millard 1997). The Roehampton Survey (1997) confirmed this, for when children aged 7–11 were given a choice between reading a book, playing a computer game or watching television, less than 20 per cent of the boys chose reading, while more than 50 per cent of the girls chose reading. The detailed picture is more complex, however, with QCA (1999) reporting that, boys differ from girls in:

- their choice of reading matter;

- their perception of reading;

'The reader's bill of rights', Daniel Pennac, from *Reads like a Novel* (translated by D. Gunn) © Quartet Books.

- their purposes in undertaking reading;

- the amount of time they give to reading;

- their enthusiasm for reading.

Differences in reading competence hold back learning and widen gaps in attainment between the sexes and this situation is perpetuated if boys' choices of private reading are not valued or recognised by the school. It is argued (Millard 1997; QCA 1998b) that boys often read non-fiction in relation to their interests and hobbies and in response to contemporary media and popular culture. However, research reports differ. For example, the WHSmith Project (Hall and Coles 1996) notes that only 2.8 per cent of their sample read solely non-fiction and while three-quarters of these were boys, this represented a minority percentage within the whole survey. This project also affirmed the clear pattern of decline in the amount of book reading from higher to lower socioeconomic groups, and noted that magazines, comics and newspapers were widely read and purchased. Boys also need opportunities to explore and develop their affective response to text, so that reading can become a journey into others' lives as well as their own (Barrs 2000). Some research suggests that boys who are weaker readers often choose non-fiction because such texts are not as obviously 'graded' as fiction, and this allows them to maintain their role in the peer group (Moss 1998).

> Non-fiction texts allow weaker boy readers to escape others' judgements about how well they read and how competent they are. They enable them to maintain self esteem in the competitive environment of their peer-group relationships.   (Moss 1998)

The boys that Moss categorised as 'can't/don't' readers worked hard to avoid reading, especially where their teacher's judgements about reading ability were made visible. Girls in the same category (of which there were fewer, however) reacted differently and seemed to accept that reading was a challenge to them. They were not as anxious to hide their failure as readers. Moss (1998) also found that girls spent more time networking and talking about books, whereas the boys' peer groups tended to work against choosing to read. It is essential, therefore, that a reading culture is established and opportunities to explore texts independently are regularly offered. Such opportunities need to include 'the education of the emotions and of the whole person' (Barrs 2000) through literature based activities, some of which may well be developed in shared and guided reading, as well as in independent reading time.

Independent reading activities

Reading is a social activity, so it is important for all children to practise reading in supportive social contexts. While reading aloud, shared and guided reading offer such social contexts, independent reading activities that are also social are essential. Some may be semi-structured opportunities such as play readings or literature circles; others may be less structured, but still interactive, such as paired book browsing or text re-enactment. All such activities are text based and seek to prompt children's independent engagement with texts in pairs or small groups. They can be set for groupwork in the literacy hour (in response to NLS objectives), or developed through a reading workshop, when a cycle of different reading activities is undertaken. Workshop activities will not usually relate to the literacy hour text, but seek to support independent personal reading and develop children's preferences, their ability to choose appropriate texts and their knowledge of a range of genres. A further purpose of reading workshop activities is to profile and develop children's enjoyment and enthusiasm about reading, and their active membership of the community of readers in the classroom. The workshop may also include attention to text, sentence and word level features of the reading material but as a secondary strand. However, in the literacy hour, focused reading activities will highlight more explicitly children's contextual, grapho-phonic and syntactic strategies.

Quiet reading

To help children cope with extended text and develop their reading stamina, some schools offer a regular silent or quiet reading period. The influence of the Extending Beginning Reading Project (Southgate *et al.* 1981) prompted this practice, which can help readers handle longer stretches of continuous prose. It is not, however, an overt instructional context and has been criticised by OFSTED (1996) as lacking purpose and direction. However, children need the chance to become lost in a book and to read on their own in the company of others who are also comfortably engaged in developing the reading habit, for what keeps readers going is 'a legacy of past satisfactions' (Britton 1977). The importance of a teacher providing a model of quiet reading is highlighted by several researchers (e.g. Perez 1986; Wheldall and Entwistle 1988), and spontaneous or planned sharing is recognised as part of the process (Campbell 1990). Quiet reading during registration time, however, reduces children's concentration due to the number of distractions, and fails to provide sufficient time to develop in-depth reading and involvement in the text. A good routine is likely to include the children's prior selection of texts, an extended time to read and a time to discuss, retell sections, share extracts, talk about characters or information gathered and so on. So the resources available need to be varied and attractive, providing the opportunity for rereading a shared text, for accessing a wide range of texts over time, and for quiet reading with partners. Children also need to practice browsing, selecting and rejecting texts.

In 1996, a survey of 50 primary schools found that 95 per cent practised silent reading (Fenwick and Reader 1996) but this situation has not been maintained. Some schools include a guided group reading session in quiet reading time, while others have sought to reorganise it into a reading workshop (which may include a guided reading group). Several schools now offer silent reading half-termly, alternating with a readers' workshop, which offers a more socially supported instructional context. However, there are still too many children who can read, but choose not to, partly because they do not like to (Brooks *et al.* 1996), so teachers must make provision to develop independent reading.

Some advantages of quiet reading

- It can foster personal choice of text (albeit, guided and supported).
- It develops children's own preferences and awareness of their reading habits.
- It can retain an interactive element.
- It can increase personal involvement and confidence.
- It offers time to develop reading stamina.
- It can increase children's experience of a wide range of texts.
- It helps to sustain and enrich the community of readers.

The texts

> Reading development is not some step by step progress through progressive mastery of mechanical skills. Rather it is a process of taking experience of the world, as well as knowledge and expectations about how stories work and finding a book that offers enough promise of emotional satisfaction in the light of those expectations and that experience to make it worthwhile to persist with reading it.
>
> (Sarland 1991)

Independent reading activities may focus on the wide range of literary genre and non-fiction text types identified in the NLSF and listed in the National Curriculum, but a much wider range of reading material needs to be overtly included and valued in the classroom, to support independent reading, enrich personal choices and foster satisfaction. Book boxes arranged according to themes or genre (e.g. fairy tales, science fiction, adventure or animal stories), including boxes of non-fiction books and everyday publications (e.g. comics, magazines, newspapers, catalogues) pass clear messages to children about the range of texts that are recognised as valid reading resources. This may particularly encourage boys, since some boys and their fathers do not consider themselves to be readers because they are not reading novels. Conversely, however, assumptions about boys' or girls' interests and preferences in reading must be avoided and each class of children treated as individuals whose interests need to be established and built on.

What is clear is that teachers' knowledge of individual children's interests and reading habits should guide their personal recommendations and suggestions. New adventures in print need to be offered to help extend individual repertoires and build confidence. Teachers' knowledge of 'new' authors (e.g. Hugh Lupton, William Nicholson, and Nancy Sweetland) or the new books published by established authors (e.g. Henrietta Branford, Nina Bawden and Martin Waddell) is critical in fostering independence and being able to offer recommendations. In trying to keep up to date, *Books for Keeps*, the children's book review magazine, is highly recommended as a school resource, in order to maintain quality book stock. The teacher's own enthusiasm for literature undoubtedly influences the attitudes, interests and engagement of readers and needs to be acknowledged as a factor influencing independence. Teachers want to avoid the flat-earth readers' syndrome (Chambers 1991), when readers are not challenged by reading beyond their competence and are unadventurous, although for some newly fledged readers being hooked on, for example, Dick King Smith or Jacqueline Wilson could be advantageous in the short term. Likewise, teachers' own views about the literary merits of particular texts may need to be put to one side and the popularity of, say, Point Horror or Babysitters Club recognised. The challenge of choice and honouring children's tastes needs to be handled carefully. Peer group culture is very influential and in a reading community fads and fashions influenced by the media, popular culture, television and film will come and go. The teacher's role is not to fight these trends but to recognise them, work with them and seek to offer growing paths and opportunities that stretch beyond them. These should expand the children's repertoires in directions that complement the features of the currently popular texts and enable contrasts and comparisons to be made, without denigrating their choice of material.

At home

> Talking well about books is a high value activity in itself. But talking well about books is also the best rehearsal there is for talking well about other things. So in helping children to talk about their reading, we help them be articulate about the rest of their lives.   (Chambers 1993)

Home–school links make a significant contribution to children's attitudes and attainment as independent readers, as the influential Haringey and Belfield reading projects showed in the early 1980s. Most schools make arrangements for children to take books home to read with their parents (Wragg *et al.* 1998), although the nature of the actual reading experience prompted by school and undertaken at home is less well researched and documented. Homework guidelines (DfEE 1998a) state that KS1 homework should largely consist of regular reading *with* parents and carers, but whatever their perceived parental responsibilities in relation to homework, parents need to know that the first vital ingredient of success in reading is children's personal response and enjoyment from texts. This enjoyment emerges from two sources: the enjoyment of the text that is read and the enjoyment of the shared experience of reading it. Such enjoyment is a critical motivator in learning to read and developing as a reader, so parents need to understand the full significance of reading *to* their children, as well as *with* their children and of encouraging their youngsters to read *by* themselves.

Reading at home

Reading *to* your child	• challenging books, newspapers, magazines, fiction and non-fiction • whole texts or extracts of interest • discussing the text
Reading *with* your child	• their school book/library book/own text • reading together a page, paragraph, chapter each • discussing and sharing the text
Prompting your child to read *by themselves*	• their school/library book/own text • to find out information and for pleasure • discussing the text

---

Explaining that reading is much more than the accurate decoding of words is essential if parents are to be encouraged to talk about texts, interpreting, responding and making sense of them with their children. Explaining the levels of inferential reading and deduction required for the SATs at all key stages may help, and innovative ways of recording joint child and parent involvement in reading and responding may help to encourage conversing (Greenhough and Hughes 1999). As these researchers acknowledge, changing parental behaviour is most likely to succeed through involvement that builds on parents' current practice and expertise and convinces them of the rationale for talking about reading and making meaning together. With the inevitable reduction in one-to-one, teacher–child reading sessions in school as a consequence of the NLS, parents are arguably playing a more significant role in supporting individual conversations about texts. Parents and teachers need to work together to use this time most fruitfully.

Developing 'story sacks' for use at home can prompt young readers to re-enact, retell and reread texts with action and increasing understanding. A more recent innovation targeted at struggling and reluctant boy readers at KS2 are curiosity kits, which are non-fiction book bags. Research has indicated that these kits had a marked and positive impact on home reading, increased the number of shared readings in the home and widened the range of adults and siblings who took part in these interactions (Lewis *et al.* 2000). In fact the curiosity kits were used for multiple readings, with fathers, mothers, brothers and sisters choosing to read the kits themselves as well as share them. Further principles and ideas for parental involvement are noted in 'Working collaboratively with parents' (p. 125) and 'Working collaboratively with LSAs' (p. 130).

Independent reading: Institutional self-review

- What provision is made for independent reading: in the literacy hour, in workshop oriented sessions or in a quiet reading time?

- How are children's reading preferences and attitudes monitored and developed?

- Does the range of texts available reflect the breadth introduced in shared reading and include everyday publications?

- How are parents involved in their child's reading development?

- How is reading assessed, recorded and shared with parents?

Independent reading: Ideas for action

- *Review independent reading habits and preferences*: Use the questionnaire in 'Assessment and target setting – class, group and individual: Ideas for action' (p. 42). Such information can be used to plan activities building on and extending the class's current reading choices.

- *Analyse home–school contact books*: Monitor parent and child involvement through these books. Trial alternative strategies that focus on recording involvement, engagement and conversation about the text, or model a focus on textual characteristics (e.g. characters, plot, language etc.).

- *Review quiet reading time with the class*: Through discussion and involvement establish what the class wants from quiet reading, their attitudes towards it and their suggestions for improving the quality of this time.

- *Establish reading partners*: This may be within the class or across year groups with regular opportunities for partners to meet and read together. The older readers may also make comments in their partners' home–school reading record.

- *Order* Books for Keeps, *the children's book magazine:* Use this to keep up to date, to order new books and find out about authors and book events (BFK, 6 Brightfield Road, Lee, London, SE12 8QF. Tel: 020 852 4953).

- *Create an A–Z of authors or poets*: Groups generate a list of authors and collect books by authors from their part of the alphabet. Make a class list so that popular authors or poets can be seen at a glance.

- *Undertake surveys of favourite writers, books or magazines:* Encourage different groups to survey the class or year group and create graphs to show, say, the top ten poets or magazines.

- *Display the teacher's or a child's own favourite books*: Prepare the display, and create book cards about each text. Share one or two extracts and discuss the reasons for the choice.

- *Write Post-it messages about books*: Provide Post-its for the children to offer informal initialled recommendations to others. These are stuck inside the front cover of the text and are not reviews, but often include enthusiastic responses, star ratings or page numbers of exciting parts.

- *Organise a book blanket*: This is an organised browsing and discussion session to help children make more informed choices and get to know the class library. Spread all the books (or just one genre) over the tables and undertake book activities with them (e.g. children select a book they do/don't want to read, one by an author they do/don't know. All activities involve browsing, selection *and* discussion with their neighbour (e.g. 'Tell your friend why you like that picture'; 'Why don't you want to read it?'; 'Check the blurb, does it tempt you?'). After a couple of activities encourage book selection in pairs and settle the class to read these together, choosing texts that can be tackled in one sitting.

- *Establish librarian role plays*: Each pair agrees that one of them will adopt the role of librarian. The other is not in role. Each librarian collects a pile of known or read books and their reading record and seeks to persuade the 'visiting child' that they'd like to read these.

- *Create browsing boxes*: Ensure variety by offering one group a browsing box in quiet reading time, so each year every child has the chance to browse or read, for example, poetry, non-fiction, comics or magazines, joke books, catalogues, newspapers or picture fiction. Browsing groups need to be allowed to talk and share their reading.

- *Set up squirt plus*: This involves *s*ilent, *q*uiet, *u*ninterrupted *i*ndividualised *r*eading *t*ime, *plus* a commitment to discussion time in pairs. This five minutes' focus after quiet reading can take many forms (e.g. noting text, sentence or word level features, sharing their attitude to their book or connections, predictions, questions and rich vocabulary).

- *Set up reading journals*: Children record their responses to the text they are reading and develop a dialogue about their reading with their teacher. This conversation on paper notes what children think and feel as they read, and not merely their views at the close of the book. Teachers write back regularly and may make recommendations for future reading.

- *Write a letter to the teacher*: Children write to their teacher about their current reading book or class novel, sharing their affective response, identifying questions about the text, quoting favourite phrases or descriptions and exploring their thinking about the text. Teachers reply. This is like a one-off reading journal entry. In both activities support will initially be needed.

- *Set up print walks*: Provide clipboards and, with an adult, let a small group walk around the school/classroom collecting evidence of print used for different purposes. Alternatively, print walks can focus on specific word, sentence or text level features.

- *Establish curiosity kits*: These non-fiction themed book bags might contain a non-fiction book, an adult magazine, a related wordsearch, an activity and a toy. Contained in a record bag these can be targeted at particular groups and borrowed for a week's loan to prompt shared reading at home (Lewis *et al.* 2000).

- *Create storyboxes*: These can prompt story play and storytelling in the home. They are small boxes with a theme. For example, a dinosaur storybox might contain plastic dinosaurs, a nest and eggs and a piece of red cloth (for lava), all contained in a decorated box showing the terrain (Bromley 1998).

Writing – shared, guided and independent: Principles

Teacher said ..., by Judith Nicholls

You can use
mumbled and muttered,
groaned, grumbled and uttered,
professed, droned or stuttered
    ... but *don't* use SAID!

You can use
rant or recite,
yell, yodel or snort,
bellow, murmur or moan,
you can grunt or just groan
    ... but *don't* use SAID!

You can
hum, howl and hail,
scream, screech, shriek or bawl,
squeak, snivel or squeal
with a blood-curdling wail
    ... but *don't* use SAID!
    ... SAID my teacher

The catch-22 that Judith Nicholls highlights in this poem clearly applies to the teaching of writing. Exhortations and instructions to use particular speech verbs or complex sentences for example, tend to fall on dry ground if children are not motivated to write and are not themselves involved in the process of communicating to others. Furthermore, the rules and requirements of any written genre are not only interpreted and adapted in real world texts but parodied with irony and intelligence. If teachers are to avoid creating a 'generation of clerks' (Hilton 1988) who can name a given grammatical part, but don't care to take a full part and have little to say, then a balanced writing curriculum must be offered that profiles the purpose and use of language (Frater 2000).

Through immersing children in a text type (in read aloud time), attending to purpose of the form and its features (in shared reading), and modelling these explicitly (in shared writing), children can begin to develop their writing with their teacher's support (in guided writing) and practise the genre on their own (in independent writing). Throughout, critical reflection on the choices made and the writing composed is essential, not only to help children transfer the knowledge and insight gained through text exploration, but also in order to develop a metalanguage with which to describe, analyse, synthesise and conceptualise their work and that of others. Mature writers are able to talk about their stories in a way that indicates knowledge transformation (Bereiter and Scardamalia 1987). Other research also indicates the need for children to develop metacognitive understandings of their own writing processes (Wray 1994; Corden 2000). So all opportunities to share, reflect on and evaluate their own and others' writing need to be seized, the appropriate terminology used and ways forward identified through reflection.

'Teacher said ...', Judith Nicholls, from *Magic Mirror and Other Poems for Children* (1985), reproduced by permission of Faber and Faber Limited.

Reading as a writer through:

- immersion and familiarisation in a text   *reading aloud and text-related activities*
  ↓
- analysis and attention to textual features   *shared reading*
  ↓
- modelling and articulating the conventions   *shared writing*
  ↓
- scaffolding and supporting writing   *guided writing*
  ↓
- increasingly independent writing   *independent work in hour, extended writing*
  ↓

| Critical reflection |
| What is effective? |
| What can be improved? |

throughout the writing process

The relationship between children's reading and writing has long been recognised (e.g. Clay 1980; Kress 1986; Rosenblatt 1989; Fox 1993), so this apprenticeship model of teaching writing is well founded, but needs to be augmented by independent opportunities for children to make personal choices about form, content and purpose, and must be underpinned by a commitment to developing young writers' personal voices (Clarke 2000). The teacher's challenge is to make the reading–writing relationship powerful and productive and not merely a form-led imitation of language features, without voice or emotive impact.

As the National Curriculum Cox Report (DES 1988a) stated, 'the best writing is vigorous, committed, honest and interesting. We have not included these qualities in our statements of attainment because they cannot be mapped on to National Curriculum Levels. Even so, all good classroom practice will be geared to encouraging and fostering these vital qualities'. Currently, however, progression in writing is largely perceived as increasing technical accuracy, and control over structure, organisation and a widening vocabulary. The annual QCA reports on the previous year's SAT results seem to drive the profession into teaching particular linguistic features as if they were in themselves the *raison d'être* of writing. The NLS (1999b) and QCA (1999f) both highlight structure and language features at the expense of communicating meaning through content, voice and developing style. It is not that linguistic features are unimportant, but simply teaching children to pepper their writing with more adverbs, for example, will not necessarily improve their writing. Writing takes time and much will depend on the purpose and audience of the writing, its authenticity (Medwell 1994) and children's ability to transfer and use the knowledge taught, as well as their wider experience of reading and writing. The new National Curriculum (DfEE 1999a) is however clear about purpose and readership.

The range of purposes for writing should include:
a) to communicate to others;
b) to create imaginary worlds;
c) to explore experience;
d) to organise and explain information.

The range of readers for writing should include:
teachers, other adults, children and the writers themselves.

Key Stage 1, National Curriculum (DfEE 1999a)

The range of purposes for writing should include:

a) to imagine and explore feelings and ideas, focusing on creative uses of language and how to interest the reader;

b) to inform and explain, focusing on the subject matter and to convey it in sufficient detail for the reader;

c) to persuade, focusing on how arguments and evidence are built up and language used to convince the reader;

d) to review and comment on what has been read, seen or heard, focusing on both the topic and the writer's view of it.

The range of readers for writing should include:

teachers, the class, other children, adults, the wider community and imagined readers.

Key Stage 2, National Curriculum (DfEE 1999a)

As recent surveys have shown, the schools that were most effective at raising writing standards contextualised their teaching of word, sentence and text level work and this interacted with written composition. So the teaching of language concepts and skills was woven into the process of written composition (Frater 2000). This supports research in *The Effective Teachers of Literacy* (Medwell *et al.* 1998), which showed that while less effective literacy teachers approached technical issues as skills to be learned for their own sakes, the good teachers ensured that children saw them as a means to the end of improving their actual reading and writing. The NLSF (DfEE 1998b) does not seek to mitigate against such effective practice. Indeed, in his *The National Literacy Strategy: Review of Research and Other Related Evidence*, Beard (1999) notes that this TTA commissioned research underpins the NLSF, but in making a literal interpretation of the framework, some teachers have adopted a more fragmented and less effective approach to both planning and teaching English. In their classrooms, word and sentence level work were taught separately from text level work and 'in practice these took precedence' (Frater 2000). A constructive balance between the levels and their integration in action is central to developing inclusive and effective practice in writing.

Text, sentence and word level learning

Text level work focuses on composition, the generation and structuring of ideas to produce a coherent piece of writing. This involves knowledge of literacy genres and non-fiction text types and their organisation, presentation, structure and purpose. Such knowledge is developed through rich experiences of reading aloud and interactive shared reading opportunities, as well as through modelled and shared writing. Quality composition also depends on imaginative ideas and interesting content conveyed with conviction and style by the writer. Freedom and space to develop coherent and complete compositions are as necessary to enable this as they are for creative development. The meaningful aspects of what children write are currently in danger of being ignored (D'Arcy 2000), but their thoughts, feelings, understandings and values need to be committed to paper. Genuine response to these meanings as well as to the conventions used must be made. Compositional opportunities across the curriculum also need to be seized and a more integrated thematic approach valued once again. Coherent units of work can ensure that genres are taught in sufficient depth, so increased compositional independence becomes possible, and more satisfying and rounded literacy experiences are offered.

In relation to studying texts in shared reading, learning to read like a writer and noticing how writers create their effects, it is essential that whole texts are regularly used. Decontextualised extracts cannot offer the same degree of whole text coherence and meaning that, say, picture books or short stories do to enrich and support composition. Talk, interaction and experiential approaches at text level (e.g. drama, storytelling, graphic representation of story grammars and charts) also play a significant role in the cognitive process of composition. Children can learn to extend their ideas by dwelling within texts, empathising with characters, developing viewpoints and acknowledging other perspectives. Knowledge about form is useful but is unlikely on its own to generate writing that is strongly expressed or powerfully felt. Indeed 'direct teaching of particular linguistic features is no substitute for substantial experience of reading and writing' (Barrs 2000). Both are needed in order to shape and compose meaning.

Sentence level work includes both grammar and punctuation and should enable children to:

- become aware of the variety and complexity of grammatical choices available that they can use for different purposes to clarify the meaning of texts;

- explore the effects of choosing particular grammatical forms or punctuation marks rather than others;

- know that different types of writing use different layouts, organisation, sentence structure and language features;

- relate their learning to their own reading and writing;

- build on their implicit knowledge through investigative approaches that encourage an interest in the structures and patterns of written language.

The National Curriculum (DfEE 1999a) requires that explicit knowledge of the forms and structures of language (and the necessary terminology to describe and discuss these forms) is taught, as well as knowledge about the functions of language, how it is used and for what purposes. Contemporary approaches to teaching this highlight not only what is to be covered, but also focus on how this will be taught, remembered and used. The key teaching strategies in the NLSF play a significant role in this process. The teacher's challenge is to approach the teaching of grammar and punctuation, 'not as a dull, algebraic exercise, but as a creative craft' (Rooke 1999), which is both intriguing and essential to clarify and evaluate meaning.

A sentence level teaching model

Reading aloud
Children hear the tunes and patterns of language, the grammatical organisation of texts.
↓

Shared reading	↔	**Shared writing**
Teacher and class read, notice and attend to grammar and punctuation, and discuss its use and function		Teacher models or scribes, reflecting on the grammatical choices available in composition
↓		↓
Sentence level exploration	↔	**Sentence level exploration**
Explicit focus, as a class and independently – direct instruction, investigations and discussion		Explicit focus, as a class and independently – direct instruction, investigations and discussion
↓		↓
Guided reading	↔	**Guided writing**
Teacher scaffolds syntactic strategies and may discuss grammatical features or particular punctuation		Teacher scaffolds the use of appropriate grammar and punctuation and may focus on one aspect, its use and function
↓		↓
Independent reading	↔	**Independent writing**
Child reads like a writer and is increasingly aware of the effect of grammar and punctuation in the text		Child uses knowledge of grammar and punctuation increasingly appropriately according to form and purpose – feedback and critical reflection may relate to this

Investigative approaches to teaching grammar and punctuation are recommended by many (e.g. Bain and Bridgewood 1998; Crinson 1998; DfEE 1999b), in order to encourage children to explore patterns and hypothesise rules on the basis of their investigations. Such rules can then be tested on a wider range of reading material and made explicit to others. The resultant display needs to be referred to, and used by, the teacher in shared work and revisited in guided work so that it becomes embedded and applied in independent work. For example, the children could analyse a list of nouns to work out the rules for making plurals or using capitals; or they could hunt in traditional tales for sentences that end in an exclamation mark, then categorise its use and draw out key principles to be checked elsewhere. This problem-solving, hands-on approach encourages children to take more responsibility for their own learning, although it needs careful teacher support and materials appropriate to the ability range. The quality of the shared texts chosen to teach linguistic features is critical; they should provide a meaningful context and natural language patterns (Kress 1997).

Word level work focuses on phonics, spelling, vocabulary and handwriting tailored to each key stage. In relation to spelling, the most widely held view is that children's spelling development falls into stages, so that children move from pre-literate scribbles to the use of phonetic strategies, through a transitional stage (when errors are associated with visual, structural or semantic aspects), before conventional spelling is firmly established (Gentry 1982; Temple *et al.* 1982). However, more recent work has begun to show that this process is not invariable, and that in order to spell, children draw on several different sources of knowledge: phonetic, visual, structural and semantic (Lennox and Siegal 1994; Treiman 1994; O'Sullivan 2000). Teaching spelling needs to involve explicit instruction and demonstrations, investigative approaches, intervention in writing and editing, and interactive word study sessions. Profiling children's thinking about spelling at KS2 through raising their reflective awareness of their own spelling strategies has also been shown to play a key role in spelling development (O'Sullivan 2000). Again, children need to be actively involved in the cognitive processes of hypothesising and predicting, and making inferences and analogies, since children need to be prepared to tackle unknown, irregular and complex words with confidence.

The knowledge involved in reading and spelling is obviously reciprocal (Frith 1985; Ehri 1997), yet good readers who are poor spellers tend to have a limited approach to spelling unfamiliar words and rely too heavily on phonological approaches (Frith 1980; OFSTED 1998; O'Sullivan 2000). The NLS recognises the importance of visual and aural spelling strategies and the need for morphological knowledge as well as active approaches. However, spelling development is also influenced by purposeful writing, varied experiences and the opportunity to write at length. The latter needs to be carefully planned for in addition to the literacy hour at both key stages.

The writing environment

An environment that develops writers is one of demonstration, expectation and opportunity, in which the teacher provides explicit support for writing and is a genuine reader of each child's writing. Children need to become attentive and critical readers of their own writing, but this can only happen if they take increased responsibility for the process of writing and develop the language with which to appraise their own and each other's writing. The chance to discuss writing with others at all stages of the writing process will also be a regular social feature of the classrooms that are writing communities, since the intention of sharing writing is to build a community of writers who are engaged in generating and evaluating their writing. This will enable them to both understand the nature of the writing process and improve their own writing.

Physical aspects of the effective writing environment will also be evident in a furniture arrangement that encourages verbal interaction and the use of computers, writing tables and literate role play areas, as well as the use of reference posters providing summaries of the writing process, features of particular genres, spelling rules, word families and so on. A wealth of reading materials in different formats are needed (e.g. pamphlets, advertising material, magazines, letters, instruction manuals, catalogues), as are alphabet charts, keyword cards and quality texts, both fiction and non-fiction. A variety of writing materials need to be readily available, as should access to bookmaking materials, overhead projectors (OHPs), flipcharts, tape recorders and folders. Such a plethora of resources and quality displays are next to useless, however, if they act as mere decoration and wallpaper. Teachers need to draw children's attention to such resources actively, highlight their value, model their use and encourage substantial independent use of these writing supports. This purposeful use of resources is commonly found in effective literacy environments (Medwell *et al.* 1998; Cambourne 2000), alongside an ethos and classroom culture that highlight the children's ownership of their own writing as a motivating factor. Such ownership, care and responsibility are difficult to develop if artificial, discrete writing tasks are set and independent opportunities in which a strong sense of personal commitment and choice are invested are rarely offered. As White (2000) shows, the creation of a productive classroom culture for writing in which ownership is developed through self-directed writing projects can significantly influence the quality of children's texts and their attitudes to writing.

Shared writing: Principles

Shared writing needs to be approached like any writing task, allowing time to discuss the content, time to get the ideas down on paper and then time to re-read what has been written and revise if necessary.

(Pidgeon 1990)

Shared writing is the joint construction of a text by teacher and children, which enables the class to learn collaboratively about both composition and later transcription. This context for teaching about the writing process emerged from the work of Don Holdaway (1979), and has been developed and refined by others (Smith 1982; McKenzie 1985; Laycock 1990; Browne 1993). Shared writing is frequently explicitly linked to texts encountered in shared reading and reading aloud sessions, so that examples of a particular genre can be introduced, read and attended to, in preparation for shared writing. Together, the teacher and the children collaborate to plan or develop a piece of writing that extends the children's independent writing skills. Using the children's contributions the teacher models different aspects of writing, such as structure and content, as well as grammar and spelling, redrafting and editing.

Shared writing provides an interactive demonstration of how written language works, and helps writers develop the skills they need to communicate effectively. However, it is an underused tool for teaching writing (HMI 2000). It is important to keep sight of what is involved in writing and the purpose of the writing therefore needs to remain central. Effective teachers of literacy profile purpose and meaning in their work with children, and fully explain the reasons for the work they're engaged in (Medwell *et al.* 1998). But writers not only need to know about purpose in writing; they also need to know their readership or audience. Who is the writing for? What is it trying to achieve? They also need to be aware of the process of writing and that quality written text can provide good models for writing. Through shared reading and writing children can widen their knowledge of genre, and learn to communicate more effectively (Kress 1982; Wray and Lewis 1997).

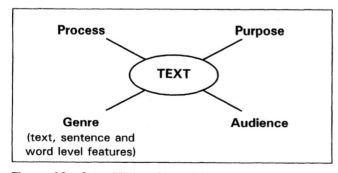

Figure 13 Searchlights for writing

Shared writing is underpinned by theories about effective learning. As Vygotsky (1978) has shown, the critical elements in learning are social and collaborative, and teachers need to provide support to scaffold children's learning (Bruner 1985; Wood *et al.* 1976) The teacher's dialogue is critical in scaffolding their developing knowledge so they learn to write independently. Shared writing is also underpinned by research that highlights the need for teachers to model what is involved and to make the literacy process explicit to children (Wray 1994). Children already have implicit knowledge about language, but need to make this more explicit, and to develop the vocabulary to talk about texts. So the craft of writing is partly taught through more conscious awareness of the strategies, skills and processes involved (Carter 1991; Corden 2000).

The advantages of shared writing

- It can help children to understand that the writer is in control and constantly has choices to make about their writing.
- It can model the use and explain the purpose of any aspect of writing.
- It can explicitly demonstrate and use the writing process: planning, drafting, revising, editing.
- It can involve the children actively in a collaborative process of composition.
- It can introduce, reinforce and extend understanding about writing at text, sentence and word level.
- It can encourage increased insight through evaluation, praise, constructive criticism and critical reflection.
- It can provide an opportunity to develop a metalanguage: a language to talk about language.
- It can highlight the relationship between reading and writing.
- It enables a text to be produced that can serve as an ongoing resource for literacy learning.

Texts for shared writing

The reciprocal links between reading and writing are well established (e.g. Clay 1991a, 1993; Tierney *et al.* 1989), and it is clear that the texts that children read and those that are read to them provide structures, themes and ideas for their writing. So, where possible, shared reading and writing should be linked, with children being helped to improve their writing by learning from experienced and talented writers. In investigating and exploring how quality writers create certain effects, and make use of various narrative or non-narrative structures, children can begin to 'read like writers'. In deconstructing the whole text or part of a text in shared reading, readers can identify some of the building blocks that the writer employed. This knowledge can be used to reconstruct a new text on the shoulders of the old. Clearly only some features of the text will be examined and should be highlighted in a manner that doesn't reduce the text's power and meaning, but seeks rather to expand it. If children are to lean on literature and non-fiction to learn about writing, it follows that the texts they meet and analyse in shared reading need to be of the highest quality. Teachers' knowledge of powerful emotive texts, rhythmic repetitive texts, and informative and illuminating texts is critical. Basic language, limited illustrations, weak characters, overly complex narrative structures and dull themes will not motivate young readers and writers. Such texts cannot provide quality models to mirror in writing, nor will such texts prompt informed discussion and interested analysis. Teachers cannot offer effective and related reading and writing sessions without quality examples of poetry, fiction and non-fiction that are really worth rereading and revisiting.

Texts need to be chosen carefully and not merely rely on what is available in big book form. A well selected, enlarged extract from a known narrative (which is being read in its entirety), or a variety of poems collected on a given theme can be very useful as models to imitate and learn from. The quality of the text must guide teacher's choices. In relation to narrative, good short story collections are needed (e.g. Joan Aiken's *A Necklace of Raindrops* and Berlie Doherty's *How Green You Are*), as are thought-provoking picture books (e.g. Philippa Butler's *Pawprints in Time* or Eugene Trivias's *The Three Little Wolves and the Big Bad Pig*). Tales that are clearly structured also need to be drawn upon (e.g. Sarah Hayes's *This is the Bear* series and Jill Murphy's *On the Way Home*), as do traditional tales (e.g. Tony Ross's *The Boy who Cried Wolf* or John Steptoe's *Mufaro's Beautiful Daughters*). In poetry, anthologies and poets need profiling, and not merely individual examples of a poetic form (e.g. Quentin Blake's *All Join In* or Susan Hill's anthology *Really Rapt*). Non-fiction choices need to include real world print and quality collections (e.g. Heinemann's Literacy World series). Novels, too, are valuable (e.g. Michael Morpurgo's *The Dancing Bear* or Jill Tomlinson's *Penguins Progress*), although these do not provide access to the short story form that children are most frequently asked to produce.

Texts for shared reading and writing need to be selected and grouped according to the genre focus of the unit of work. Planning several two- or three-week blocks to examine, for example, traditional tales or persuasive and discursive texts, enables the teacher to tackle the genre in depth and immerse the class in a range of examples, before discussion and consideration of any common features in shared reading. Later they will construct their own examples in shared writing. So the genres (and their related text level objectives) that a class experience, learn about and practise need to be planned first. The related sentence and word level work can then be woven into this plan and integrated within the writing as HMI (2000) recommend. Each term needs to work towards some kind of focused publication or event in the class. This will be introduced by the teacher and the genre studied will be read, analysed, annotated, modelled, constructed and worked on in several shared writing sessions to prompt and support guided and independent work. The medium-term writing focus needs to profile language in use and provide a purpose and a wider audience for children's writing. This gives children a reason for redrafting and editing work, and enables the essential word and sentence level skills to be taught and practised in a meaningful manner. A term or half-term's focus might include:

- a class anthology of myths and legends;
- a presentation of work on a cross-curricular theme;
- a storytelling tape with an accompanying book;
- a trip to the infants to share their animal or adventure tales;
- a poetry reading;
- a scripted television documentary shown in assembly;
- a newspaper;
- a play reading;
- a series of adverts in print and in action as commercials.

The process of shared writing

Preparation time
Preparation time and activity before the actual writing are frequently necessary and may involve the class in generating ideas in pairs or small groups before offering these to the teacher scribe. Such preparation time needs to be overtly interactive to draw children in and to enable full participation. It may involve an initial brainstorm, a brief revisitation of the text, retelling part of the tale in pairs or a more extended activity. For example, the teacher may read a brief framesetting section from the chosen text and then ask the class to extend the argument between two characters through role play. This activity creates an oral draft of the conversation, and can provoke ideas and a sense of character through intonation and language. In shared writing, these features of the interchange can be captured in words and appropriate speech verbs and adverbs chosen to reflect the role play (Grainger and Cremin 2000). Alternatively a story map (Benton and Fox 1985) or story shapes (Bentley and Rowe 1991) may be drawn to highlight the structure of the tale or the themes within it. This structure applied to June Crebbin's *The Train Ride*, for

example, may be created in KS1 through a series of sequential freeze frames to show the significant features of the journey. This can then be used as a basis for developing children's story schemas and for writing a parallel journey story. Additionally, the map can be used to teach linking words or time phrases (e.g. 'next', 'later', 'after that', 'then', 'suddenly') during sentence level work. These brief examples reflect the oral, interactive nature of preparing for shared writing and the close relationship between shared reading and writing activities. In shared writing, children realise what they can accomplish together through teacher guidance and productive collaboration. Such work should involve both 'active engagement' and 'spill over' (evidence of transferability), which Cambourne (1997) believes are useful criteria for measuring successful teaching strategies that include everyone.

Writing time

During the actual construction of the text, the class contribute ideas and comments to shape the writing as it progresses. The teacher is constantly modelling and thinking out loud, making explicit the processes that a writer has to go through to construct a text, and enabling children to reflect on their own and others' suggestions.

> Shared writing obviously requires sensitive, skilled teachers, who listen carefully and who, without forcing ideas, can help children bring together their thinking and their language into a unified text.
> (McKenzie 1985)

In shared writing the control and ownership of the piece is overtly and explicitly shared, with the teacher using every opportunity to draw in the more reticent children and to ensure that children with English as an additional language (EAL) understand what is being said. In demonstrating the problem solving, planning and decision-making nature of writing at the moment of composition, and in sharing these processes by speaking aloud their thoughts, teachers will on occasion be involved in modelled writing. This is subtly different from shared writing, in that all the ownership and control is vested in the teacher. Modelled writing sessions will often turn into shared writing sessions because the children offer ideas and suggestions. In both strategies the teacher needs explicitly to voice the multiple options available to writers and to explain the thinking underlying the choices made. Figure 14, developed from Laycock (1999), outlines this significant process: the thinking out loud about writing choices.

Reflection time

When the jointly constructed piece of writing is 'complete' the teacher will frequently review and evaluate the work with the class. Reflecting back on the original purpose of the writing and the learning objectives set for it will be central to this process. Many ongoing writer's choices will have been made explicit during the shared writing, so that reflective consideration is given at the point of composition, but a final reflection time is an opportunity to read the whole piece together as a class and to appraise its strengths and weaknesses in relation to its intention. This reflection and evaluation serves several purposes.

It is through reflection that learners begin to exercise conscious control over their learning, and in this shared context the class needs to review their work as a group, positively and affirmatively, while also acknowledging that there are potential growth points or areas for development in the writing. A

Reflection and evaluation in writing

- It assesses the extent to which the piece of writing achieves its purpose.
- It provides a model for critical reflection and constructive criticism.
- It enables the development of metalanguage: a language to talk about language.
- It connects the writing back to the text, highlighting the relationship between reading and writing.
- It can refine understandings about textual, grammatical and word level features.
- It can prepare the ground for developing, revising or editing the text.

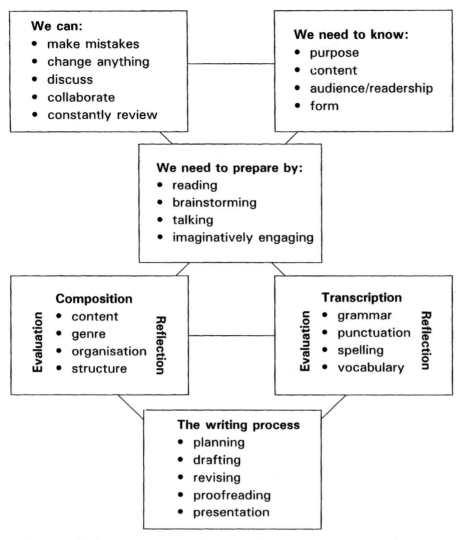

Figure 14 Shared writing: the teacher voices the process of writing (developed from Laycock, L. (1999) 'Shared reading and shared writing at Key Stage 1', in Goodwin, P. (ed.) *The Literate Classroom*. London: David Fulton Publishers)

final reflection period is not needed in every shared writing session, but it is an invaluable opportunity for modelling both critical evaluation and preparation for the next stage of the writing process. In this way the shared writing piece can be used as the basis for later development work. The National Curriculum (DfEE 1999a) requires that children reflect on and review their own and others' writing.

Working with the teacher and with others, in order to develop their writing, pupils should be taught to:
- assemble and develop ideas on paper and on screen
- plan and *review their writing, discussing the quality of what is written.*
                                                            KS1, National Curriculum (DfEE 1999a)
To develop their writing on paper and on screen, pupils should be taught to:
- plan: note and develop initial ideas
- draft: develop ideas from the plan into structured written text
- revise: change and improve the draft
- proofread: check the draft for spelling and punctuation errors, omissions and repetitions
- present: prepare a neat, correct and clear final copy
- *discuss and evaluate their own and others' writing*
                                                            KS2, National Curriculum (DfEE 1999a)

Further discussion of other reflective opportunities, such as response partnerships and conferences are discussed in 'Guided writing: Principles' (pp. 104–106) and 'Independent writing: Principles' (pp. 108–13). Through shared writing the opportunity exists to evaluate the overall text critically as well as attend to word, sentence and text level features. In classrooms where the community of writers is strong, individual children's work can also be used as the basis for this reflection and evaluation. The individual writer's own thoughts and comments need to be honoured first, before the class identify positive elements and areas for development in relation to the set of objectives or intentions. Using an overhead transparency of the child's work, enlarging it or wordprocessing it, enables all the children to read it and can help them make explicit connections between this piece and their own writing. Time to teach, model and profile reflection needs to be provided in shared writing, in order to extend children's independence and their ability to improve their written work, for a reflective learner is an effective learner.

Shared writing: Institutional self-review

- Is shared writing an interactive shared experience involving *all* the children?

- Are sufficient high quality texts available to support shared writing?

- Are the learning intentions of each piece of shared writing made explicit to the learners and used as a basis for evaluation and discussion?

- Is adequate preparation time provided to draft the piece orally, generate ideas and develop suggestions?

- Is shared writing used for both composition and transcription in a balanced and integrated manner?

- Does shared writing explicitly build on and connect to shared reading?

- Is the writing process overtly modelled and attended to in shared writing?

- Is reflection and evaluation of writing regularly modelled in shared writing time?

Shared writing: Ideas for action

While shared writing builds on shared reading, and focuses initially on composition, it is likely to be followed by sentence and word level work that flows naturally from the written text and is embedded within it. So the initial suggestions noted in this section are to make connections between text, sentence and word level work while profiling composition. The later activities noted are more explicitly focused on sentence or word level work and represent somewhat more generic activities, which are not tailored to particular literary genres or non-fiction. Many of the later activities are appropriate for whole-class work at sentence and word level. Teachers will make their own professional and flexible use of these activites and may be able to integrate them into a particular text focus. Further related ideas at text, sentence and word level are found in 'Shared reading: Ideas for action' (pp. 70–74).

Text level

Fiction

Story structure

- *Story hands:* Draw a large hand and summarise the shared text (with a beginning, trio of events in the middle and an ending, all linked). Use a story hand to plan a parallel tale, with the class generating ideas orally in pairs before writing each section. Work on connectives, link or time words that connect the narrative.

- *Skeleton summary:* As a class, create freeze frames of the significant narrative events in a shared text in sequential order. Each group agrees a phrase to describe their tableaux, and transfers it to a large skeleton outline. Work on paragraphs to put flesh on the skeleton's bones.

- *Titles:* Towards the end of a novel revisit the list of chapter titles and summarise key events in one of these. Working with a future unread chapter, map out the likely events together as a flow chart. Work on creating one or two paragraphs based on the flow chart.

- *Story cauldron:* Make a cauldron and create the ingredients of a magic story on cards (beginning, setting, characters, problem and resolution). Place them in the cauldron and use them to retell the story dramatically. Attach the cards to a flipchart and use them as a short story or planning frame. Expand on one or two to create paragraphs. Work on sentence construction and conjunctions.

Character

- *Role play a tense moment in a text*: Read from the text, then role play two characters at a moment of significance and tension in the tale. The conversation can be captured in speech bubbles as a playscript or as dialogue. Work on, say, speech verbs, adverbs or inverted commas. New lines and narrative action can be integrated as appropriate over time.

- *Decision alley:* Use this to consider a critical decision-making moment from one character's point of view. Half the class face the other half and as one child, in role as the character, progresses down the alley, their thoughts for and against a course of action are voiced by the class. Record these views as a list of pros and cons or retell that part of the tale as an interior monologue. Work on emotive vocabulary to reflect the difficulty involved in making the decision.

- *Hot-seat a character:* Prepare to question a character, generating possible questions (maybe writing them down) and ask several children to operate as the character. This is more effective if the other members of the class have roles too (e.g. as police, journalists or neighbours). Summarise what has been learnt about the character and feed this into a piece of shared writing about the character from another character's viewpoint, or list the questions and answers and write up the interview for a magazine or newspaper. Work on adapting writing style and tone.

- *Create a parallel description:* Reread a quality character description and draw a quick shared visual of the person painted in words. Imitate this description by producing one that operates in reverse, working from a visual (of another character in the text, magazine, painting or picture book). Work on descriptive vocabulary, synonyms and shades of meaning.

Setting

- *Observe and record ideas:* Focus on a quality picture book illustration of a setting and generate a list of events that could happen there, characters who are likely to be present, and words and phrases that describe the setting. List them. Enrich these setting descriptors, adding adjectives and creating noun phrases, a sense of atmosphere and so on. Weave these words together in an evocative and atmospheric paragraph. Compare this with how the author describes the setting.

- *Identify the language of settings in a pile of books:* Revisit a couple of familiar books with the same setting and collect words, phrases and sentences that the author uses to describe it. Write a paragraph explicitly borrowing from these texts and blending ideas together. In independent work children can collect more words, phrases or sentences, or can list the settings in a pile of, say, traditional tales. Work on synonyms or similes.

- *Whole group improvisation:* Reread an extract, and improvise the scene described. This could be created as a freeze frame (e.g. a market, a funfair, a castle) and then be brought to life. The noises and action, atmosphere and imagined sense of the place can then be captured in shared writing. Work on using all the senses in the paragraph.

- *Changing the atmosphere:* Using a well-crafted extract from the shared text, discuss the atmosphere created by a particular setting. Evoke an alternative atmosphere in the same setting (e.g. a more sinister atmosphere), mirror some sentences carefully and explore which words dramatically alter the sense of the place.

Non-fiction

- *Find real purposes for the writing:* For example, follow the instructions on a seed packet and sow the seeds, play a maths board game, respond to a local issue or let children write the class newsletter to their parents.

- *Use real audiences for writing:* Seek out opportunities to write letters to parents or museums, instructions for a new game, articles or reports to the local newspaper or radio station, and school booklets. Such authenticity supports redrafting and profiles the need for teaching careful proofreading and editing with the whole class.

- *Use the children's issues and interests:* For example, in working towards discursive writing, children can identify issues of concern (personal or social) and in shared writing select one, brainstorming the pros and cons as they perceive them. These can be shaped through a writing frame into a piece on, for example, wearing jewellery in school, playing football on the playground, privacy.

- *Write instructions for response partners:* This procedural text could be targeted at younger pupils or for use in class and serves a dual purpose.

- *Focus on comics*: After analysis of the text types, children can create their own adverts, games, crosswords, puzzles, reports, articles, letters or cartoons in shared writing. Work on ellipses, onomatopoeia, contractions, pronouns or unusual adjectives.

- *Use writing frames:* These can scaffold shared writing of different text types and provide structural support. Model these carefully and differentiate them according to need.

- *Use shared writing for cross-curricular work:* This enables more frequent referral to text structure and facilitates reinforcement throughout the curriculum.

- *Move across genres:* Use literary genre to revisit non-fiction, assessing what the children have retained from previous work (e.g. write Harry Potter's formal acceptance letter to Hogwarts

School of Wizardry). Likewise, non-fiction work on, say, food, Victorians, or rivers can prompt literary writing, particularly poetry. Alternatively transform a local news item into a poem, playscript or narrative.

- *Produce class criteria for writing different text types:* Write the 'rules' for writing a particular text type, as an advice sheet for new journalists, authors, or historians.

Poetry

- *Create one-liners:* Generate one-liners with starting frames (e.g. 'In my rainbow box I will put …', 'I would like to …', 'In my magic shoe I can …', 'If I left my house I would miss …', 'I would like to paint …', 'What I hate about …', 'In a politician's/teacher's/parent's head there is …'). Evaluate these on a continuum from ordinary and interesting, to extraordinary and powerful. Challenge the class to use abstract and emotive ideas.

- *Assembling verse:* Use the 'one-liners' produced on a single subject. Stick several to the easel, read them and discuss how they might be grouped (e.g. by themes, as contrasts, in rhyming pairs, etc.). Some will be left out and new ones will be created. Agree a final 'collected' class poem. Read and evaluate it.

- *Influence the reader:* Having read and studied examples on a theme, create free verse with self-set intentions (e.g. 'We want to make the reader laugh/feel surprised/afraid/see the subject in a new light/…'). Model this through shared writing and evaluate the piece.

- *Improvisation and imitation:* Through whole-class performance of a poem the structure is physically felt, the words repeated and the meanings made manifest. This leads easily into imitative shared writing leaning on the structure and patterns in the text. It can also highlight punctuation, the role of choral refrains, rhymes and so on.

- *Percussion and performance:* Perform the poem prepared in shared reading, using the body or musical percussion to highlight the syllabic beats, the structure and rhyming patterns. Use this as a structure for class composition, writing a piece that can fit the same accompaniment and work on onset and rime and spelling patterns.

- *Using figures of speech:* In working on, for example, similes or alliterations in poetry, collect examples over time (e.g. Roger McGough's *The Writer of this Poem*). Write these on paper strips, display them and create a shared poem that includes at least two or three from the collection. Select a subject together and weave the borrowed similes in, as well as generating new ones.

- *Narrative verse and paragraphs:* Subtitle verses or groups of verses to highlight the narrative events and structure. Take one subtitle and turn it into a shared prose paragraph. Compare and contrast the poetic and the prose versions.

Sentence level

- *Revisit the shared writing:* In producing, reflecting on and discussing the shared writing focus on particular sentence level objectives and explore, say, sentence construction, punctuation or connectives.

- *Play punctuation detectives:* Get the children to hunt through picture books or magazines in pairs to note where and why particular punctuation marks are used. In recording and quoting several examples they can categorise and speculate on their function and purpose.

- *A washing line for sentence construction:* Show children how to construct simple or complex sentences with punctuation by making cards with individual words, punctuation, phrases, clauses, connectives or blanks, and working together to make choices. This generates a close examination and discussion of sentence construction.

- *Make unfolding sentences:* Fold a piece of paper eight times evenly so a fanned shape is created. Each child adds one word to an unfolding sentence and passes it on. Retrospectively these can be annotated as parts of speech, or an order could be agreed prior to sentence construction (e.g. article–adjective–noun–verb–preposition–article–adjective–noun). A larger class example could model this.

- *Targeted cloze procedure:* Focus on a particular passage from the shared text and cover or delete particular words (e.g. adverbs, adjectives, connectives). Read the page or two leading up to the passage to provide a context and then generate and record alternatives for each missing word, agreeing one together through discussion. Compare these to the author's word choices.

- *Play the connective game:* Write connectives on card and aim to create an oral story in the group, with a connective in each sentence offered. The children can either select their connective freely or be challenged to pick from the top of the pack. A variation called the 'never ending story' can be played, when tellers offer a sentence that has to begin with a connective.

- *Noun sorts:* Provide untitled lists of nouns (e.g. abstract, proper, common collective) from a current text and ask the children to discuss what they have in common and to describe the different groups. Later produce a passage from the text with, for example, the different types of nouns highlighted in different colours so the children read them in context.

- *Make an A–Z of parts of speech:* Create an instant class book with a simple sentence on each page containing alphabetically ordered nouns or verbs. Write these in a different colour.

- *Play the adverb game:* A couple of children leave the room while the class agree on an adverb (e.g. carefully, lazily). The pair return and watch individuals who can be asked to do any actions 'in the manner of the word'. A few examples can be recorded in print to identify the attached verb. Challenge the children to use these adverbs in their work.

Word level

- *Establish class and individual spelling journals:* These create a record for spelling work and can include class or personal spelling lists, resumés of spelling conventions, high frequency word lists, spelling investigations, brainstorms of particular kinds of words, class mnemonics and so on. A large class version is a useful model and a valuable reference text.

- *Create class mnemonics:* Useful for persistently challenging words (e.g. said, because, friends), mnemonics can be a fun way to encourage children to use these strategies.

- *Play Shannon's game:* This is similar to Hangman, but works on serial probability. The first letter is given and successive letters are added in strict order; e.g. C _ _ _ _ _. It draws on children's knowledge of spellings and can easily be contextualised.

- *SACAWAC words:* This is a variation on 'look, cover, write, check', stressing visual strategies: study and cover and write and check. Personally difficult words could undergo this more intensive scrutiny.

- *Make morphemic word webs:* Raise awareness of word structure, spelling patterns and relationships between words. Add related words to a root word from the shared text (e.g. sign).

- *Compose word clines or ladders:* Based on meaning, create word clines to show the subtle differences in word meanings. This is also useful for work on synonyms.

    For example:

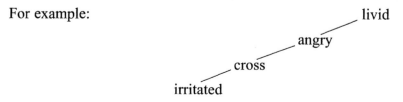

- *Make a washing line of hot words:* List new vocabulary encountered in a text. Decide on 'hot words', discuss and check their meanings, hang them on the line, and encourage and celebrate their use in children's writing.

- *Create keyword placemats:* Make large, brightly coloured, illuminated placemats that contain keywords in alphabetical order. These operate as prompts in writing activities. They can be topic related.

- *Word of the week:* Take a word of the week from a text or theme. Display it, discuss its meaning and challenge children to include it in their writing. Synonyms could also be generated. Each word could be illustrated and explained in a class dictionary.

- *Collect onomatopoeic words:* Hunt for these in cartoons, adverts and poems and collect a variety. Sort them and invent new ones to use in a radio advert or add them to a cartoon where the original sounds words have been removed.

- *Create an A–Z of alliteration:* Generate alliterative sentences, perhaps as a counting rhyme, and illustrate the resultant alphabet book.

- *Use a word wall*: Create a laminated word wall (Figure 15) as a poster. Encourage the class to identify interesting or significant words, phrases or lines that enrich a text that has been read/ written. Discuss the placement of these words, phrases or lines on the word wall. Create synonyms for some of them and use some of them in writing.

Can you find words, phrases or sentences in the text that are ...?

Amusing		Repeated		
	Scary			
			Puzzling	
Frightening				
	Rhythmic			
Memorable			Strange	
		Descriptive		
				Poetic
Sad				

Figure 15 A word wall

Guided writing: Principles

These writing sessions should be to teach pupils to work independently. The work will normally be linked to reading, and will often flow from work in the whole-class shared writing sessions. These sessions should also be used to meet specific objectives and focus on specific aspects of the writing process, rather than on the completion of a single piece of work.

NLS (DfEE 1998b)

Guided writing involves the teacher supporting children as they move from the security of group shared writing and respond to the challenges of independent writing. Guided writing provides the teacher with good opportunities to teach writing in small groups, to scaffold the children's learning and, as with guided reading, it creates a bridge to independence.

In the context of shared writing, the teacher models and demonstrates key aspects of writing such as audience, purpose and text organisation according to the chosen form. The writing process of planning, drafting, revising and editing the work will also be explicitly taught in shared writing. In the context of guided writing, this will all be revisited over time, with brief demonstrations if appropriate and the opportunity for the children to apply their knowledge, skills and understanding. Before, during or after some writing has been produced the teacher will intervene to guide the learners through the process, encouraging them to reflect on and evaluate their own work and that of others. Guided group work can become a zone of proximal development (Vygotsky 1978) in which, working on a piece of writing with the guidance of their teachers, the children are able to discuss particular aspects of writing and shape and reshape their writing accordingly.

Some advantages of guided writing

- The teaching focus and the teacher's intervention can be tailored in response to particular needs.
- Children are given the opportunity to practise writing in a supported group context.
- Children learn to share and problem solve aspects of writing with others.
- Reflection, evaluation and improvement are taught and practised.
- Its flexibility allows for individual, paired or collaborative group writing.

The focus of each guided writing group will depend on need and any particular areas of difficulty identified by the teacher, as well as NLS objectives. Some aspects chosen to focus on will specifically relate to a text form, while others may relate to the actual process of writing and revising. Both the linguistic and the process based features of writing need to be explicitly developed through guided sessions. For example, a form session might focus on guiding children to use connectives to structure an argument, or using link phrases, imperative verbs, and subheadings in an instructional text. In a process based session the teacher might focus on guiding children to evaluate and revise their work, or on the skill of planning and generating ideas for a piece of writing. There is, however, no clear separation between linguistic and process based paradigms for writing and, as D'Arcy (2000) argues, they are both complementary and essential.

Peer collaboration in guided writing

Working in a group, children are able to explore and develop their understanding about writing, take risks in safety and refine their use of particular features. Children can work alone or in pairs, on work that may have begun in independent work in the literacy hour, or on work that may be extended later in literacy hour. Collaborative writing in guided work can be particularly helpful for students who have learning difficulties, as Fine (1989) has noted: 'Collaborative writing is the key to unlocking the silences of children'.

Some children, given the opportunity, will spontaneously engage in collaborative interaction while writing (Carr and Allen 1987; Schultz 1997), but others need training in order to work effectively together. Recent research by Topping *et al.* (2000) has shown that practical use of their paired writing framework scaffolded clear improvements in writing attainment and attitude of primary children. The metacognitive and interactive components of the framework provided structured and beneficial support for writers. Such procedures for peer-assisted learning in writing can be introduced and used within guided group work.

Children can also learn to assist one another as response partners; sharing, supporting, and responding constructively to each other's work. As the National Writing Project (1978–93) showed (Whittaker and Salend 1991; Dyson 1995) genuine feedback from a peer can be very influential in helping writers to focus on the strengths of a piece and aspects that could be developed. However, for this to work effectively, children need to perceive their views as valid and be able to assert, argue and articulate these views in an appropriate manner. Guided writing represents a good opportunity to teach children how to make constructive comments on each other's work. Modelling the process can take place in shared or guided writing sessions. The teacher can use an OHT or photocopy of a child's piece of work, or copy it out on the whiteboard, to demonstrate the process. If a specific learning objective was identified for the piece of writing, then this will naturally focus the discussion, although the writer's intentions and the content and meaning of their writing need to be responded to first. Much will depend on the maturity and experience of the writers but, with support, peers can successfully appraise each other's writing, and give quality developmental feedback.

Response partners can be helped to discuss:
- The writer's intentions.
- Their response to the content and meaning.
- Two or three aspects of the writing that are well executed (these might relate to named learning objectives).
- Two or three aspects of the writing that could be improved (with specific recommendations).
- The personal writing targets of the writer and evidence of these in the piece.

Tentative or generously accepting children can learn to become more constructively critical in their responses, praising and celebrating their partner's writing and noting areas of confusion or weakness. The response is likely to be oral, but brief specific comments could also be recorded in written form. Children appreciate the responsibility of reading each other's work and respond seriously, articulating and developing their own knowledge about writing in the process. When response partnerships are well established, suitable questions can be framed to guide the children in scrutinising the content, organisation and technical accuracy of their work. Such questions may be genre specific or process related and can be modelled by the teacher, displayed on posters and made use of by response partners. By discussing their own written texts with others, children can refine and extend their knowledge in 'a conscious and deliberate manner' (Wells *et al.* 1990). In working with response partners and giving and receiving swift feedback before discussing their work with their teacher, children are able to develop a metalanguage with which to talk about writing. This is important because metacognitive understanding of their own writing processes is recognised as a feature of compositional maturity (Bereiter and Scardamalia 1987; Wray 1994).

Teacher intervention in guided writing

In guided writing, the quality of the dialogue between the teacher and the children is particularly critical. Through focused group discussion children can be made aware of how texts are constructed. They can reflect on their own knowledge about linguistic features and the writing process and use this in their own work. Successful interventions will, at various times, involve interaction before writing, during writing and after writing so writers learn self-help strategies for each of these 'stages'. The teacher will adopt different roles, for example, demonstrating and instructing, giving constructive and specific feedback, or structuring and encouraging discussion of particular content, organisation or language features. As the NLS (DfEE 1999b) notes 'if the role of the teacher is unclear or redundant, it probably shouldn't be a guided writing session at all'. Guided writing allows the teacher to both support children and monitor their use of the range of skills and processes involved. Close observation is helpful and can enable appropriate interventions to be made in response to the pupils' needs and the nature of the task. If the session is about planning and preparing to write, the teacher will focus on helping the group review the task, connect to the genre and identify a way forward. Then working together, they might generate ideas in a brainstorm, or organise these through word webs or mindmaps. Intervention at this point is essentially forward looking, helping children to generate alternatives and begin to sort and choose from among these.

If the session is undertaken with children who have already begun their writing, the teacher may focus on the processes of sharing, improving and appraising their work – again, helping the children review the task, connect to the genre and identify content organisation and language features that are well handled, as well as areas for development and revision. This may be undertaken as a group with the teacher using one child's photocopied piece as an example, or may involve the teacher conferencing with individuals. The organisation of guided writing will vary to suit the nature of the task set, and interventions too will be tailored accordingly. In guiding the children through the act of composition, the teacher may concentrate on specific elements or the more difficult moments of application. If the session is undertaken with children who have completed a piece of writing, then the teacher is likely to review the purpose of the writing and the genre. If the group work together they could be asked to read and share the parts of which they are proud and to compare and contrast them with one another's. Weaknesses should also be highlighted and areas for improvement identified and worked on. If response partners have already read and appraised each other's work the teacher can discuss the writing of both the children together, drawing on their views and comments. Specific teacher feedback in relation to the learning objectives will be an integral part of this discussion.

In all teacher interventions, critical reflection on the key elements of writing will be foregrounded in discussions with the children. Such reflection will relate to: the purpose of the writing; the form (and its features); the audience; and the writing process.

Guided writing:
Institutional self-review

- Do the guided writing activities relate to the genre focus of the unit of work (e.g. traditional tales, instructional texts)?

- Do guided writing sessions retain an explicit teaching objective, tailored by the teacher in response to group need?

- Is there a balance between guidance in relation to linguistic features and forms and in relation to the writing process?

- Are the children actively involved in reflecting on and evaluating their own and others' writing?

- Do guided writing sessions form supportive opportunities to reflect on complete pieces of writing as well as short, focused pieces?

Guided writing: Ideas for action

- *Establish response partners:* Create prompt sheets for discussion. These could be generic, genre specific, or related to the particular audience for the writing.

Response partner prompt sheets

General

- Remind each other of the intention of the work.
- Listen as your partner reads their work.
- Ask your partner their view of the work.
- Tell your partner two aspects you particularly liked and explain why.
- Comment on two aspects that could be improved on.
- Suggest particular ways of improving these two aspects.
- Discuss these together.

Specific

Before you read, ask your partner what the learning objective of the work is, and if there is anything else they want you to check.

As you read, look out for evidence of the learning objective and think of one way in which the work could be improved in order to meet the objective.

After you have read, tell your partner about one good aspect of their writing and show your partner where they could make changes to meet the objective set.

- *Widen the repertoire of questions and comments used*: These teacher questions should help writers extend their work and draw children into the discussion. For example: 'Tell me how you could extend ...; 'Say a little more about ...'; 'What do you think about ...?; 'You could try ... or ...'; 'What could you say/use ...?'

- *Provide positive and specific oral feedback:* Identify elements you like and explain why you like, say, this particular phrase, sentence or paragraph. Make your views explicit.

- *Use appropriate terminology:* Use linguistic terminology in the discussion when reflecting on their written text. Prompt the children to use this also.

- *Encourage regular collaborative writing opportunities:* Observe these, monitor and review their use and involve the children in reflecting on their value.

- *Evaluate guided writing:* Over a half term take note of the groups' activities and review the breadth, balance and integrated nature of the activities undertaken.

Independent writing: Principles

> When we invite children to choose their form, voice and audience as well as their subject, we give them ownership and responsibility for their writing. This transforms writing from an assigned task into a personal project.
>
> (Calkins 1986)

Such personal projects are often invested with meaning for the writer, and since good writing involves a close relationship between meaning and form, attention must be focused first and foremost on the content of texts and on composition, while not ignoring their linguistic structure (Medwell *et al*. 1998; D'Arcy 2000). Children need extended opportunities to write independently and use the skills and techniques they have been taught and had reinforced in shared and guided writing. There are limits to what can be achieved through direct instruction and demonstration however, and regular time needs to be set aside for concentrated composition. Child writers need to develop a real voice and engage in rewarding and rounded activities where the content of their work is emphasised and responded to individually (Hall 1998). While some independent writing activities will properly take place in the literacy hour, these will practise skills taught earlier and the tight time frame does not offer sufficient time to plan, develop, revise and edit a complete text. Sustained time for written composition is central to children's progress and development as writers, and needs to be balanced with time spent on the overt teaching of language features (Frater 2000). Many teachers extend the literacy hour or offer separate writers' workshops of an hour or more to achieve this. Children regularly need to focus on composition and content in a sustained piece of writing, attending to orthographic accuracy at the editing stage. In separating transcription from composition in this way, and by profiling meaning making, writers can be given more choice over the content, form and purpose of their writing and really develop their independence.

The National Curriculum (DfEE 1999a) requires that pupils at KS2 are taught to 'choose form and content to suit a particular purpose'. In addition, KS1 children need opportunities to produce sustained pieces of writing and make some, albeit more supported, choices (in both key stages extended writing is a requirement within the SATs). Children have a right to select their own content, form and purpose, to choose from the genres they have met, and to develop their skills, voice and style by writing about subjects they care about and are personally engaged with. In a writing workshop they will also be involved in reviewing their work with response partners, shaping and polishing their writing, conferencing with their teacher and publishing selected pieces. In the early years 'redrafting' may take the form of changing a few surface details. Later, however, full drafting will be introduced and modelled. This will involve reshaping the text and clarifying the meaning; working on the composition itself. Shared writing sessions as well as opportunities in writers' workshop will need to be used to teach this process. However, children need considerable support and guidance to make their own writing choices, which will involve answering the following questions.

	Choices writers need to make
Content:	What do I want to write about?
Purpose:	Why am I going to do this?
Form:	What genres could I use?
	What are the features of the chosen form?
	• at text level
	• at sentence level
	• at word level
Audience:	Who will read my writing?
	What effect do I intend it to have?

Organising a writers' workshop

A writers' workshop is an approach to writing that encourages children to see themselves as writers and enables them to develop their skills through working in a community of writers. This approach, pioneered by Graves (1983) and Calkins (1986, 1991), provides a balance to direct instruction, offers time to write and can be comfortably established alongside the literacy hour, enabling children to integrate the skills they have been taught, demonstrate the transferability of their growing orthographic knowledge and compose self-chosen pieces of writing. The teacher may guide and limit the choices available to the children in response to their maturity and ability as writers, but making a choice about content and/or form and purpose remains a significant feature (Rowe and Goodwin 1999). In infant classrooms, while a writers' workshop is still valuable, the full process will be adapted to suit the class, so the children may not, for example, all be working at different stages of the writing process, but work together in a single session on writing, discussing and sharing their work.

The advantages of writers' workshops

- They provide time and support for extended independent writing.
- They allow children to demonstrate their developing skills as writers.
- They enable children to revisit particular forms of writing.
- They make clear the role of purpose and audience in writing.
- They encourage independence through increased choice.
- They prompt evaluation and appraisal of their own and others' writing.
- They enable the teacher to assess independent competence and confidence.

Key features of writers' workshops

- *Preparing to write:* Children choose the content, form and purpose of their writing and take time to prepare to write. This may be with guidance during the workshop at KS1. Discussion of the choice is essential to think about the subject and generate ideas. Notes/a plan/a brainstorm may be made.

- *Quiet writing:* Children write in a period of quiet. The teacher also writes. Children may be working at different stages of the writing process. If they are at the initial stages they need not worry about spellings; these can be worked on later.

- *Response partners share:* Children work with their response partner to share, discuss and develop their work. The teacher/class may share some first drafts, modelling the tentative process of selecting and rejecting ideas, and the mess likely to be involved. Redrafting and revision will follow.

- *Teacher conferences:* Children reflect on their work with their teacher during the drafting stage and negotiate ways forward. This may take place in the workshop, individually or in small groups or in guided writing in the literacy hour.

- *Proofreading and publication:* Children check carefully and consider spelling and punctuation, choosing how to share/publish their work. This may be through reading it aloud, or in a class/ individual anthology, or as a booklet, pamphlet, poster, taped text with a print copy, letter in the post, posted on a website, etc.

Choosing content, form and purpose

While giving children more responsibility and freedom over *what* they choose to write and *how* they write it, teachers must provide appropriate support for them to make some/all of these choices. Records need to be kept, particularly at KS2, where more choice may be offered both to inform the teacher and to provide the children with a resource bank of four or five possible options and ideas. Careful monitoring and support of children's choices must be maintained, in order to ensure that some work is followed through to editing and publication. Children may choose not to develop or publish each piece, selecting those they are most proud of in consultation with their response partner and teacher. It is likely however, that the children will be prepared to work on, and want to publish in some form, the pieces of writing that they become very involved in.

My writing choices				
I might choose to write about …	Which form of writing might I choose?	Date started	Date finished and form of publication	What do I think about my finished work?/Why didn't I finish it?

Choosing the subject matter

If time is given to prepare for extended independent writing the writing itself flows more easily. Initially a range of activities needs to be undertaken to prompt memories, ideas, concerns and emotions and generate possible themes, which the children can record in their options list. Selecting from these options may take place at the start of the session with younger learners, or the previous day with more experienced writers, so that oral and written preparation can encompass homework and some time for incubation of ideas and discussion is offered. This allows more time for the actual writing and ensures that older children come to the workshop ready to write.

With younger writers preparation time may need to be set aside at the start of the extended writing session to help children select from two or three writing opportunities, or suggest their own alternative. The initial activity needs to capture the children's imaginations, connect in some way to their lives and energise their emotions, so a desire to write is developed and their inner voices are activated through engagement and response. The list of writing choices will need to be added to regularly to provide possible options. In creating such a list for themselves and helping the children create theirs, teachers can help children lean on their interests and lives, on literature and on non-fiction. Children need to realize that *their lives* are worth writing about and that their memories and feelings can be captured effectively, triggered perhaps by autobiographical anecdotes, timelines or objects. As Calkins (1986) noted, 'We need to say to others "This is me, my story, my life, my truth". We need to be heard'.

Children deserve to be heard and to develop their inner voices through recalling incidents and events in their lifes, both in school and out. These are their very own writing frames, which structure and scaffold the writing. Also *their views and concerns* about current issues in their lives, the community and the world need to be heard and are often committed to paper with strength and passion. Subjects that are important to individual children are also frequently selected, when prompted through evocative literature. Some of the children's choices in writing will be influenced by *popular culture* and current film releases (Hilton 1998); others may be developed through *imaginative activity* in drama and role play (Grainger 1997). All such choices need to be valued, honoured and affirmed if children are to develop as writers in this context. Teachers, too, may add options to individual lists, such as visitors or visits made. This encourages only those children who were, for example, really motivated by the trip to the Science Museum to produce a follow up piece of writing. Equally, teachers may on some occasions choose the form to reinforce literacy hour work and model this text structure, letting the children choose the content for themselves.

In guiding the children to keep a list of possible options and adding to this at regular intervals, or in starting the lesson with an interactive focus to generate involvement and possible options, the teacher is setting aside quality preparation time, to ensure that the children have something to say and are motivated to commit it to paper. As Graves (1983) argues, voice is 'the dynamo' in writing, the part that pushes the writing ahead, 'the imprint of ourselves on our writing'. To develop this, children need to value and revisit their lives, speaking from the inside out, and to encounter other perspectives through the lived experience of drama or the vicarious experience of literature. Writing produced through empathetic engagement with others, is likely to be more focused, strongly felt and emotively expressed (Barrs 2000).

In selecting the subject matter, children can also identify its purpose and audience. They should be able to write for their teachers as people, rather than for teachers as teachers, and expect a human response as well as an educator's perspective. By encouraging children to write about things that mean something to them, and by responding personally and professionally, teachers help them see that writing has a purpose (Calkins and Harwayne 1987). The regular use of response partners for shared writing in the classroom is important in this respect. In addition, knowing the publishing options and being able to send a real letter, see their work in print or read it on a website can make a significant difference to a writer. More energy and commitment is offered to such writing, as the National Writing Project (1987–93) repeatedly demonstrated. Indeed, the NLS affirms this view, although from an accuracy based, not a meaning based perspective.

> Without genuine opportunities to write for different audiences and to read each other's writing, the real need for revision, accuracy and using grammar appropriately is lost.
>
> NLS (DfEE 1998b)

Choosing a form

Primary children are gradually introduced to a wide range of literary genres and non-fiction text types via the NLSF, so it is primarily from these genres that they will choose a form to suit their content and purpose, although they will also draw on other models with which they are acquainted (Bearne 1999). So when freedom of choice is offered, children will often adapt forms for their own purposes, and in such child-initiated writing are likely to revisit the features of layout, presentation and organisation that were recently taught. It is therefore helpful for individuals to have access to a class list of forms and a range of posters that summarise the key features of particular forms. As shown in a summary of the NLS range, such lists can name all the various genres which have been studied, and operate as a resumé of the repertoire of text types tackled. Teachers may, however, decide to revisit particular text types in writing workshops and colour code a more limited number of forms for the children to choose from, as well as suggest forms not included in the NLSF. If the class generate a list themselves as an 'A–Z of different kinds of writing' (Figure 16), teachers can ascertain their collective 'remembered' repertoire and add to this over time.

I can choose many different forms for my writing

A adverts
  anecdote
  autobiographies
  alphabet poems
  adventure stories

B book reviews
  brochures
  biographies
  ballads
  birthday cards

C concrete poetry
  cartoons
  cinquains
  couplets
  calligrams

D discursive writing
  debates
  directions
  diary entries
  descriptions

E editorials
  epitaphs
  explanations

F free verse
  fairy tales
  fables
  fliers
  fantasy stories
  flow charts

G graffiti

H haiku
  historical stories
  horoscopes

I instructions
  information texts
  invitations

J jingle
  journal
  jokes
  journalistic writing

K kennings

L legends
  limericks
  leaflets
  labels
  letters

M myths
  menus
  memos
  mystery stories

N news reports
  notes
  nursery rhymes
  nonsense poems
  notices

O opinions
  obituaries

P parables
  playscripts
  persuasive writing
  postcards
  puns
  parody
  posters
  prayers

Q quizzes

R recounts
  reports
  riddles
  rules
  recipes

S sonnet
  science fiction stories
  synopsis
  songs

T traditional tales
  travelogues
  tongue twisters
  tanka

U

V viewpoints

W

X

Y

Z

Figure 16 A–Z of different kinds of writing

Teacher conferences and response partners

Response to work in progress is important to allow the writer to receive swift feedback and praise and identify areas to develop and revise. A more detailed examination of response partners is given in 'Guided writing: Principles' (pp. 104–107), although this peer group support is valuable in a range of contexts. Talking with a partner can be reassuring and helps children develop a metalanguage to talk about writing and increase their awareness of the writing process. In conferencing with the child (in a guided session or in a writers' workshop), the teacher is listening carefully, finding out about the child's intentions in the piece, responding as a genuine reader and discussing the stage reached in the process. When children have chosen their subject matter, as they often do in writers' workshops, they tend to be more involved and interested in feedback. Whether the feedback is oral or written, or comes from the teacher or a child, will depend in part on the stage the writing has reached. Over time feedback needs to be balanced and should acknowledge the significance of a personal and human response to writing alongside response to the craft displayed by the writer. D'Arcy (2000) argues for a two-layered response to stories and suggests that teachers should initially respond to their *engagement* in the story, focusing on the meaning. Secondly, she suggests that teachers should focus on *appreciation,* considering how the story was written and the techniques used that enabled engagement to take place. Areas of strength and areas for development will also be identified and negotiated through the conference discussion. Supportive feedback may include responses to:

- *the writer as a person:* 'what a shame about your hamster'; 'you really made me laugh'; 'I enjoyed this piece'; 'I hadn't realised you felt so strongly about the environment'.

- *the writer as a writer:* 'I can see how your concept map helped you structure the argument'; 'do you want to publish this?'

- *the learning objectives of the piece:* 'you achieved the summary in 50 words – well done!'

- *the content and ideas:* 'I liked the idea of the castle in the clouds'; 'your point about the homeless is well made'.

- *the genre and the language features:* 'your imperative verbs make it clear what to do'; 'I think that if you state the moral of the fable it will help'.

- *the spelling and proofreading:* 'these words need attending to; you'll need to check this very carefully, and look out for …'.

Independent writing: Institutional self-review

- Is sufficient dedicated time given to extended independent writing?

- Is there a balance between teacher initiated and child initiated writing?

- Do the children make any choices about content, form and purpose in their writing?

- Are the children motivated and keen to communicate as writers?

- To what extent are the writing skills and techniques that are taught in the literacy hour transferred and used in more independent contexts?

- To what extent do children use each other to share, review, evaluate and improve on their work?

- Is feedback in writing balanced? Is the content and meaning responded to as well as language features in the text?

- How does the school profile, publish and promote children's finished work?

Independent writing: Ideas for action

Ideas from the children's personal lives

- *Share autobiographical incidents:* Share a personal story and ask the children to pair up and tell a friend about an incident in their life. Regroup so the children retell their tale again and listen to another anecdote. Create interesting titles for the tales.

- *Create timelines of life:* Children note significant memories across the years. These will need to be completed with help from home and will prompt stories to be told and retold, one or more of which can be written.

- *Create mood/emotion graphs*: The vertical axis represents the emotions (low and high), the horizontal axis a period of time. Children note emotive/sad memories, and include a key to symbols used. Once complete the graphs are used to prompt retellings in pairs with the children reserving the right to privacy over particular events.

- *Photographs:* Children bring in photographs of an event, occasion or place they might like to write about. These should not be baby photographs for display, but snaps that become prompts for oral storytelling and reminiscing in pairs and small groups. Stories, descriptions or advertising pamphlets might follow.

- *Objects/personal possessions:* Children bring in objects or personal possessions from home that remind them of someone or some event in their lives. These are used not for whole-class 'show and tell', but for paired discussion and to help planning. The pros and cons of being a member of a particular club, poems or stories might follow.

- *Create a class timeline*: Create a timeline to cover a term/year and note memorable events in school. Use it as a basis for retelling tales of school or creating vignettes for a school magazine.

- *Families: leaning on literature:* Focus on families using quality literature (e.g. John Birmingham's *Grandpa*, Margaret Wild's *Our Granny*, Laurence Anholt's *Magpie Song*, and Ted Hughes's *Meet My Folk*). Prompt discussions, connections, anecdotes and character portrayals to be shared about significant family members. Letters, character descriptions, poems or short stories could follow.

- *Views and concerns:* Share your personal and passionate views about an issue and ask the children to pair up and articulate their opinions about issues they feel strongly about. These may be personal, community or wider world concerns. Persuasive, discursive or journalistic writing or diary entries might follow.

- *Issues: leaning on literature:* Focus on issues of community concern to individuals, using local news items or literature (e.g. Libby Hawthorne's *Way Home* on homelessness, Clarke Taylor's *The House that Crack Built*, on drugs). Letters to the newspapers or discursive writing might follow.

Ideas from popular culture

- *Watch videoshorts*: Watch a few minutes from one child's favourite film or television programme, followed by a discussion or role play. A playscript of the scene, poster or review of the film for a class magazine might follow.

- *Share personal interests and enthusiasms:* Children bring in objects or items they'd like to share and write about (e.g. Beanie Babies, Pokémon, fishing tackle). Mini research projects, magazines, pamphlets, stories, labelled diagrams and fact files might all follow.

- *Use favourite comics or magazines:* Children bring in a favourite comic or magazine to share with others and explain their interest in it or parts of it. Writing in the same style or sending letters, views or competition responses to the magazine might all follow.

Ideas from drama and role play

- *A magic carpet ride:* Unroll a magic carpet and take a ride to another land where adventures befall you and problems need solving before you return home safely. Cards, letters and postcards might all follow.

- *Fairy dust:* Bring in a magic 'box' or small container, and explain that the contents are fairy dust (sea salt), which when sprinkled over the class will transport them, say, to the Kingdom under the Sea or to Egypt or into the past. Through classroom drama and the use of conventions such as teacher in role, hot seating or decision alley, respond to the challenges set for you. Diaries, letters, maps and diagrams might follow.

- *New jobs*: Receive a letter addressed to the class asking for their help or offering them jobs as part of new enterprise (e.g. a museum, a health centre, or a park). In role as a manager, hold a meeting to plan the building work and develop the drama from there. Publicity leaflets, posters, letters, press releases and newspaper reports might follow.

- *Imaginary characters:* Bring in a soft toy and establish an imaginary character for it. Explain where it has come from (e.g. Lucy Lamb is doing a project on humans and wants to find out all she can). The character can write letters, leave messages, share their fears and pose questions, all of which can be responded to by the children. The character can also visit homes (accompanied by their diary), be invited to tea and so on.

- *Classroom drama from a text:* Develop a whole-class drama exploring the themes in a text before reading it. Empathetic and emotive writing in role in a character's diary or in letter form might follow.

Ideas from literature

- *Complete the story:* Read or tell the first part of a powerful narrative and group the children to generate possible endings, using suspense, surprise or introducing a twist in the tale.

- *Explore picture fiction:* Develop in-depth explanations of challenging picture books through a variety of open-ended response to text activities and offer writing choices emerging from this work (e.g. Kathy Henderson's *The Year in the City*, Jenny Koralek's *The Boy and the Cloth of Dreams*, Michael Rosen's *Rover*, Michael Morpurgo's *Blodin the Beast*).

- *Explore characters' uses of literacy:* Reread a known text, or the next chapter in a novel, and talk about the characters, brainstorming the 'literacy events' in their lives. Are the characters in Sylvia Waugh's *The Mennyms* or Jan Brett's retelling of *Goldilocks and the Three Bears* likely to receive or send letters, plan journeys, need instructions, write recipes or keep diaries? Children can select from the characters and the possible genre.

- *Borrow book titles:* Cover the tables in books, and let the class peruse them in pairs, collecting three or four possible titles for a piece of writing. They do not have to know the text and can regroup after selection to work with others on generating ideas for writing from one of the titles (e.g. Gene Kemp's *The Hairy Hands*, Pat Hutchins's *Follow that Bus*, Shirley Hughes's *It's Too Frightening for Me*, or Jane O'Connor's *The Bad Luck Penny*).

- *Create poetry presentations:* Read, explore and create small group presentations of several poems on a given emotive theme (e.g. fear, bullying, nightmares, parents). Let individuals select the poem they want to perform, watch the others and then write their own verse or prose about the theme collaboratively or individually.

ICT, enabling literacy and learning: Principles

The Computer's First Christmas Card, by Edwin Morgan

jollymerry	mollymerry
hollyberry	jerryjolly
jollyberry	bellyboppy
merryholly	jorryhoppy
happyholly	hollyhmoppy
jollyjelly	berrymerry
jellybelly	jarryhappy
bellymerry	happybobby
hollyheppy	boppyjolly
jollymolly	jollymerry
marryJerry	merrymerry
merryHarry	merrymerry
hoppyBarry	merryChris
heppyJarry	ammerryayasa
bobbyheppy	Chrismerry
berryjorry	asMERRYCHR
jorryjolly	YSANTHEMUM
moppyjelly	

Developments in the use of ICT have been rapid and have impacted on the way in which we conduct our everyday lives. The impact in schools, however, in both the content and the methods by which pupils are educated, has been far less profound. Recent government initiatives, *Circular 4/98, Teaching: High Status, High Standards* and the expected outcomes of the New Opportunities Fund Training Initiative, is a centralised attempt to change this. The focus of recent developments at a national level involve ICT in: *generally* supporting learning in subject teaching; s*pecifically* raising standards in the key skills of literacy and numeracy; and raising awareness, skill and confidence of teachers in the effective uses of ICT. The underlying philosophy of these proposals is that:

- ICT gives us the ability to do the same things in different ways. This type of approach is only part of the story, as it is based on a view of the curriculum, which is print, paper and pencil based. ICT resources add a further dimension to the teaching–learning cycle. To be fully literate in the digital age, schools must enable pupils to take full advantage of all the possibilities that the developing technologies allow. Such developments are, however, built on a sound framework of national and international research and of practical experience within school settings. An appreciation of both of these elements allows us to add a further dynamic dimension to that proposed.

- ICT gives us the ability to do different things in different ways. Where effective, it should not simply raise pupil standards against traditional measures of success. It should cause teachers to question what it is to be truly literate in an electronic age. It is argued that the rapid growth of technology moves text based material into a category better termed 'letteracy' (Papert 1993). This short section cannot contend with this issue fully, however, the perspective from which it is written is that, while paper based technology is presently pre-eminent, and while pupils must be efficient and effective text based communicators, the expansion of digital technology is a crucial issue for teachers and fundamentally challenges what it means to be truly literate in an electronic society.

'The Computer's First Christmas Card', Edwin Morgan, from *Collected Poems* (Carcanet 1982), reproduced by permission of Carcanet Press Limited.

This chapter takes a wide view of ICT resources: they can only be used effectively through careful selection and utilisation within a planned, systematic, interactive, supportive and inclusive teaching–learning environment. Teachers need to examine the three elements, and interactions between those elements, of the inclusive educational process through which ICT resources can enable literacy learning to progress such that ICT serves an enabling rather than a compensatory purpose (Figure 17).

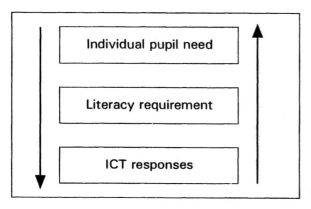

Figure 17   Dimensions of the educational process

Four key principles underpin all that follows:

- ICT resources provide a range of powerful strategies to support and scaffold literacy learning;

- a single ICT resource will not suffice – teachers require the facility to use a small, well-chosen range of flexible programs;

- ICT resources must be incorporated into the overall language and literacy provision;

- ICT should provide a constant challenge for pupils and teachers.

If a person only has a hammer, the whole world looks like a nail. Adding new tools to the carpenter's toolkit changes the way the carpenter looks at the world. So, too, with computational paradigms: new paradigms can change the way computer users think about the world.

(Resnick 1999)

The TTA (1999) has provided a model of the functions of ICT that teachers should consider when making decisions about its possible effectiveness to support literacy. The principal features outlined are:

- *speed and automatic functions:* including synthetic speech, which supports a reader's engagement with complex text, and word processing features, such as spell checker, thesaurus, copy and paste, which give greater control of the editing of a written passage.

- *capacity and range:* the rapid introduction of CD-ROM technology allows pupils to access a breadth of information in a variety of forms. Effective use of the Internet through refined searching enables both teachers and pupils to select and gather material from a wide variety of sources.

- *provisionality:* material can be rapidly changed and modified, for example allowing text to be modified for differing audiences by changing font style and size, highlighting keywords or changing colour and layout.

- *interactivity:* software may provide feedback to pupils depending on their actions. By clicking an icon pupils could hear text spoken or see a video clip. The use of email and video-conferencing extends pupils' opportunities to work collaboratively with groups outside their immediate environment.

The Centre for Applied Special Technology (CAST) proposes a simpler series of features, which highlight the key quality of computers including *flexibility, versatility* and capacity to be *customised.* They are multipurpose machines that change fundamentally through the use of differing software.

CAST has developed a series of universal design principles that take advantage of the inherent flexibility of computer systems. When coupled with suitable software they allow the creation of appropriate learning environments for pupils at three levels:

- representation of information: adjusting to the needs of all students, including children with learning disabilities, visual or auditory impairments, physical disabilities, and diverse learning preferences.

- expression of information: supporting pupils' differing motor and strategic systems.

- affective systems: adjusting to students' differing interests and needs for challenge, support and novelty.

Examining software

Bearing these preceding principles in mind, it is useful critically to examine some types of software that are designed for use in the language classroom. Due to the rapid changes in this field we only mention specific software titles as examples.

Integrated Learning Systems (ILS)

Such systems are reminiscent of the teaching machines of old. They are an ICT means of delivering curriculum content via an individualised learning programme and are designed to provide immediate feedback and detailed records for both pupils and teachers. Schools mainly use them to raise pupil attainment in basic skills. In making decisions about whether the use of such systems is appropriate, teachers need to consider the inherent model of teaching and learning that underpins their design. (*The UK ILS Evaluations – Final Report* (NCET 1998b)). While some evidence suggests that pupils do make gains in basic skills, such gains do not seem to automatically transfer to other contexts nor do they appear to have any impact on examination grades. When used by pupils designated as having SEN, enhanced motivation is shown, although gains are in line with initial performance levels.

Flexible learning environments

This general term covers all systems in which a range of media is orchestrated to support learning. The non computer-using classroom, in which broadcast material in the form of television and video is combined with audio tapes, printed matter and, most importantly, adult and pupil interaction, is an example of one such environment. Coupled with this, ICT systems provide a potent setting for learning. The developing capacity to provide material in the form of text, sound, still and moving graphics has led to the coining of the new broad description of 'multimedia'. Heppell (1993) offers a helpful extension to the term, centres it on pupil action and suggests that such programs support learning through three modes of activity:

- narrative – involving watching and listening;

- interactive – involving browsing, exploration, navigation, making choices;

- participative – *as interactive* with added ability to originate and present (Heppell 1993).

Subject-specific software

Reference to any computer catalogue provides evidence of the plethora of software designed directly to support literacy. On deciding on the purchase of such software look for programs that:

- engage pupils and provide motivation;

- emphasise language patterns;

- allow pupils to practise language in meaningful contexts;

- address individual differences.

The evolvement of high quality graphics and CD-ROM technology can allow children to play and replay stories, poems or songs, complete language tasks and both see and hear the result. Such activities can be stimulating, highly motivating and repeated as often as required by the ever-patient computer. Packages that allow pupils to input their own voices are particularly useful. Such a facility, particularly if it allows the pupil to manipulate the sound by slowing it down without lowering the pitch, or seeing it reproduced visually on screen, provides a valuable addition to the language toolkit. However, pupils do not learn language skills in the same way or in the same sequence, and are taught by teachers and not by technicians. The only solution is to be highly selective and gather a range of software, matched to the specific needs of pupils.

CD-ROM books

The generically named 'talking stories' are so ubiquitous as to need little further explanation. These are an easy to use extension to traditional print based text and allow pupils to interact with the text and images, and can provide useful motivation. Their power to support and motivate can be enhanced if they are used *with* the pupil rather than simply *by* the pupil. CD-ROM technology is also used within a fact based context with information books and dictionaries benefiting from the use of electronic features. Such electronic books should be a standard feature in the ICT-using literacy classroom. As with Internet facilities, pupils work best when a specified task has been planned.

Text disclosure packages

The skilled reader uses their knowledge of syntax and context to engage effectively with the meaning of text. ICT systems can be used to support pupils' development of such strategies through text disclosure programmes. These present children with partially or completely missing text in which absent items are replaced by a symbol. At a simple level this can be thought of as an electronic cloze procedure. Such software allows pupils the opportunity to develop and consolidate a range of language strategies to recreate the missing items. The power of this software is its simplicity, openness and transparency, which allows learners to engage with text rather than with software about text. Also, teachers can modify the content and focus of this work. This type of package functions effectively when small groups use the screen as the focus for collaborative work; such an activity reinforces the use of computers for the development of oral language within meaningful contexts.

Intranet, Internet and email

The selective use of Web technology by pupils and teachers extends the available opportunities for research, publication and communication.

> The Internet offers novel opportunities to enhance teaching and learning processes by opening up the world to classrooms and vice versa.
>
> (Joo 1999)

Modern word processing programs, for example Microsoft Word and Multimedia TextEase, together with specific authoring programs such as FrontPage, HotMetal Pro and Netscape Composer, allow teachers and pupils to create their own Internet content. The possibilities of video communication in classrooms and email allow pupils to work collaboratively at a distance and share the results of learning with a wider audience. To see two groups of hearing impaired pupils communicating at a distance through a video link, or 10-year-old pupils downloading the electronic photographs of the devastation caused by an earthquake sent to them by Japanese schoolchildren prompts an increased awareness of the possibilities that such new forms of communication allow.

The word processor

Despite the obvious value of using the word processor to support independent and collaborative work it must be noted that with a pen and paper you can write anywhere you want and in any direction. The program TextEase allows such flexibility: words and phrases can be placed anywhere on the screen then rotated and dragged around. This facility is particularly useful in supporting procedural writing or labelling diagrams.

Overlay keyboards and voice recognition software are useful as another form of text input from the use of word banks or wordlists. These take the form of lists of words that appear in cells on the screen below or within the work area. Pupils can select the words with a mouse click and so speed the process of typing. As with paper overlays these virtual overlays can contain key vocabulary, part words, complete phrases, sequences or computer actions. Some forms allow the use of embedded or dynamic overlays in which links trigger the display of further choices. A final form of input comes from the use of predictors. As pupils type, a range of possible words or phrases are presented on screen, which predict what the user is about to type. What is predicted can be tailored for the individual user or is automatically based on what the user has previously typed. Items can be selected from the presented list, so speeding the input process. The addition of such features to word processors can be used alongside the standard keyboard input to make the package available to a far wider range of pupils. Graphics and photographs can also enrich presentation. An interesting development that extends the traditional word processors is programs providing an 'expert system' in which pupils select the writing genre in which they are to work and are then provided with key prompts. SCET's Writer's Toolkit is a prime example of such a package.

Graphics packages

Graphics packages fit into one of two rough categories: packages that produce vector based graphics, such as Microsoft Word, are useful for diagrams, charts and forms; and paint packages that allow a rather more natural approach, often copying traditional paint and drawing tools. When combined with a graphics tablet, a small flat pad that allows input from a pen-like device, pupils can engage with 'handwriting' activities in a unique and often motivating way. One useful feature of graphics packages is the slideshow capability, which allows a series of screens to be completed then shown in sequence.

Multimedia authoring

A fully featured multimedia authoring package, such as HyperStudio, allows pupils to create the type of interactive product of which they are normally only users. Such packages provide more flexibility than presentation packages in that areas of the computer screen, termed *buttons* or *hotspots,* can trigger a wide range of actions; perhaps allowing the user to move to another screen, to play an animation, a clip of video, reveal text and so on. Providing the appropriate hardware requirements are met they also allow pupils to record their own voices directly into the programs. By their nature they provide immense, creative flexible potential for work in literacy. Their power lies in the compelling and motivating potential for pupils of creating rather than simply using multimedia products. Software, while time consuming, allows pupils to create their own personalised and interactive books. A key principle when using a complex computer package is, *it is not necessary to use every available feature to make its use worthwhile.* For example, a presentation package can be used by a group of pupils to present their science findings. The potential for language work within a collaborative context is immense. The computer program acts in this situation as the focus for the activity rather than the mechanism by which content is provided. Similarly, a whole-class could be involved in the production of their own talking dictionary, in which pairs of children construct a single page each.

Whiteboards

A key aim of effective ICT usage is to make the technology as transparent as possible. Interactive whiteboards are tremendously useful for this. Computer images can be displayed on the board and directly interacted with. Text and pictures can be highlighted, changed and moved, words can be spoken and images animated – all from the surface of the screen and all with the movement of a hand. Some even come with word recognition software, allowing you to write on the board and watch it immediately turn into 'typed' text. Through the coupled use of a computer, data projector and whiteboard, teachers can, for example:

- model the writing process by highlighting, cutting and moving blocks of text literally at the pass of a hand;

- use a presentation package to demonstrate the development of spelling patterns with moving text and speech output.

Teacher responsibility

'Whatever the role of the computer the teacher is key to its success' (Sitko and Sitko 1996). Individual teachers are responsible not only for pupil development within their own classrooms but also for pupils' ongoing intellectual and skill development. Decisions about how and when ICT key skills are developed have to be made at a school level, as activities carried out in individual classrooms form the essential foundations for later work. When planning for the use of ICT to support pupils, teachers have to identify which are ICT objectives and which are related to the subject: the two should not be confused. The approaches adopted at school and individual class level, force teachers to contend with issues of how pupils learn and whether all pupils learn in the same way.

ICT, enabling literacy and learning: Institutional self-review

- Are all adults who are supporting literacy development with ICT provided with appropriate training?
- Are all pupils provided with equal access to ICT resources?
- Is the use of ICT resources integrated within literacy sessions?
- How are ICT resources used to support and extend the school's teaching of literacy?
- Is an informed balance achieved between ICT in literacy at an individual, group and class level?
- Is the effectiveness of ICT resources to support literacy objectives regularly monitored?

ICT, enabling literacy and learning: Ideas for action

ICT resources can be used at a variety of levels to support language and literacy learning.

Ideas for adults

- *Become familiar with more than one search engine*: try AltaVista, 'Ask Jeeves for Kids', and so on. Decide which you feel most comfortable with.
- *Locate and bookmark important sites:* As you find important sites add them to your favourites so that you can look at them off-line. Some useful sites are listed at the end of this section to get you started. Many have work material that you can print, some of which is useful.

- *Join a discussion board:* The Web is not just a source of material. Some sites allow you to 'post' electronic messages to other professionals; try the special educational needs coordinator (SENCO) forum at www.cant.ac.uk/xplanatory as a starting point.

- *Use computer packages to prepare materials:* These can be printed, as with traditional worksheets, or, better still, saved as 'interactive materials'. For example, text with punctuation removed can be edited by pupils on screen; a sequenced activity recorded as a series of key sentences can be reordered by pupils using the software's cut and paste facility; Talking TextEase allows words to be matched and sorted directly on screen

- *Use the school website:* Download the 'hotpotatoes' software, which allows you or children to create jumbled sentence exercises, crosswords, cloze procedures, matching-ordering and multiple-choices activities, all of which can be used on screen. It is excellent software and it's free!

- *Use the computer as a blackboard:* Link the system to a large monitor, data projector or whiteboard, or conversely use this with a smaller group of pupils. Pupils can collaboratively write text using the screen to draft and redraft. Experiment with screen colours.

- *Use a presentation package:* Such programs are ideal for presenting material in motivating ways. For example, on work related to letter strings (e.g. ight, ough) initial letters can be made to fly in to produce complete words.

- *Try out software first:* Many companies allow you to try software before you buy it. Keep an eye on magazines. When software companies bring out new versions of titles they often give away current versions as an incentive to buy. You should have the NLS 'Progression in Phonics' CD-ROM, which was free to schools.

Ideas for pupils

- *Set up an Internet search for pupils:* How you do this depends on the way you are accessing the Web from school. 'Ask Jeeves for Kids' and 'Yahooligans' will only return kid-safe sites. If possible try the search out yourself, or use an existing Web resource with its own search tools. See the Internet sites at the end of this chapter.

- *Use reference CD-ROMs:* If your computer has a CD-ROM drive, install a talking dictionary that can be left switched on to be used as a constant source of reference. A range of further reference software should be used to extend the variety of sources available in the classroom. Set a specific task (e.g. create a book of favourite animals) in which children have to search for and locate appropriate text and an image that can be compiled into a class book, with each child being responsible for the completion of a single page.

- *Use the computer as a spell checker:* You can use the spell check facility of programs as a class resource when the system is not being used for independent or group work. Simply switch on the system, load appropriate software and allow the children to use it as a supplement or extension to traditional reference forms.

- *Use a floor turtle:* Floor turtles are an excellent context for developing the skills of giving and understanding precise instructions. Such work can be linked with literature, for example *Rosie's Walk* by Pat Hutchins, and activities in physical education to support the use of prepositional language. Children can create their own walks for a fictional character or an actual guide to walk around the school/local environment.

- *Use a multimedia authoring package:* Use a range of real activities (e.g. making biscuits, constructing a model, doing a physical education activity, etc.) as a starting point for multimedia work. Use a digital camera to record the key points of the activity. Children write instructions to accompany the images, or let children draw the images on blank OHPs, which can be shown in sequence along with the commentary. Allow children to research a specific topic, a period in history, information about a country, and so on. Each group can create a single page of information including an image, some text, sound and a button that links their page to a contents page. The teacher or capable child should create this page with links to all the others. If time and hardware are available, children could embark on a longer authoring project; their own fictional story. Talking books give the added advantage of children hearing their own voices reading the stories.

- *Use a branching database*: Files can be constructed on a variety of topics (e.g. characters in stories, musical instruments, customs). Children then create a branching diagram using appropriate software. Use real objects from which a range of questions can be generated and create categories.

- *Use a standard database*: Create a book file in which children can enter specific information (e.g. name of book, author, main characters, genre, story structure). Children can gather this information throughout the year and use it as a valuable focus for book reviews and selections.

- *Use a word processor with word banks*: Sets of words can be prepared in advance and key items of vocabulary can be reinforced. Clicker 4 (Crick Software), provides a range of readymade files covering history, topics and high frequency words and allows the incorporation of clipart and synthetic speech.

- *Use a word processor*: Try to use the key features of packages rather than simply using them as an alternative to typewriters. Set a word limit (e.g. mini-sagas of 50 words). Take one or two printouts as the work develops and use these as a focus for discussion. Focus on word presentation. Give children a set of words around which text must be written. Create a file of single words. Ask the children to use differing font sizes, typefaces, colours, font effects, position and orientation on screen to match their meaning. Try 'dazzle', 'explode', 'shrink', 'snail', 'dash' and 'fall'. Develop email exchanges.

- *Use writing frames*: Writing frames emphasise the structure of specific text types. More useful are electronic versions, which act as expert prompts to pupil writing. A range of suitable contexts are provided by Lewis and Wray (1998).

- *Visit author websites*: Many key authors and illustrators have their own websites. Set a challenge to visit one of these and, using information gathered elsewhere too, get groups to develop an 'author focus' presentation.

Useful websites

Literacy and ICT

The National Grid for Learning (NGFL)	ngfl.gov.uk/ngfl/index.html
The Virtual Teacher Centre (VTC):	vtc.ngfl.gov.uk
The literacy site:	vtc.ngfl.gov.uk/resource/literacy/index.html
BECTa Educational Software Database:	vtc.ngfl.gov.uk/resource/esr/
BECTa CD-ROM reviews:	vtc.ngfl.gov.uk/resource/information/cd-roms/
SEMERC:	www.granadalearning.co.uk/special_needs/index.html
	cast.org/LearningToRead/ch_1/2_computers.html

Web resource sites

The Standards site:	www.standards.dfee.gov.uk/schemes/it
The Amazing Picture Machine:	www.ncrtec.org/picture.htm
Berit's Best Sites for Chidren:	Db.cochran.com/li_toc: theoPage.db

Kathy Schrock's Guide for Educators:	www.capecod.net/schrockguide
BBC Education Web Guide:	Db.bbc.uk/education-webguide/pkg_min.p_home
Hotpotatoes software:	www.halfbackedsoftware.com

Software suppliers

Crick Software:	www.cricksoft.com
Inclusive Technology:	www.inclusive.co.uk
IANSYST Ltd:	email: sales@dyslexic.com
Xavier Software:	147.143.96.183/xavier
Topologica Software:	www.topologika.demon.co.uk
Sherston Software:	www.sherston.com

Working collaboratively with parents: Principles

Working collaboratively with parents

> The only other factor (apart from 'the peer group effect') which in valid longitudinal research appears to mitigate the comprehensive effects of social class upon children's attainment – is the degree of parental interest and involvement in their child's education.　　　　(Hilton 1998)

Parents play a substantial role in supporting their children's literacy development (e.g. Harste *et al.* 1984; Hall *et al.* 1989; Adams 1990), and this often happens as part of everyday family activity rather than as something separate. The literacy developed in the home environment has been shown to have a direct and influential bearing on later literacy achievement (Wells 1986; Tizard *et al.* 1988; Snow *et al.* 1991). Elements of the home environment may include familiarity with books, stories, nursery rhymes and songs, the availability of literacy materials, parents' expectations of their child and of schooling, frequency of library visits, and the child's preschool knowledge of letters. It is clear that by observing their parents and others using literacy in their lives, children build up a picture of what it is to be literate in a print environment and enter school with different literacy histories, learned socially and culturally at home (Brice-Heath 1983; Minns 1990; Gregory 1996).

However, there has been some evidence to suggest that teachers underestimate what parents are doing related to literacy at home (Hannon and James 1990), that teachers tend to work more with the parents who already know most about literacy practices (Toomey 1989) and that teachers need to

'Letter from a Parent', Kenneth Kitchen, from *Teacher's Features*, reproduced by permission of Gerald Duckworth & Co. Ltd.

understand further the challenges of parents' particular circumstances (Paratore 1995). Morrow (1995) noted that even parents who lack knowledge about the school's practices did not lack interest in both their child's schooling and learning how to help them at home. The overwhelming majority of parents are involved and interested in their children's literacy (e.g. Weinberger 1996), so work on expanding home–school relationships will benefit children's development. Developing parental partnerships and home–school dialogues with *all* parents is essential, so that information flows in both directions in order to most effectively support the young learners. There is much to be gained by acknowledging the strengths of home and school as contexts for literacy learning. It is the values placed on literacy and not on social status, race or economics, that make for a home rich in literacy (Morrow 1995).

However, research indicates that the types and forms of literacy practised in homes can be very different to that encountered by children in schools (Brice-Heath 1983; Au 1995; McCarthey 1997; Cairney and Ruge 1998). Both school and home/community uses of literacy need to be recognised and understood, so that enhanced home–school relationships can be shaped accordingly and the curriculum can be developed in a more inclusive manner.

Teachers' expertise	Parents' expertise
• Detailed knowledge about children at a particular age.	• Detailed knowledge about their own child or children.
• Knowledge of ways of helping children with particular literacy problems.	• Knowledge of how literacy is used in their particular home and community.
• Knowledge of the curriculum, and what has previously been taught in school.	• Knowledge of their own child's personal history.
• Relationships with children during school hours and activities, including literacy practices.	• Relationship with their child out of school hours, including literacy practices.
• Showing children about what literacy means in a school setting.	• Showing children about what literacy means in a home setting.

(Reprinted by permission of Paul Chapman Publishing, a Sage Publications company, from J. Weinberger, *Literacy Goes to School: The Parents' Role in Young Children's Literacy Learning*, Copyright J. Weinberger 1996)

If schools are to meet the needs of families from diverse social, cultural and language backgrounds, then teachers need to find out more about the home language and literacy practices of their children, and use this knowledge to broaden their conceptions of literacy, building on home literacy practices. Commitment to family literacy continues to grow. A variety of family literacy programmes that value diverse family backgrounds exist. These seek to establish regular interactions with parents to understand their beliefs, attitudes, challenges and perceptions of the roles they play in their children's literacy development. Many also succeed in working with parents to improve their children's literacy (Swap 1993; Robinson 1994; Nistler and Maiers 2000). Strong personal relationships can be built between teachers and parents and between parents and parents, and a range of strategies can be employed to ensure that all families believe they are among friends in the school community.

The presence and use of parent noticeboards or billboards for each class, and regular class newsletters (sometimes written by the children) can contribute to a sense of involvement, as can personal professional feedback and response to children's and parents' effort on homework tasks. Parents can be encouraged to comment on any written and investigative homework, making observations about how their child undertook it, difficulties encountered, help given and so on. This becomes a way of conversing with the teacher and needs in turn to be responded to. Whatever strategies are employed, teachers need to see recruitment for increased parental involvement as an ongoing element in inclusive educational practice.

Working collaboratively with parents: Institutional self-review

- How does the school find out about and build on the diverse language and literacy practices in the homes and community it serves?
- To what extent are parents involved in a reciprocal home–school partnership?
- What strategies and activities are regularly employed to enhance this partnership?
- How are home–school partnership initiatives evaluated?
- How is parental knowledge of their children as literacy learners gathered?
- To what extent is this knowledge integrated into teaching, learning and assessment?
- Is anyone responsible for developing effective home–school partnerships?

Working collaboratively with parents: Ideas for action

- *Regularly invite parents into classrooms*: Both for 'formal' presentations and more informal 'observation', free from the expectation that they should help with instruction in some way. This could provide time to observe and practise quality interactive story sharing, writing, role play and so on.
- *Offer home–school visits*: Before schooling in particular these can establish early and effective relationships.
- *Produce a weekly or monthly class newsletter*: Note the particular genres taught or about to be taught, significant teaching objectives, texts studied and incidental events in the life of the classroom community. This can prompt conversations and keeps parents informed.
- *Create a loan box*: Include pamphlets, magazines, articles, book based games and spelling activities that parents can browse and borrow from.
- *Organise interactive sessions*: Provide a crèche, and make the sessions on aspects of literacy more engaging and gradually negotiable. You might include a bookshop or examination of resources and plenty of small group purposeful browsing to generate questions and discussion.
- *Establish parent–teacher two-way conferences*: These actively seek knowledge and information about individual learner's home language and literacy practices as well as offer teachers' perspectives.
- *Establish a family reading group*: In liaison with the public library, meet regularly to share, read and discuss texts.
- *Provide booklists and recommendations*: These might include authors, websites, audio tapes and CD-ROM lists, to prompt buying. Useful for Christmas or the summer vacation.

- *Make differentiated bookmarks*: These prompt different kinds of reading encounters and ensure that reading to children, with children and encouraging them to read by themselves happens over a term. (These are most easily used with weekly library choice books and can be colour coded for easy reference.)

Reading *to* your child

Please can you read this to your child.

Do not expect him/her to join in, but if they wish to, encourage them to read with you.

Please talk about the text and any pictures.

**Fiction
Reading *with* your child**

Your child has chosen this story.

Please share the reading of it, a sentence or page each.

Please talk about the story and any pictures.

What does the tale remind you both of?

**Non-fiction
Reading *with* your child**

Your child has chosen this information book.

Using the contents, find an interesting section or agree a subject you would like to know more about.

Read the relevant visuals and the print and discuss what you have found out.

**Poetry
Reading *with* your child**

Your child has chosen this poetry book.

Please choose some poems between you that you'd like to read to each other.

Talk about the poems.

Which was a favourite?

Reading *by* themselves

Your child should be able to read this book by him/herself.

He/she may wish to tell you about it, or to ask for your help.

Do encourage him/her.

- *Provide a resumé of reading principles*: On the back of the bookmarks, or in reading newsletters or pamphlets, remind parents of the significance of talking about the text, as well as reading skills and strategies (Figure 19). Different summaries can be made for both key stages or different year groups.

- *Make the learning intentions of homework activities clear*: This should mean that parents are better informed and can help their child focus on and evaluate their learning.

- *Create home–school writing packs*: These can contain a variety of writing materials (e.g. blank picture postcards, shopping lists, invitations, preprinted class stationery), and allow parents to choose an activity that fits in with what is happening at home. Comments can be noted in homework books.

Reading support

Whether you are reading *to* your child, *with* your child or are encouraging them to read *by* themselves he/she will need your support.

1. *Before the reading:* Talk about the book. Look through the pictures and predict together.

2. *During the reading:* Talk about the book. You could chat about the story, the characters, the information, the words and pictures and make connections between the book and your own experience.
   If they come to a word they don't know, *pause–prompt–praise*.

3. *After the reading:* Talk about the book. You could chat about the story, the theme, favourite parts so far. You could retell the story together or list the information found out.

Enjoy reading together!

Figure 18   Remind parents of reading principles

- *Set joint parent/child homework*: This might include choosing, watching and reviewing a television programme; collecting, discussing and describing junk mail; or writing joint instructions for making hot chocolate, toast or a boiled egg.

- *Create storysacks or curiosity kits*: These can be fiction or non-fiction book bags, containing, for example, props, activities, adult reference material and text related toys. See 'Independent reading: Ideas for action' (pp. 86–7). These generate activity and interaction about reading.

- *Gather information*: Arrange for information to be collected from parents and grandparents (e.g. oral histories, memories of toys, books, playground rhymes, films, songs).

- *Develop language and literacy surveys*: Survey the range of reading, including newspapers, magazines, television viewings underataken in one day at home or the range of writing for different purposes.

- *Offer community arts events*: Design these for families (e.g. storytelling, poetry and music, drama), to which children contribute and invite the wider community.

- *Make a parents' noticeboard*: Profile different aspects of literacy each half term on the board (e.g. learning in drama), and use it for communication about school events. Encourage parents to use the space for their own purposes too (e.g. adverts, fliers, reminders, requests).

Working collaboratively with LSAs: Principles

In recent years there has been a dramatic increase in the number of LSAs working in mainstream schools mainly with pupils with SEN. The Green Paper 'Meeting the Challenge of Change' (DfEE 1998d) prepares the ground for further increases in the number of LSAs by targeting the recruitment and training of 2,000 literacy assistants in the short term, with projected targets for 2002 being a further 20,000. In any one classroom there could be LSAs funded by their LEA to support pupils with statements, those employed by the school to support groups of pupils with SEN and those who are designated to support literacy teaching for all pupils.

A research report commissioned by the DFEE (Farrel Balshaw and Polat 1999) reveals the following findings:

- *The role of LSAs*: Their role is varied, complex and challenging, with no clear distinction between the role of LSAs working with SEN pupils and other general classroom assistants. Lack of planning time is consistently recorded as a key factor that can reduce effectiveness of work. In contrast, LSAs employed to support the NLS do have clear prescribed objectives. Most LSAs were enthusiastic and committed to their work

  Management issues: Most LSAs felt that they were supported by senior management and regarded as members of a team. Most were concerned about low levels of pay and an almost non-existent career structure.

  Training: Virtually all trainers recognised the need for a nationally recognised and accredited training programme – only 20 per cent of LSAs want to become teachers.

Recommendations from this research for the development of effective practice suggest that their role should be directed towards: fostering the participation of pupils in social and academic processes of the school; seeking to enable pupils to become more independent learners; and helping to raise standards in schools. In relation to these issues, prior research (Moyles 1997) suggests that while teachers tend to direct attention to learning processes, LSAs focus on outcomes of children's activities. This may reflect issues of time in that it is quicker for the class teacher to use an outcomes model for planning individual support than it is to plan to achieve learning processes. In addition, training for LSAs, particularly for the NLS Additional Literacy Support (DFEE 1999e), is prescriptive in relation to outcomes and methodology. Training for LSAs in SEN tends to be based on categories of need (behaviour, learning, physical/sensory, language and communication) and may foster the development of a deficit remedial model of support using some 'specialist' teaching methods rather than one that focuses on individual differences in learning.

LSAs are themselves monitored and they also monitor pupil responses to individual education plans (IEPs). As SMART targeting is central to the accountability function of IEPs, and given that LSAs have very little time to undertake monitoring activities, there is a tendency for schools and LEAs to design brief manageable monitoring sheets, which may encourage the efforts of both LSAs and pupils to be directed towards 'task completion' rather than aspects of attitude and understanding: 'surface' learning. Moyles also reported that teachers used more strategies to encourage children to think, understand and reflect on their own learning. In concentrating on 'task completion and outcome', LSAs tend to help children physically and by verbal prompts such that independent learning and self-evaluation are not being fostered. LSAs who support IEPs for pupils with behavioural difficulties are directed towards concentrating on outcomes that are concerned with access, compliance and control: targets for developing social relationships, peer interaction, collaborative working and so on are not fostered by an emphasis on narrow behavioural targets delivered via an individual learning programme. Similarly, pupils with language and social communication difficulties need opportunities to develop communication in a social context that extends outwards from one-to-one situations in order to function in social settings with peers.

The issue is whether LSAs give individuals support or support learning and participation for all learners. Are they helpers or enablers? Do they have a responsibility for social as well as academic aspects of the curriculum? Starting from the positive aspects that LSAs enjoy their jobs, can anticipate the development of national training and career progression and are regarded as valued members of the school team, the time seems right to examine how LSAs can best be supported to develop their roles in contributing to inclusive educational practice.

Working collaboratively with LSAs: Institutional self-review

- Are medium-term learning intentions shared explicitly with LSAs?

- Are LSAs given opportunities and guidance on how to contribute to learning and the monitoring of learning outcomes?

- Are LSAs included in the development and evaluation of strategies to develop independent learners?

- How is their knowledge of literacy learning built upon and extended?

- Is the LSAs' knowledge about individual children's learning preferences, interests, friendship groups and culture used to assist in planning appropriate provision?

- Is there a balance between focused individual support and supporting participation in collaborative and inclusive activities?

- Do monitoring sheets for use by LSAs encourage them to reflect on children's learning, their participation and involvement?

- Are there opportunities for LSAs to spend time in more informal interactive contact with children to support literacy and language such as reading stories, role play and discussion?

- Are LSAs clear about their roles in relation to working with parents or caretakers to support literacy and language?

Working collaboratively with LSAs: Ideas for action

Work with LSAs and teachers to design an assessment sheet to identify how best to enable learners to make progress. Questions could include (taken from Elliott 2000) :

- Under what conditions does the child function at his or her best?

  - type of task (short, structured, etc.)
  - type of presentation: (visual, verbal)
  - with other peers or on his or her own
  - with an adult close by or an adult available when needed
  - response (choice of answers, ICT, etc.)
  - pace: under pressure or time allowed

- What is the pupil's response to difficulty?

  - give up
  - seek help
  - persist with same strategy
  - other
  - mess around
  - wait for help
  - try something else

- What forms of assistance seem to be most helpful?

  - direct help
  - praise
  - mediation
  - working with a peer
  - prompts
  - promises of rewards
  - suggestions of strategies

- Does the child:

  - reflect on his or her own learning and solve problems
  - self-assess his or her own learning
  - talk to himself or herself
  - discuss learning with LSA or teacher
  - problem solve with peers
  - seek to get 'done and finished' by the easiest and quickest means
  - engage with the task – how do you know?

- What are the implications of your findings for prioritising learning targets for the child? How can staff work collaboratively to enable the child to move forward?

Finally

In this endnote we wish again to encourage teachers to capitalise on their informed intuition, their deep commitment to the children and their knowledge and experience of language, literacy and learning. As previously stated, all learners are entitled to a rich and interactive language and literacy curriculum that is affectively engaging and effectively enriching. While raising standards is significant, the context in which this is undertaken and the long-term consequences for individuals must not be jeopardised. If we want to develop confident, competent, curious and communicative adults who are thoughtful and imaginative members of society, we need to be sure that both our medium and our message reflect the spirit of inclusion.

References

Adams, M. J. (1990) *Beginning to Read: Thinking and Learning about Print*. Cambridge, MA: MIT Press.

Ainscow, M. (2000) 'The next step in special education: supporting the development of inclusive practices', *British Journal of Special Education* **27**(2), 76–80.

Airasian, P. (1988) 'Measurement driven instruction: a closer look', *Educational Measurement: Issues and Practice*, Winter, 114–38.

Alexander, R. *et al.* (1992) *Curriculum Organisation and Classroom Practice in Primary Schools*. London: HMSO.

Anderson, H. *et al.* (2000) 'Hourwatch: monitoring the inception of the NLS', *Reading* **34**(3), 113–18.

Armstrong, F. and Barton, L. (2000) Advertisement for the University of Sheffield – Department of Educational Studies Distance Learning Programme MEd. Dip Inclusive Education, course directors Armstrong, F. and Barton L., *British Journal of Special Education* **27**(2), 66.

Arnold, H. (1982) *Listening to Children Reading*. London: Hodder and Stoughton.

Attfield, R. (2000) 'Target setting performance pointers', *Special Summer 2000*. Tamworth: National Association for Special Educational Needs (NASEN).

Au, K. (1993) *Literacy Instruction in Multicultral Settings*. Fort Worth: Harcourt Brace Jovanovich.

Au, K. (1995) 'Multicultural perspectives on literacy research', *Journal of Reading Behaviour* **27**(1), 18–27.

Bain, R. (1998) *The Primary Grammar Book: Finding Patterns – Making Sense*. Sheffield: National Association for the Teaching of English (NATE).

Bain, R. and Bridgewood, M. (1998) *The Primary Grammar Book: Finding Patterns – Making Sense*. Sheffield: National Association for the Teaching of English (NATE) and York Publishing Services.

Barnes, D. and Todd, F. (1977) *Communication and Learning in Small Groups*. London: Routledege and Kegan Paul.

Barrs, M. (1990) *Words not Numbers: Assessment in English*. Sheffield: National Association of Advisers in English (NAAE)/National Association for the Teaching of English (NATE).

Barrs, M. (2000) 'Gendered literacy', *Language Arts* **77**(4), 287–93.

Barrs, M. and Pidgeon, S. (eds) (1998) *Boys and Reading*. Southwark: Centre for Language in Primary Education.

Barrs, M. and Thomas, A. (1991) *The Reading Book*. London: Centre for Language in Primary Education.

Barrs, M. *et al.* (1988) *The Primary Language Record Handbook for Teachers*. London: CLPE.

Barton, B. (1986) *Tell Me Another: Storytelling and Reading Aloud at Home, at School and in the Community*. Ontario: Pembroke.

Barton, D. (1994) *Literacy: An Introduction to the Ecology of Written Language*. Oxford: Blackwell.

Barton, D. and Ivanic, R. (1997) *Writing in the Community*. London: Sage.

Baynham, M. (1995) *Literacy Practices: Investigation, Literacy in Social Context*. London: Longman.

Beard, R. (1993) *Teaching Literacy: Balancing Perspectives*. London: Hodder and Stoughton.

Beard, R. (1999) *The National Literacy Strategy: Review of Research and Other Related Evidence*. London: DfEE.

Bearne, E. (1997a) 'Miscue analysis: part one', *Primary English Magazine* **3**(1), 17–20.

Bearne, E. (1997b) 'Teaching writing, miscue analysis: part two', *Primary English Magazine* **3**(2), 18–22.

Bennett, N. and Dunne, E. (1992) *Managing Classroom Groups*. London: Simon and Schuster.

Bennett, N. and Turner-Bisset, R. (1993) 'Knowledge bases and teaching performance', in Bennett, N. and Carré, C. (ed.) *Learning to Teach*. London: Routledge.

Bentley, D. and Rowe, A. (1991) *Group Reading in the Primary Classroom*. Reading: Reading and Language Information Centre, University of Reading.

Benton, M. and Fox, G. (1985) *Teaching Literature 9–14*. Oxford: Oxford University Press.

Bereiter, C. and Scardamalia, M. (1987) *The Psychology of Composition*. Hillsdale, NJ: Lawrence Erlbaum.

Bielby, N. (1998) 'How to teach reading: a balanced approach', in Moustafa, M. *et al.* (eds) *Whole to Part Phonics*. Leamington Spa: Scholastic.

Black, P. *et al.* (1988) *National Curriculum Task Group on Assessment and Testing: A Report (TGAT)*. London: HMSO.

Black, P. and William, D. (1998) 'Assessment and classroom learning', *Assessment in Education* **5**, 7–76.

Booth, T. (2000) 'Inclusion and exclusion policy in England: who controls the agenda?', in Armstrong, F. *et al.* (eds) *Inclusive Education: Policy, Contexts and Comparative Perspectives*. London: David Fulton Publishers.

Bradley, L. ad Bryant, P. (1983) 'Categorising sounds and learning to read: a causal connection', *Nature* **301**, 419–21.

Brice-Heath, S. (1983) *Ways with Words*. Cambridge: Cambridge University Press.

Britton, J. (1977) 'The nature of the reader's satisfaction', in Meek, M. *et al.* (eds) *The Cool Web: The Pattern of Children's Reading*. London: Bodley Head.

Britton, J. (1982) *Prospect and Retrospect*. London: Heinemann.

Broadfoot, P. (1998) 'Don't forget the confidence factor', *Times Educational Supplement*, 6 November, 25.

Bromley, H. (1998) 'In which we are introduced to the boxes and some children, and the stories begin', in Beavne, E. (ed.) *Use of Language Across the Primary Curriculum*. London: Routledge.

Brooks, G. (1998) 'Trends in standards of literacy in the United Kingdom', *Topic* **19**, 1–10.

Brooks, G. *et al.* (1996) *Reading Performance at Nine*. Slough: National Foundation for Educational Research.

Browne, A. (1993) *Helping Children to Write*. London: Paul Chapman.

Browne, A. (1996) *Developing Language and Literacy*. London: Paul Chapman.

Bruner, J. (1985) 'Vygotsky: a historical and conceptual perspective', in Wertsch, J. (ed.) *Culture, Communication and Cognition: Vygotskian Perspectives*. Cambridge: Cambridge University Press.

Bruner, J. (1986) *Actual Minds, Possible Worlds*. Cambridge, MA: Harvard University Press.

Bryant, P. and Bradley, L. (1985) *Children's Reading Problems*. Oxford: Blackwell.

Bunting, R. (1997) *Teaching about Language in the Primary Years*. London: David Fulton Publishers.

Bussis, A. *et al.* (1985) *Inquiry into Meaning: an Investigation of Learning to Read*. Hillsdale, NJ: Lawrence Erlbaum.

Button, K., and Johnson, M. (1997) 'The role of shared reading in developing effective early reading strategies', *Reading Horizons* **37**(4), 262–73.

Byers, R. (1999) 'The national literacy strategy and pupils with SEN', *British Journal of Special Education* **26**(1), 8–11.

Cairney, T. and Ruge, J. (1998) *Community Literacy Practices and Schooling: Towards Effective Support for Students*. Sydney, Australia: Department of Employment, Education, Training and Youth Affairs.

Calkins, L. (1983) *Lessons From a Child*. London: Heinemann.

Calkins, L. (1986) *The Art of Teaching Writing*. Portsmouth, NH: Heinemann.

Calkins, L. (1991) *Living Between the Lines*. London: Heinemann.

Calkins, L. and Harwayne, S. (1987) *The Writing Workshop: A World of Difference*. London: Heinemann.

Cambourne, B. (1995) 'Towards an educationally relevant theory of literacy learning: twelve years of enquiry', *The Reading Teacher* **49**(3), 182–90.

Cambourne, B. (1997) 'Key Principles of good literacy teaching'. Keynote and unpublished conference paper, United Kingdom Reading Association *Literacy Learning*, July, Manchester.

Cambourne, B. (2000) 'Conditions for literacy learning', *The Reading Teacher* **53**(6), 512–15.

Campbell, R. (1990) *Reading Together*. Milton Keynes: Open University Press.

Campbell, R. (1998) 'A literacy hour is only part of the story', *Reading* **32**(1), 21–3.

Campbell, R. (1999) 'Four blocks for literacy', *Reading* **33**(1), 29–32.

Carr, E. and Allen, J. (1987) 'Peer teaching and learning during writing time in kindergarten'. Paper presented at the National Reading Conference, St Petersburg, December.

Carter, R. (ed.) (1991) *Knowledge about Language and the Curriculum: The LINC Reader*. Sevenoaks, Kent: Hodder and Stoughton.

Centre for Language in Primary Education (CLPE) (2000) *The Core Book List*. London: CLPE.

Centre for Studies in Inclusive Education (CSIE) (1995) *Inclusive Education: The Right to Belong to the Mainstream*. Bristol: CSIE.

Centre for Studies in Inclusive Education (CSIE) (2000) *Index for Inclusion*. Bristol: CSIE.

Chambers, A. (1991) *Booktalk: Occasional Writing on Literature and Children*. London: Bodley Head.

Chambers, A. (1993) *Tell Me: Children Reading and Talk*. Stroud: Thimble Press.

Clark, C. *et al.* (1999) 'Theorising special education – time to move on?', in Clark, C. *et al.* (eds) *Theorising Special Education*. London : Routledge.

Clarke, L. (2000) 'Lessons from the nursery: children as writers in early years education', *Reading* **34**(2), 68–73.

Clark, M. (1976) *Young Fluent Readers: What Can They Teacher Us*. London: Heinemann.

Clarke, S. (1998) *Targeting Assessment in the Primary Classroom*. London: Hodder and Stoughton.

Clay, M. (1972) *Reading: The Patterning of Complex Behaviour*. Auckland: Heinemann.

Clay, M. (1980) 'Early reading and writing: reciprocal gains', in Clark, M. and Glynn, T. (eds) *Reading and Writing for the Child with Difficulties*. University of Birmingham: Education Review Occasional Publications, no. 8.

Clay, M. (1991a) *Becoming Literate: The Construction of Inner Control*. Portsmouth, NH: Heinemann.

Clay, M. (1991b) 'Introducing a new storybook to young readers', *The Reading Teacher* **45**, 264–73.

Clay, M. (1993) *Reading Recovery: A Guidebook for Teachers in Training*. Auckland: Heinemann.

Cliff Hodges, G. *et al.* (2000) *Tales, Tellers and Texts*. London: Cassell.

Clough, P. (1998) *Managing Inclusive Education: From Policy to Experience*. London: Paul Chapman.

Clough, P. (1999) 'Exclusive tendencies: concepts, consciousness and curriculum in the project of inclusion', *International Journal of Inclusive Education* **3**, 163–73.

Cole, M. J. (1995) 'Critical thinking, talk and a community of enquiry in the primary school', *Language and Education* **9**(3), 161–77.

Corden, R. (2000) *Literacy and Learning through Talk: Strategies for the Primary Classroom*. Buckingham: Open University Press.

Corker, M. (1998) 'Disability discourse in a post-modern world', in Shakspeare. T. (ed.) *The Disability Reader*. London: Cassell.

Cox, B. (ed.) (1998) *Literacy is not Enough: Essays on the Importance of Reading*. Manchester: Manchester University Press and Book Trust.

Cremin, M. and Grainger, T. (2000) *Resourcing Classroom Drama 8–14*. Sheffield: National Association for the Teaching of English (NATE).

Crinson, J. (1998) 'The verb phrase; past, present and future', *The Primary English Magazine* **3**(4), 14–15.

Croll, P. and Moses, D. (2000) 'Ideologies and utopias: education professionals' views of inclusion', *European Journal of Special Needs Education* **15**(1), 1–12.

Cummins, J. (1986) 'Empowering minority students: a framework for intervention', *Harvard Educational Review* **56**, 18–36.

Dadds, M. (1999) 'Teachers' values and the literacy hour', *Cambridge Journal of Education* **29**(1), 7–20.

D'Arcy, P. (2000) *Two Contrasting Paradigms for the Teaching and Assessment of Writing: A Critique of Current Approaches in the NC*. Loughborough: National Association of Advisers in English, National Association for Primary Education and National Association of Teachers of English.

Department for Education and Employment (DfEE) (1997) *Excellence for All Children: Meeting Special Educational Needs*. London HMSO.

Department for Education and Employment (DfEE) (1998a) *Homework: Guidelines for Primary and Secondary Schools.* London: DfEE.

Department for Education and Employment (DfEE) (1998b) *The National Literacy Strategy Framework for Teaching.* London: DfEE.

Department for Education and Employment (DfEE) (1998c) *Meeting Special Educational Needs: A Programme of Action.* Sudbury: DfEE Publications.

Department for Education and Employment (DfEE) (1999a) *Looking for Patterns*, NLS flier. London: DfEE.

Department for Education and Employment (DfEE) (1999b) *The NLS: Progression in Phonics.* London: DfEE.

Department for Education and Employment (DfEE) (1999c) *All our Futures: Creativity, Culture and Education*, Report of the National Advisory Committee on Creative and Cultural Education. London: DfEE.

Department for Education and Employment (DfEE) (1999d) *Writing in the Literacy Hour*, Flier 4. London: DfEE.

Department for Education and Employment (DfEE) (1999e) *National Literacy Strategy Additional Literacy Support: Modules 1–4.* London: DfEE.

Department for Education and Employment (DfEE) (2000a) *Draft revised SEN code of practice*, www.dfee.gov.uk/sen/standard.htm (accessed 20 August 2000).

Department for Education and Employment (DfEE) (2000b) *Grammar for Writing*, CD-ROM. London: The Stationery Office.

Department for Education and Employment (DfEE) and Qualifications and Curriculum Authority (QCA) (1999) *The National Curriculum Handbook for Primary Teachers in England Key Stages 1 and 2.* London: DfEE and QCA.

Department of Education and Science (DES) (1975) *A Language of Life: Report of the Committee of Inquiry Appointed by the Secretary of State for Education and Science* (Bullock Report). London: HMSO.

Department of Education and Science (DES) (1978) *The Education of Handicapped Children and Young People* (Warnock Report). London HMSO.

Department of Education and Science (DES) (1988a) *The National Curriculum: English for Ages 5 to 11.* London: HMSO.

Department of Education and Science (DES) (1988b) *National Curriculum Report of Task Group on Assessment and Testing.* London: HMSO.

Derewianka, B. (1990) *Exploring How Texts Work.* Newtown, New South Wales: PETA.

Dickenson D. (1995) *Bridges to Literature: Children, Families and Schools.* Oxford. Blackwell.

Doddington, C. (1998) 'Significant speech', in Bearne, E. (ed.) *Use of Language Across the Primary Curriculum.* London: Routledge.

Dombey, H. (1988) 'Partners in the telling', in Meek, M. and Mills, C. (eds) *Language and Literacy in the Primary School.* London: Falmer Press.

Dombey, H. (1998a) *Whole to Part Phonics: How Children Learn to Read and Spell.* London: Centre for Language in Primary Education.

Dombey, H. (1998b) 'Changing literacy in the early years of school', in Cox, B. (ed.) *Literacy is not Enough: Essays on the Importance of Reading.* Manchester: Manchester University Press and Book Trust.

Dombey, H. (1999) 'A balanced approach to phonics teaching', *Reading* 33(2), 52–8.

Dombey, H. (2000) 'Book review of *Understanding Literacy Development*, Geekie, P. *et al.*', *Reading* 35(3), 138–9.

Doonan, J. (1993) *Looking at Pictures in Picture Books.* Stroud: Thimble Press.

Durkin, D. (1966) *Children Who Read Early: Two Longitudinal Studies.* New York: Teacher's College Press.

Dyson, A. (1995) 'Writing children: reinventing the development of childhood literacy', *Written Communication* 12, 4–46.

Edwards, A. and Mercer, N. (1987) *Common Knowledge: The Development of Understanding in the Classroom.* London: Methuen.

Edwards, A. and Furlong, V. (1978) *The Language of Teaching.* London: Heinemann.

Ehri, L. (1997) 'Learning to read and learning to spell are one and the same, almost', in Perfetti, C. *et al.* (eds) *Learning to Spell: Research, Theory and Practice Across Languages.* Mahwah, NJ: Lawrence Erlbaum.

Elliot, J. G. (2000) 'The psychological assessment of children with learning difficulties', *British Journal of Special Education* 27(2), 59–66.

Ellis, S. and Barrs, M. (1996) *The Core Book: A Structured Approach to Using Books within the Reading Curriculum.* London: Centre for Language in Primary Education.

Ewing, J. and Kennedy, I. (1996) 'Putting co-operative learning to good effect', *Reading* 30(1), 15–19.

Farrell, P. *et al.* (1999) *The Management, Role and Training of Learning Support Assistants.* Research report no. 161. London: HMSO.

Fenwick, G. and Reader, P. (1996) 'Sustained, silent reading', unpublished paper from a primary school survey. Liverpool: John Moore's University.

Fine, E. (1989) 'Collaborative writing: key to unlocking the silences of children', *Language Arts* 66(5), 501–508.

Fisher, R. (1998) 'Thinking about thinking: developing metacognition in children', *Early Child Development and Care* 141, 1–13.

Fisher, R. and Lewis, R. (1999) 'Anticipation or trepidation? Teachers' views on the literacy hour', *Reading* 33(1), 23–8.

Flanders, N. (1970) *Analysing Teacher Behaviour.* Reading, MA: Addison Wesley.

Fountas, I. C. and Pinnell, G. S. (1996) *Guided Reading: Good First Teaching for all Children.* Portsmouth, NH: Heinemann.

Fox, C. (1993) *At the Very Edge of the Forest: The Influence of Literature on Storytelling by Children.* London: Cassell.

Fox, G. (1996) 'Reading picture books ... how to?', in Styles, M. *et al.* (eds) *Voices Off: Texts, Contexts and Readers.* London: Cassell.

Fox, R. (1994) 'Assessing developing writing and writers', in Wray, D. and Medwell, J. (eds) *Teaching Primary English: The State of the Art.* London: Routledge.

Fox, R. (2000) 'Assessing writing at KS1: Some problems and suggested solutions', *Reading* **34**(1), 24–33.

Frater, G. (2000) 'Observed in practice. English in the NLS: some reflections', *Reading* **34**(3), 107–12.

Freire, P. (1985) *The Politics of Education*. London: Macmillan.

Frith, U. (1980) 'Unexpected spelling problems', in Frith, U. (ed.) *Cognitive Processes in Spelling*. San Diego, CA: Academic Press.

Frith, U. (1985) 'Developmental dyslexia', in Patterson, K. *et al.* (eds) *Surface Dyslexia*. Hillsdale, NJ: Lawrence Erlbaum Associates.

Furlong, T. (1998) 'Reading in the primary school', in Cox, B. (ed.) *Literacy is not Enough: Essays on the Importance of Reading*. Manchester: Manchester University Press and Book Trust.

Geekie, P. *et al.* (1999) *Understanding Literacy Development*. Stoke on Trent: Trentham.

Gee, J. P. (1996) *Social Linguistics and Literacies' Ideology in Discourses,* 2nd edn. London: Taylor and Francis.

Gentry, J. R. (1982) 'An analysis of developmental spelling in GNYS AT WRK', *The Reading Teacher* **36**, 192–200.

Goddard, A. (1997) 'The role of individual education plans/programmes in special education: a critique', *Support for Learning* **12**(4), 170–3.

Goodman, K. (1973) 'Miscues: windows on the reading process', in Goodman, K. (ed.) *Miscue Analysis: Application to Reading Instruction*. Urbana, IL: ERIC Clearing House on Reading and Communication, NCTE.

Goodman, K. and Burke (1972) *The Reading Miscue Inventory Manual: Procedures for Diagnosis and Evaluation*. London: Macmillan.

Goodwin, P. and Routh, C. (2000) 'A brief history of timing: the impact of the NLS on the marketing and publishing of resources to support literacy teaching', *Reading* **34**(3), 119–23.

Goswami, U. (1999) 'Phonological development and reading by analogy: what is analogy and what is not?', *Journal of Research in Reading* **18**(2), 217–40.

Goswami, U. and Bryant, P. (1991) *Phonological Skills and Learning to Read*. Norwood, NJ: Lawrence Erlbaum Associates.

Graham, J. (1990) *Pictures on the Page*. Sheffield: National Association for Teaching of English (NATE).

Graham, J. (1999) 'The creation of readers, or Mr Magnolia meets the literacy hour. Will he survive?' in Goodwin, P. (ed.) *The Literate Classroom*. London: David Fulton Publishers.

Graham, J. (2000) 'Creativity and picture books', *Reading,* **34**(2), 61–7.

Graham, J. and Kelly, A. (eds) (1997) *Reading Under Control: Teaching Reading in the Primary School*. London: David Fulton Publishers in association with the Roehampton Institute.

Graham, L. (1995) *Writing Development: A Framework: Early Years and Key Stage 1 and 2*. Croydon: Schools Advisory Service.

Graham, L. (1999) 'Changing practice through reflection: the KS 2 reading project, Croydon', *Reading* **33**(3), 106–13.

Grainger, T. (1997) *Traditional Storytelling in the Primary Classroom*. Leamington Spa: Scholastic.

Grainger, T. (2000) 'The current status of oracy: a cause of (dis)satisfaction?', in Davison, J. and Moss, J. (eds) *Issues in English Teaching*. London: Routledge.

Grainger, T. and Cremin, M. (2000) *Resourcing Classroom Drama 5–8*. Leicester: National Association for Teaching of English (NATE).

Graves, D. (1983) *Writing: Teachers and Children at Work*. London: Heinemann Educational.

Greenhough, P. and Hughes, M. (1999) 'Encouraging conversing: trying to change what parents do when their children read with them', *Reading* **33**(3), 98–105.

Gregory, R. (1996) *Making Sense of a New World*. London: Paul Chapman Publishing.

Hall, A. and Robinson, A. (eds) (1996) *Learning about Punctuation*. Clevedon: Multilingual Matters.

Hall, C. and Coles, M. (1999) *Children's Reading Choices*. London: Routledge.

Hall, N. (ed.) (1998) *Writing with Reason: The Emergence of Authorship in Young Children*. London: Hodder and Stoughton.

Hall, N. and Robinson, A. (1995) *Exploring Writing and Play in the Early Years*. London: David Fulton Publishers.

Hall, N. *et al.* (1989) *Parental Views on Writing and the Teaching of Writing*. Manchester School of Education, Manchester Polytechnic.

Halliday, M. (1985) 'Three aspects of children's language development: learn language, learn about language, learn through language', unpublished manuscript, Department of Linguistics, University of Sydney, Australia.

Hannon, P. (1995) *Literacy, Home and School: Research and Practice in Teaching Literacy with Parents*. London: Falmer Press.

Hannon, P. and James, S. (1990) 'Parents' and teachers' perspectives on preschool literacy development', *British Educational Research Journal* **16**(3), 259–72.

Hansen, J. (1987) *When Writers Read*. Portsmouth, NH: Heinemann.

Hardman, F. and Beverton, S. (1993) 'Co-operative group work and the development of metadiscoursal skills', *Support for Learning,* **8**(4), 146–50.

Harding, D. W. (1977) 'Psychological processes in the reading of fiction', in Meek, M. *et al.* (eds) *The Cool Web*. London: Bodley Head.

Harlen, W. and James, M. (1997) 'Assessment and learning: differences and relationships between formative and summative assessment', *Assessment in Education*, **4**(3), 365–80.

Harsle, J. *et al.* (1989) *Creating Classrooms for Authors: The Reading–Writing Connection*. London: Heinemann.

Harste, G. *et al.* (1984) *Language Stories and Literacy Lessons*. Portsmouth, NH: Heinemann.

Hawke, J. (1989) 'Aspects of dialogue and learning in a junior school', unpublished MA thesis, Canterbury Christchurch University College.

Haworth, A. (1992) 'Towards a collaborative model of learning', *English in Education* **26**(3), 40–49.

Heppell, S. (1993) 'Teacher education, learning and the information generation: the progression and evolution of educational computing against a background of change', *Journal of Information Teachnology for Teacher Education* **2**(2): 229–37.

Her Majesty's Inspectorate of Schools (HMI) (2000) 'The teaching of writing in primary schools: could do better', a discussion paper by HMI, www.standards.dfee.gov.uk/literacy (accessed October 2000).

Hilton, M. (1994) '"The Blowing Dust": popular culture and popular books for children', in Styles, M. *et al.*, *The Prose and the Passion*. London: Cassell.

Hilton, M. (ed.) (1996) *Potent Fictions: Children's Literacy and the Challenge of Popular Culture*. London: Routledge.

Hilton, M. (1998) 'Raising literacy standards: the true story', *English in Education* **32**(3), 4–15.

Hoffman, J. V. (1998) 'When bad things happen to good ideas in literacy education', *The Reading Teacher* **52**(2), 102–13.

Holdaway, D. (1979) *The Foundations of Literacy*. Ashton: Scholastic.

Holdaway, D. (1982) 'Shared book experience: teaching reading using favourite books', *Theory into Practice* **21**(4), 293–300.

Hornby. G. (1999) 'Can one size fit all?', *Support for Learning* **14**(4), 184–8.

Hughes, T. (1970) 'Myth and education', *Children's Literature in Education* **1**(1), 12–24.

Iser, W. (1978) *The Act of Reading: A Theory of Aesthetic Response*. Baltimore, MD: Johns Hopkins University Press and London: Routledge and Kegan Paul.

Jones, J. (1999) 'The implementation of the NLS: a response to Stainthorp', *The Psychology of Education Review* **23**(1), 9–10.

Joo, J. (1999) 'Cultural issues of the internet in classrooms', *British Journal of Educational Computing* **30**(3), 249.

Kress, G. (1982) *Learning to Write*. London: Routledge and Kegan Paul.

Kress, G. (1986) 'Interrelationships of reading and writing', in Wilkinson, A. (ed.) *The Writing of Writing*. Milton Keynes: Open University Press.

Kress, G. (1997) *Before Writing: Rethinking the Paths to Literacy*. London: Routledge.

Kress, G. and Van Leween, T. (1996) *Reading Images: The Grammar of Visual Design*. London: Routledge.

Lankshear, C. (1997) *Changing Literacies*. Buckingham: Open University Press.

Laycock, L. (1990) 'Shared writing – "People working together"', in Centre for Language in Primary Education (CLPE), *Shared Reading, Shared Writing*. London: CLPE.

Laycock, L. (1999) 'Shared reading and shared writing at Key Stage 1', in Goodwin, P. (ed.) *The Literate Classroom*. London: David Fulton Publishers.

Leavers F. (2000) 'Forward to basics! Deep level learning and the experiential approach', *Early Years* **20**(2), 20–29.

Lennox, D. and Siegal, P. (1994) 'The role of phonological and orthographic processes in learning to spell', in *The Handbook of Spelling: Theory, Process and Intervention*. London: John Wiley and Son.

Lewis, M. and Wray, D. (1995) *Developing Children's Non-fiction Writing: Working with Writing Frames*. Leamington Spa: Scholastic.

Lewis, M. and Wray, D. (1998) 'New technology and new literacy', *Educational Computing and Technology*, May, 28–9.

Lewis, M. *et al.* (2000) *Curiosity Kits: Innovative Non Fiction Reading Kits: an occasional paper*. Royston: United Kingdom Reading Association.

Lingard, T. (1966) 'Why our theoretical models of integration are inhibiting effective integration', *Emotional and Behavioural Difficulties* **1**(2), 39–45.

Literacy Task Force (1997) *The Implementation of the National Literacy Strategy*. London: DfEE.

Lloyd, S. R. and Berthelot, C. (1992) *Self-empowerment: How to Get What you Want from Life*. London: Kogan Page.

Mandler, J. and Johnson, N. (1977) 'Remembrance of things parsed: story structure and recall', *Cognitive Psychology* **9**(2), 111–51.

Marshall, B. (1998) 'What they should be learning and how they should be taught', *English in Education* **32**(1), 4–9.

Martin, T. (1989) *The Strugglers*. Milton Keynes: Open University Press.

Martin, T. (1999) 'Responding to fiction', in Goodwin, P. (ed.) *The Literate Classroom*. London: David Fulton Publishers.

Martin, T. and Leather, B. (1994) *Readers and Texts in the Primary Years*. Milton Keynes: Open University Press

McCarthey, S. (1997) 'Connecting home and school literacy practices in classrooms with diverse populations', *Journal of Literacy Research* **29**(2), 145–82.

McGuiness, C. (1999) *From Thinking Skills to Thinking Classrooms*, DfEE Research Brief, Research Report no. 115. London: DfEE.

McGuiness, D. (1998) *Why Children Can't Read and What We Can Do About It*. London: Penguin.

McKenzie, M. (1985) 'Shared writing', in *Language Matters. Nos 1 and 2*. London: Centre for Language in Primary Education.

McMahon, S. and Goatley, V. (1995) 'Fifth graders helping peers discuss texts in student led groups', *The Journal of Educational Research* **89**(1), 23–34.

McTear, J. (1981) 'Towards a model for the linguistic analysis of conversation', *Belfast Working Papers in Language and Linguistics* (Ulster Polytechnic, Belfast), **5**, 79–92.

Medwell, J. (1994) 'Contexts for writing: the social construction of written composition', in Wray, D. and Medwell, J. (eds) *Teaching Primary English: the State of the Art*. London: Routledge.

Medwell, J. *et al.* (1998) *Effective Teachers of Literacy*. Exeter: University of Exeter.

Meek, M. (1988) *How Texts Teach What Readers Learn*. Stroud: Thimble Press.

Meek, M. (1991) *On Being Literate*. London: Bodley Head.

Meek, M. (1992) 'Literacy redescribing reading', in Kimberley, K. *et al.* (eds) *New Reading Contributions to an Understanding of Literacy*. London: A. & C. Black.

Mercer, N. (1995) *The Guided Construction of Knowledge: Talk Amongst Teachers and Learners*. Clevedon: Multilingual Matters.

Millard, E. (1997) *Differently Literate: Boys, Girls and the Schooling of Literacy*. London: Falmer Press.

Millum, T. (1989) *Warning, Too Much Schooling Can Damage Your Health*. Cheltenham: Stanley Thornes.

Minns, H. (1990) *Read it to Me Now*. London: Virago.

Moon, C. (1984) 'Making use of miscues when children read aloud', in National Association of Teachers of English (NATE) (ed.) *Children Reading to their Teachers*. Sheffield: NATE.

Mooney, M. (1994) *Exploring New Horizons in Guided Reading*. Australia: Thomas Nelson.

Mooney, M. (1995) 'Guided reading: the reader in control', *Teaching Pre K-8*, **25**(8), 54–8.

Mooney, M. (1990) *Reading To, With and By Children*. Katonah, NY: Richard C. Owen.

Morrow, L. (1995) *Family Literacy: Connections in Schools and Communities*. Newark, DE: International Reading Association.

Moss, G. (1998) *The Fact and Fiction Research Project. Interim Findings*. Southampton: University of Southampton.

Moss, G. (2000) 'Raising boys' attainment in reading: some principles for intervention', *Reading* **34**(3), 101–106.

Moustafa, M. and Maldonado-Colon E. (1999) 'Whole- to part phonics instruction: building on what children know to help them know more', *The Reading Teacher* **52**(5), 448–58.

Moyles, J. (1997) 'Jill of all trades?': Classroom Assistants in KS1 Classes. London: Association of Teachers and Lecturers (ATL) Publications.

National Council for Educational Technology (NCET) (1998a) *Integrated Learning Systems: A Report of Phase Two of the Pilot Evaluation of ILS in the UK*. Coventry: NCET.

National Council for Educational Technology (NCET) (1998b) *The UK ILS Evaluations: Final Report*. Coventry: NCET.

National Writing Project (1989) *Audiences for Writing*. Walton on Thames: Nelson.

Nistler, R. and Maiers, A. (2000) 'Stopping the silence: hearing parents' voices in an urban first grade family literacy program', *The Reading Teacher* **53**(8), 670–80.

Norman, K. (1990) *Teaching, Talking and Learning in Key Stages 1 and 2*. Sheffield: National Association of Teachers of English (NATE) and National Curriculum Council (NCC).

Norwich, B. (1966) 'Special needs education or education for all: connective specialisation and educational impurity', *British Journal of Special Education* **32**(3), 100–104.

Nutbrown, C. (1999) 'Purpose and authenticity in early learning assessment', *Reading* **33**(1), 33–40.

Office for Standards in Education (OFSTED) (1996) *The Teaching of Reading in 45 Inner London Schools*. London: OFSTED.

Office for Standards in Education (OFSTED) (1998) *Report on 1997 KS1/2 SATS*. London: OFSTED.

Office for Standards in Education (OFSTED) (1999) *Educational Inclusion and School Inspection: Briefing for Inspectors, Inspection Providers and Schools*. London: OFSTED.

Office for Standards in Education (OFSTED) (2000) *Educational Inclusion and School Inspection*. London: OFSTED.

Olsen, D. (1984) 'See! Jumping! Some oral antecedents to literacy', in Goelman, H. *et al.* (eds) *Awakening to Literacy*. Portsmouth, NH: Heinemann.

O'Sullivan, O. (2000) 'Understanding spelling', *Reading* **34**(1), 9–16.

Palinscar, A. S. (1986) 'The role of dialogue in providing scaffolded instruction', *Educational Psychologist* **21**, 73–98.

Pahl, K. (1999) *Transformations, Making Meaning in Nursery Education*. Stoke on Trent: Trentham.

Palinscar, A. S. and Brown, A. L. (1984) 'Reciprocal teaching of comprehension, fostering and comprehension monitoring activities', *Cognition and Instruction* **2**, 117–75.

Papert, S. (1993) *The Children's Machine: Rethinking Schools in the Age of the Computer*. New York: Basic Books.

Paratore, J. (1995) 'Implementing an intergenerational literacy program: lessons learned', in Morrow, L. (ed.) *Family Literacy Connections in Schools and Communities*. Newark, DE: International Reading Association.

Park, B. (1982) 'The big book trend – a discussion with Don Holdaway', *Language Arts* **59**(8), 815–21.

Pennac, D. (1994) *Reads like a Novel*, Gunn, D. (trans.). Reading: Quartet Books.

Perera, K. (1984) *Children's Writing and Reading*. Oxford: Blackwell.

Perera, K. (1993) 'The good book: linguistic aspects' in Beard, R. (ed.) *Teaching Literacy: Balancing Perspectives*. London: Hodder and Stoughton.

Perez, S. (1986) 'Children see, children do: teachers as reading models', *The Reading Teacher* **40**(5), 460–72.

Pidgeon, S. (1990) 'Shared reading and shared writing', in *Shared Reading and Shared Writing*. London: Centre for Language in Primary Education.

Pinnell, G. *et al.* (1995) *Listening to Children Reading Aloud: Data from NAEP's Integrated Reading Performance Record (IRPR) at Grade 4*. Report no. 23-FR-04. Washington: Office of Educational Research and Improvement, US Department of Education.

Plant, C. (1999) 'Guided reading', in Fisher, R. with Arnold, H. (eds) *Understanding the Literacy Hour*. Royston: United Kingdom Reading Association.

Pollard, A. and Filer, A. (1996) *The Social World of Children's Learning*. London: Cassell.

Pye, J. (1988) *Invisible Children: Who are the Real Losers at School?* Oxford: Oxford University Press.

Qualifications and Curriculum Authority (QCA) (1998a) KS1 SATS. London: QCA.

Qualifications and Curriculum Authority (QCA) (1998b) *Can Do Better: Raising Boys' Achievement in English*. London: QCA.

Qualifications and Curriculum Authority (QCA) (1998c) *Supporting the Target Setting Process: Guidance for Effective Target Setting for Pupils with Special Educational Needs*. London: QCA.

Qualifications and Curriculum Authority (QCA) (1999a) *Target Setting and Assessment in the National Literacy Strategy*. London: QCA.

Qualifications and Curriculum Authority (QCA) (1999b) *Teaching Speaking and Listening in Key Stages 1 and 2*. London: QCA.

Reading Recovery National Network (1998) *Book Bands for Guided Reading: Organising Key Stage One Texts for the Literacy Hour*. Longfield, Kent: Orchard Publishing.

Reid, J. *et al.* (1982) *Small Group Work n the Classroom*. Perth: Western Australia Education Department.

Resnick, M. (1999) el.www.media.edu/groups/el/Papers/mres/new_paradigms.html

Riddell, S. (2000) 'Inclusion and choice: mutually exclusive principles in special educational needs?', in Armstrong, F. *et al.* (eds) *Inclusive Education: Policy ,Contexts and Comparative Perspectives*. London: David Fulton Publishers.

Robinson, F. and Sulzby, E. (1984) 'Parents and children and "favourite" books: an interview study', in Niles, J. and Harris, L. (eds) *Changing Perspectives on Research iin Reading and Language Processing Instruction*, 33rd yearbook of the National Reading Conference.

Robinson, M. and King, C. (1995) 'Creating communities of readers', *English in Education* **28**(2), 26–40.

Roehampton Children's Literature Research Centre (1994) *Contemporary Juvenile Reading Habits*. London: Roehampton Institute (British National Bibliography Research Fund Report 69).

Rogoff, B. *et al.* (1996) 'Models of teaching and learning: participation in a community of learners', in Olson, D. and Torrance, N. (eds) *Handbook of Education and Human Development: The New Models of Learning, Teaching and Schooling*. Cambridge, MA: Blackwell.

Rogoff, B. (1990) *Apprenticeship in Thinking: Cognitive Development in Social Context*. Oxford: Oxford University Press.

Rooke, J. (1998) 'Going in for grouping', *The Primary English Magazine* **3**(3), 27–9.

Rosenblatt, L. (1978) *The Reader, the Text, the Poem*. Carbondale, IL: Southern Illinois University Press.

Rosenblatt, L. (1989) 'Writing and reading: the transactional theory', in Mason, J. (ed.) *Reading and Writing Connections*. Boston, MA: Allyn and Bacon.

Rowe, A. and Goodwin, P. (1999) 'Writer's workshops in action', in Goodwin, P. (ed.) *The Literate Classroom*. London: David Fulton Publishers.

Rowe, D. (1987) 'Literacy learning as an intertextual process', *National Reading Conference Yearbook* **36**, 101–12.

Rumelhart, D. (1976) 'Towards an interactive model of reading', *Technical Report no. 56*. San Diego Center for Human Information Processing, University of California at San Diego.

Sainsbury, M. (1998a) *Evaluation of the National Literacy Project Cohort 1 1996–1998*. Slough: NFER.

Sarland, C. (1991) *Young People Reading: Culture and Response*. Milton Keynes: Open University Press.

School Curriculum and Assessment Authority (SCAA) (1995) *Consistency in Teacher Assessment: Exemplification of Standards Key Stages 1 and 2*. London: SCAA.

School Curriculum and Assessment Authority (SCAA) (1997) *Teacher Assessment in Key Stage 2*. London: SCAA.

Schulz, K. (1997) '"Do you want to be in my story?" Collaborative writing in an urban primary classroom', *Journal of Literacy Research* **29**(2), 253–88.

Scott, A. (1997) 'No quick fixes', *The Primary English Magazine* **3**(1), 24–5.

Sheeran, Y. and Barnes, D. (1991) *School Writing: Discovering the Ground Tules*. Milton Keynes: Open University Press.

Sheridan, C. (1982) *Introduction to Miscue Analysis*. Australia: Wester Australia College of Advanced Education.

Sitko, M. C. and Sitko, C. J. (eds) (1996) *Exceptional Solutions: Computers and Students with Special Educational Needs*. Ontario: The Althouse Press.

Smith, C. and Whitely, D. (2000) 'Developing literacy through the literacy hour: a survey of teachers' experiences', *Reading* **34**(1), 34–8.

Smith, F. (1978) *Reading 3–13 Years*. Cambridge: Cambridge University Press.

Smith, F. (1982) *Writing and the Writer*. London: Heinemann.

Smith, F. (1988) *Joining the Literacy Club*. London: Heinemann.

Snow, C. *et al.* (1991) *Unfulfilled Expectations: Home and School Influences on Literacy*. London: Harvard University Press.

Solity, J. (2000) 'The early reading research: applying psychology to classroom practice', *Educational and Child Psychology* **17**(2), 46–65.

Solity, J. *et al.* (1999) 'The early reading research: implications for word level work within the NLS', paper presented at an invited conference on the Importance of Phonics in Learning to Read and Write. London: OFSTED.

Southgate, V. *et al.* (1981) *Extending Beginning Reading*. London: Heinemann Education Books.

Stannard, J. (1997) Keynote address to the UKRA regional conference, Homerton College, Cambridge, 15 March.

Street, B. (1997) 'The implication of the "new literacy studies for literacy education"', *English in Education* **32**(3), 45–59.

Street, B. V. (1993) *Cross Cultural Approaches to Literacy*. Cambridge: Cambridge University Press.

Strickland, D. S. and Morrow, L. M. (1990) 'Sharing big books', *The Reading Teacher?* **43**(5), 342–3.

Sulzby, E. (1985) 'Children's emergent reading of favorite storybooks: a developmental study', *Reading Research Quarterly* **20**(4), 58–81.

Swap, S. (1993) *Developing Home-School Partnerships*. New York: Teachers' College Press.

Swindal, D. N. (1993) 'The big advantage: using big books for shared reading experiences in the classroom', *The Reading Teacher* **46**(8), 716–17.

Taylor, M. (1994) 'What children's books tell us about teaching language', in Styles, M. *et al.* (eds) *The Prose and the Passion*. London: Cassell.

Teacher Training Agency (TTA) (1999) *National Special Educational Needs Specialist Standards*. London: TTA.

Temple, N. *et al.* (1982) *The Beginnings of Writing*. Boston: Allyn and Bacon.

Tiernay, R. *et al.* (1989) 'The effects of reading and writing upon thinking critically', *Reading Research Quarterly* **24**(2), 134–73.

Tizard, B. and Hughes, M. (1984) *Young Children's Learning, Talking and Thinking at Home and at School*. London: Fontana.

Tod. J. *et al.* (1998) *IEPs – Implementing Effective Practice*. London: David Fulton Publishers.

Toomey, D. (1989) 'How home–school relations policies can increase educational inequality', *American Journal of Education* 33(3), 284–98.

Topping, K. (1985) 'Parental involvement in reading: theoretical and empirical background', in Topping, K. and Wolfendale, S. (eds) *Parental Involvement in Children's Reading*. London: Croom Helm.

Topping, K. *et al.* (2000) 'Paired writing: a framework for effective collaboration', *Reading* 34(2), 79–90.

Treiman, R. (1985) 'Onsets and rimes as units of spoken syllables: evidence from children', *Journal of Experimental Child Psychology* 39, 161–81.

Treiman, R. (1994) 'Sources of information used by beginning spellers', in Gordon, D. *et al.* (eds) *Handbook of Spelling*. Chichester: John Wiley and Son.

Tuxford, P. and Washtell, A. (1990) '"There's them things again": shared writing and the exploration of linguistic awareness', in Centre for Language in Primary Education (CLPE), *Shared Reading, Shared Writing*. London: Inner London Education Authority (ILEA)/CLPE.

United Nations Educational, Scientific and Cultural Organisation (UNESCO) (1994) *The Salamanca Statement and Framework on Special Needs Education*. Paris: UNESCO.

Vygotsky, L. S. (1978) *Mind in Society*. Cambridge, MA: Harvard University Press.

Watson, J. and Johnson, R. (1998) *Accelerating Reading Attainment: The Effectiveness of Synthetic Phonics*. Interchange 57. Edinburgh: The Scottish Office.

Waugh, D. (1998) 'The NLS: a sense of urgency or indecent haste', *Curriculum* 19(2), 55–60.

Weaver, C. (1980) *Psycholinguistics and Reading: From Process to Practice*. Cambridge, MA: Winthrop Publishers.

Wegerif, R. and Mercer, N. (1996) 'Computers and learning through talk in the classroom', *Language in Education* 10(1), 47–64.

Weinberger, J. (1996) *Literacy Goes to School: The Parents' Role in Young Children's Literacy Learning*. London: Paul Chapman.

Wells, G. (1986) *The Meaning Makers: Children Learning Language and using Language to Learn*. London: Hodder and Stoughton.

Wells, G. *et al.* (1990) 'Creating classroom communities of literate thinkers', in Sharan, S. (ed.) *Cooperative Learning: Theory and Research*. New York: Praeger.

Whaley, J. (1981) 'Readers' expectations for story structures', *Reading Research Quarterly* XVII(1), 90–112.

Wheldhall, K. and Entwistle, J. (1988) 'Back in the USSR', *Educational Psychology* 8, 51–6.

White, C. (2000) 'Strategies are not enough: the importance of classroom culture in the teaching of writing', *Education 3–13* 28(1), 16–21.

Whitehead, F. *et al.* (1977) *Children and their Books*. Basingstoke: Macmillan.

Whitehead, M. (1997) *Early Literacy: Taking Stock*. L'Oganisation mondiale pour l'education préscolaire (OMEP) Update No. 88.

Whitehead, M. (1999) 'A literacy hour in the nursery? The big question mark', *Early Years* 19(2), 51–61.

Whittaker, C. and Salend, S. (1991) 'Collaborative peer writing groups', *Journal of Reading, Writing and Learning Disabilities International* 7(2), 125–36.

Wilde, S. (2000) *Miscue Analysis Made Easy: Building on Student Strengths*. New York: Heinemann.

Wilkinson, A. *et al.* (1965) 'Spoken English', *Education Review*, occasional publication, no. 2, University of Birmingham, School of Education.

Wilkinson, G. (1997) 'Teaching grammar: a tense situation?', *The Primary English Magazine* 2(4), 2–14.

Wilkinson, I. and Anderson, R. (1995) 'Socio-cognitive processes in guided silent reading: a microanalysis of small group lessons', *Reading Research Quarterly* 30(5), 710–40.

Williams, M. (2000) 'The part which metacognition can play in raising standards in English at KS2', *Reading* 34(1), 3–8.

Wing Jan, L. (1991) *Write Ways, Modelling Writing Forms*. Oxford: Oxford University Press.

Wood, D. (1988) *How Children Think and Learn*. Oxford: Blackwell.

Wood, D. (1992) 'Teacher talk', in Norman, K. (ed.) *Thinking Voices: The Work of the National Oracy Project*. London: Hodder and Stoughton.

Wood, D. and Wood, H. (1989) 'Questioning student initiative', in Dillon, H. (ed.) *Questioning Student Initiative*. Northwood, NJ: Ablex.

Wood, D. *et al.* (1976) 'The role of tutoring in problem solving', *Journal of Child Psychology and Psychiatry* 17, 89–100.

Wragg, E. *et al.* (1998) *Improving Literacy in the Primary School*. London: Routledge.

Wray, D. (1994) *Literacy and Awareness*. London: Hodder and Stoughton.

Wray, D. and Lewis, M. (1997) *Extending Literacy: Children Reading and Writing Non-Fiction*. London: Routledge.

Zipes, J. (1996) *Creative Storytelling: Building Community, Changing Lives*. London: Routledge.